the rise and fall of jenny goodguts

the rise and fall of jenny goodguts

jennifer hole

lovesong press

First edition

ISBN: 978-1-7337055-7-8

Cover design by LucidCreative.co
Cover illustrations and book design by Jennifer Hole

Lovesong Press

www.jenniferhole.com

dedicated to the vast ocean of possibility

and to my first 35 readers,

thank you for the gift of your time, and for your encouragement

CONTENTS

Dear reader,

When I started writing this, four years ago, typing a number of the first entries in the driver's seat of my car while pulled over on the side of the road, I was writing for myself. I think I thought writing might be a way of drawing a map to get from where I was to an imaginary place I thought I should be. I didn't know how I had come to be so *serious*. At the same time, I had this unacknowledged script of self-criticism constantly murmuring. I thought *I have untapped potential*. I thought *look what other people can do*. I thought *I haven't given my all, done my best*. Or think of any quote you've ever read about attitude and altitude.

At the beginning of this adventure, I contemplated a quote from *Walden* "Most men live lives of quiet desperation and go to the grave with the song still in them." Writing this now, this seems so bleak, such a dark rallying cry. But the sentiment these words convey is what moved me to start writing. Four years ago, I felt the song a hoarse, croaky whisper inside me, but with a force that felt no longer containable. I had worked for years in a field I cared about, frequently giving my almost very best effort, but that work didn't feel like my song. For ten years I had played no music. I had untuned, unstrung instruments, wasting away in cases (figuratively and literally) (until my son stepped on one but that is another story). So I started blogging, because it felt like a thing to do. A feasible, acceptable outlet for this uncontainable urge.

I thought I was writing to figure out my song. To remove obstacles to singing it. To fix myself. Maybe help fix you too. I also thought that figuring out how to be happy, fulfilled, and peaceful in this world sets a good example if you wish happiness, fulfillment, and peace for your children. You can't hope that for them and run around like a crazy banshee having road rage all day and think they aren't going to start watching the cars going by and yelling at drivers for they aren't sure what.

The book shares my journey from no blog to blogger, salaried to not, from renter to owner, from not-yet-forty to forty-plus, from babies to children, from Obama to Trump. While it pulls in real world events and the trajectory of history, much of the action is a slow circling inside of one six-inch noggin. Around and around, digging and scraping and looking for some secret recipe. Something like watching a slow-motion makeover where, at times, it might be pretty clear that is definitely not my shade.

What I'm nervous about is also what I think makes the book worth sharing. I learn as I go. Starting in October of 2016 the writing shifts into a more authentic, maybe a more original, voice. But it doesn't start that way. I think it may be interesting—maybe even helpful—to see the change. But to do that you have to start from the beginning. I tried to be brave enough to share the before and the after but I did cut—just a bit—some of the before. You have your own life to live and there are only so many lists a person can read! If you find yourself terribly aggravated during the beginning, consider skipping to October 2016 or to April 2017 when I find a lucky quarter in the Trader Joe's parking lot and turn my life around.

I don't want to give away the ending, what happens, everything I might have learned—not here at the beginning. I do think I've learned about setting up a life that enables me to sing the song. And maybe all of these steps and tests and trials, the checklists and experiments, were necessary.

I guess, for me, they were.

the jenaissance

IN WHICH SHE STARTS TO BLOG

The beginning

November 3, 2014

My pants are too big. Not because I've lost weight — *au contraire*. Because they are maternity pants, technically built to fit two people, and I am only one person who hasn't been pregnant in two years. They're comfortable pants. They protect me from the elements and from anyone knowing how long it's been since I last shaved. They are black so they look somewhat professional. They were clean. They fasten.

I'm sure there are additional criteria that many people consider when they get dressed, but do I have to? Is it going to get in the way of living a good life if I don't think about those other criteria?

I know the guys who wrote and directed *The Lego Movie* — they are my inspiration this week (two guys I knew in college, normal kinds of folk, and two days ago in my local newspaper there was a picture of a swarm of kids dressed up as characters from the movie. These guys *made* that). Do they put a lot of thought in the morning into which pants they are wearing?

Why am I writing this? And why this topic? This afternoon I was walking back to my office from lunch. And by "from lunch" I mean from buying a sandwich that I was planning to eat at my desk, per usual. I was thinking about climate change and snakes, about YouTube videos and songs, about comedy, about very seriousness. I was thinking about my pants, and about standards and to-do lists. Thinking about how to do less, to be okay with doing less. I was thinking about an Isabelle Allende quote I read yesterday: *Once a writer is born into a family, the family is over.*

Is it fair to my family to blog?

I feel a deep longing to *do something*. And by do something I don't mean make a donation or sign a petition or post something on social media. I don't want to tweet a URL to raise a dollar and I don't want to replace a lightbulb. And I don't want to just *not do* something—I don't want to focus on what to avoid or on the harm that I'm doing through this choice or that choice.

What I want is to DO something. To create something, to try something, to meet someone, to inspire someone, to change myself, to reinvent something, to improve something, to learn something. To live and to make a difference through what I do, not through what I avoid or how I consume.

So that's where I am today.

Fear

November 4

In my late twenties I had a job organizing scientific expeditions to remote parts of the world. A group of scientists—and me—would go live in tents for a month at a time and catalog everything we could find, every butterfly, bird, primate, frog, vine, ant. All of my expeditions were in West Africa and I was usually the only woman or one of two women (thank goodness for Ilka) out of a group of about twenty.

The thing about unexplored forests is that they are unexplored for some reason—difficult access, political instability, predatory insects. At times, we set up camp only a few miles from the border with Liberia or Côte d'Ivoire, which during my first expedition was in the middle of a political coup.

Now tents, while they may keep insects at bay, are not that effective at repelling invaders. So if a military caravan toting semi-automatic weapons were to drive by and decide they want whatever is in my tent (which could include just me, my little female self), there's not a whole lot that the canvas walls can do to protect me. And I love biologists, but my herpetologist friend is no match for the Liberian army. Or worse, the guys the Liberian army might be looking for.

I was also financially responsible for the expeditions. And that required cash—only way to pay for food, camp assistance, palm wine, live goats (aka dinner). And $1,000 USD in Guinea in 2002 was around 500 million Guinean francs. So I slept in my tent each night, a little, blonde-ish southern girl, with an enormous backpack full of smelly Guinean cash. Everyone in the camp knew I was the sugardaddy. The guys in the village knew it too.

Was I afraid? Well, I think I vomited from fear one time. But I had also taken some prophylactic antibiotics on an empty stomach the same night the military convoy drove past, waking me from sleep. I did cry in my hotel room sometimes before a trip and think: *My friends are not doing this. I don't have to do this.* But I did it. I loved it. It was unbelievable to be out there, discovering the world.

But today I needed to *get my laptop from the office* (dun dun dun, cue scary music track, this is the stuff nightmares are made of). I needed to park somewhere, temporarily, and there were no street spaces. There's a huge driveway outside of the office building. Cabs park here and wait for people all the time. So I'll just pull up, park the car for two minutes, off the street, not in a reserved space, not in anyone's way, grab the computer and be back lickety-split.

My heart is racing. *Is this against the rules? What are the rules here?* I feel palpable fear as I leave the car to walk inside. I don't even know what I'm afraid of. Afraid someone is going to think I'm doing something wrong? I have someone singing in my head *you're not supposed to do that, you're not supposed to do that.*

It's a car, parked in a safe place. It's not hurting anyone, not blocking anyone. I'm running inside. Am I the same person who slept in a tent on the Liberian border? (This occurs to me as I'm pushing open the building door, the impetus for this car-penned post.) And why am I now sitting in the car typing as if my life depended on it when I have a list, six miles long, of shoulds.

I don't know. I guess I'm writing to find out.

Day three

November 5

I just signed up for guitar lessons. It wasn't a planned thing. I walked by the shop that I've passed seven hundred times but today I turned around. I walked in the front door, and I asked them *do you teach guitar to adults*? They do and I start on Sunday.

Two days ago I had an idea and I wanted to write about it—to consider it, to give it space. That has been happening to me for a while (not long, maybe just twelve years or so), getting ideas and then moving on to whatever is in my inbox or whatever someone else's deadline and priority might be. But this time, when I got back to my desk and tried to focus on "the list," it was like a golden retriever who has decided he's done walking, like my hands had stopped working, nothing was working. All I could think about was writing down that idea. It overcame me.

Then I sent what I had written to a few friends and they liked it. Or they said they did which was, apparently, all I needed. And that set off a chain reaction of having seven million ideas of things to write about. So I'm driving down the road, pulling over frequently to write down all of these ideas. Laughing out loud. Sobbing to random songs.[1]

In case you are wondering, yes, I am writing this in my car. It's not going to be a thing, it is pretty uncomfortable. But it's quiet.

---

1 Think "Wake Me Up Inside" by Evanescence or "What About Now" by Daughtry.

And it gets me away from "the list." And it's a semi-solution while I work out some other life details to make the Jenaissance possible.

I also pulled out my guitar last night. I used to write songs, a lifetime ago. So I dug up the lyrics for some of my old songs. I wrote that?? Not bad. My kids even kind of like it. I think I'm kind of funny. I think my songs are kind of funny. And slightly painful. That idea I had a few months ago about dusting off some of the old songs and putting them on YouTube, why not? Why the heck not??

Well, I'm actually not that strong a guitarist. I am also not at the top of my game in the pants department which is a non-veiled metaphor for this whole physical part of me that includes what you see and what it wears. I can do the songs, but does it have to be me in the video? Also, who's going to record the video? Seems like there would be a lot of steps in getting a song recorded and posted. Or I could just, you know, do it. Just like I made a blog yesterday. I signed up for a guitar class so that I can write a rock opera. I'm not planning to wait to be a good guitar player before I post a song.

I've had some ideas about criticism. I think I'll write about that next but let's see what the universe sends my way.

Parenting principle #1: the poop ratio

November 6

As a relatively new mom, I find myself constantly uncertain. Perpetually questioning. So when I come up with a hard and fast principle to guide me in parental decision making that's a good day. Today has been a good day.

My daughter came home from preschool yesterday pretty fussy (not atypical) but also with a runny nose and, I don't know, overdressed? Just sat in the sun? She seemed a little low of spirits/ energy but I never know how to tell.

I put her to bed, thinking she'd either wake up better or worse and we'd take it from there. Not a great night of sleep so I'm guessing it is moving into the "worse" category. She wakes up sleepy and warm (and cuddly) and it's decided, the thermometer will come out after breakfast. Not because I'm concerned that there's anything major going on, but just so I know if she's to be quarantined away from all sentient beings or if I can let her lick other toddlers with impunity.

So we sit down to breakfast, pretty normal morning, she eats like a horse (maybe thermometer not required), nose not running (check), and then I hit gold. She starts singing. I feel like this is a pretty good sign. And in a matter of moments, the mystery is solved. She's singing about poop!

And that's when I discover the principle. A child singing about poo at the breakfast table is not sick. I call it the *poop ratio*. If one of every ten words in a given one-hundred-word span is *poop* or *poo*, your kid is fine.

Maybe this should be included in training for people who answer the phone at the doctor's office:

MOM:　Hi, my child is acting fussy and she may have a fever, should I bring her in?

NURSE ON PHONE: Have you checked her poop ratio?

MOM:　Excuse me?

NURSE:　Is she lying comatose on the couch not chasing her brother or asking you to play voices?

MOM:　No.

NURSE:　She's not sick. But just to be sure, let's check the poop ratio. Try introducing the word *poop* into a conversation. Or put something in her vicinity that could resemble poop.

MOM:　Okay.

NURSE:　And?

MOM:　Huh—she's singing about poop.

NURSE: Give me a percentage.

MOM: I'd go with around 8% of the words coming out of her mouth right now are either *poop* or *poopy*.

NURSE: Too close to call. What if you include *poo…* and *mouth*?

MOM: Around 25%. And if we include *your, my,* and *eat* then we're at about 50%.

NURSE: What if you add non-words that rhyme with *poopy*?

MOM: With that we're up around 85%.

NURSE: Try saying something like *potty words are for the bathroom* or try *poop is not a word for breakfast time*. Now?

MOM: We're at a full 100% of constant *poop, poo, poopy,* or a non-word rhyme. What should I do?

NURSE: With a 100% poop ratio I usually suggest Bailey's, grain alcohol, whatever you've got. But is there a pharmacy nearby?

MOM: Yes.

NURSE: Okay, try a handful of Excedrin and two hours of soft play. If she doesn't recover to a reasonable 20–25% soon, just give up and watch *Frozen*. You know you want to anyway.

Another potty blog

November 9

I can count the number of times I have slept through the night in the past six months on one finger. I woke up suddenly this morning. There was a tiny bit of light coming through the window and it didn't seem supernatural leading me to the delightful and startling conclusion that I had slept through the night. The house was silent. *I SLEPT THROUGH THE NIGHT AND BOTH OF MY KIDS ARE STILL ASLEEP! Wait, both of my kids are still asleep. Why am I awake?* My eyes were again closed, hoping that I could nurse this sleepy state back into gorgeous, luxurious, blissful sleep for as long as possible when I heard something like a tiny sheep being strangled very quickly somewhere in my house. *ARE YOU KIDDING ME? THE &^%&*$@# FIRE ALARM BATTERY? AGAIN??*

You see, the only other night in the past two months in which I was almost destined to get a full night of sleep with no interruptions was *also* brutally destroyed by a fire alarm battery.

But there is a silver lining to my tale of woe. I'm lying there, while my husband creeps downstairs with the stealth of a fox (a fox wearing heavy shoes or with an ear infection leading to a balance problem) to dismantle the fire alarm, thinking to myself surely there's an answer to this terrible dilemma. Most people are not woken by their fire alarm batteries twice in two months. What do they know that I don't? And then a path appears. Sure, most bloggers have something to share with readers. Resources, tips for saving money. BUT I HAVE QUESTIONS! I have questions all the time. I never run out of questions. I know I might not like all the answers, but I've thought a bit about online criticism and here's where I landed: it's highly unlikely anyone is going to criticize me in a way that's extremely different or more cutting than that little voice in my head. (That said, I don't need to test it, I get plenty of practice.)

So I'm lying there thinking about being the blog that asks questions and people can send me answers and my life will improve and I can share helpful answers with others when I realize that I need to use the bathroom. Desperately. But I don't dare move a muscle as both of my kids are still silent. Then I start wondering if you can do damage to yourself if you really need to use the bathroom (we're just talking about #1 here) and you hold it for a long, long time. Does that mess with your internal organs? Then I remember that there's not much more that can be done to my internal organs than has already been done.

I've had two kids. My internal organs have been stretched out, literally ripped from my body and put onto an operating table, and then squished back in. I had a C-section and my husband watched the whole thing. He saw my guts on the table and he saw them squishing them all back in. He's a biologist and those are the terms he uses—one of the doctors, using both of his arms, picked all of the organs up off the table like a pile of leaves and just dropped them back in the cavity, kind of pushed it down to make it all level and then sewed it up—and by it, I mean me. As a note to millennials, don't let your husband watch your C-section, that curtain is there for a reason.

So, fire alarm battery wakes me up, have to urinate, hear son gurgling to himself, tell husband I have an idea for a post, he tells me to grab son and head downstairs to write. Um, I'm sorry honey, grab son and write? I believe this is known as a paradox. So I grab son, come downstairs, and device upon which I was planning to write has no batteries, bring son to "office" (glorified closet) desk. So here I am.

I have read some great mom bloggers, but I didn't want that to be my thing and I'm not sure anyone can do that better than The Honest Toddler. But I'm a mom. And most of the funny things that occur to me (if the things that occur to me are funny) have something to do with who I am. Also, apparently, a lot of the things that occur to me have to do with the potty. So maybe I'll just be a potty blog that asks a lot of questions.

Introducing... word of the day

November 10
So far, the categories I have considered for the *Jenaissance* blog include:

Soul searching: See posts 1, 2, and 3.

Mommy blogs: See posts 4 and 5. Objective is 25% or fewer of posts, current reality 33%.

Stone soup: Possibly my favorite potential category but I can't spill the beans yet.

In the news: My first post in this category will be on snakes and climate change. I've been waiting to write this for about two years, it's a doozy.

Product reviews: This is where I write about products that I highly do not endorse. I haven't worked out the business model for this yet since many blogs monetize themselves by providing product endorsements. I, on the other hand, want to tell you how furious I am with a small number of products and/or corporate policies. My first review will be for the Kensington Key Folio 2, an iPad holder and wireless keyboard that has become a key factor in my huge success as a blogger. I am furious with Kensington in that they do not offer replacement parts for this iPad accessory. So if I lose a charger, for example, I have to buy a whole new case. THIS IS AN OUTRAGE! I know that unfortunately in posting this non-endorsement I am telling readers that I use and adore this product. BUT I WILL FIND A SUBSTITUTE IF I EVER LOSE MY CHARGER, THIS I SWEAR TO YOU KENSINGTON. I WILL SEE THIS BLOG BURN TO THE GROUND BEFORE I EVER BUY AN ENTIRE NEW DEVICE JUST TO GET A NEW CHARGER, YOU SCOUNDRELS. YOU MIGHT CHARGE ME $20 FOR THE CHARGER, THIS I EXPECT. BUT IT IS A CRIME AGAINST HUMANITY AND LANDFILLS EVERYWHERE IF YOU DO NOT OFFER A REPLACEMENT CHARGER. (Now, if someone from Kensington, who I admittedly have not called, wants to refute this claim and let me know how I might obtain a replacement charger, I will publicly apologize for these praise-filled yet maligning and defamatory remarks.)

Brief aside: Have you noticed that I really like to use parentheses? (I do.)

Guest blogger — a real-life scientist: This is where a real-life scientist I know weighs in on some of the day's most controversial subjects and breaks it down for us simple folk. I know a lot of scientists and some of them can be funny (looking—ha ha).

And drumroll please...The final category that I have in mind for now is....

Word of the day: This is where I introduce a word or phrase to which I plan to refer frequently throughout the life of this blog.

Word #1: <u>Ham crust</u>. This is the term I have created for what has become my favorite breakfast. Imagine a sandwich made of artisanal multigrain bread, organic, free-range ham, Emmentaler cheese, creole mustard, and a generous slathering of Hellmann's mayo. This is the sandwich I make each day for my three-year-old's lunchbox. I then remove the crusts per client specs and what remains is what has come to be, for me, a substantial, filling, and emotionally satisfying breakfast treat. I found myself, this very morning, celebrating the fact that: *It's Monday! Hooray for ham crusts!*

Word #2: <u>Crypothesis</u>. This is like the game chicken and hypothesis-testing rolled into one. Imagine your child has woken from a nap. She's upstairs. The babygate is locked. She can't unlock it. You are downstairs on the couch taking a nap (for the first time in three months—don't think I sit around napping all of the time). You hear her making little noises to try to get someone's attention to let her downstairs. BUT there is a chance if no one responds she will return quietly to her room and happily play in there for another 20–30 minutes. You think to yourself, *is this a testable crypothesis*? Either she will go play quietly and I can rest, or she'll start making weird animal noises right outside of her brother's room and they will both be awake (leading to me crying, just a little bit). The end result of any crypothesis testing is usually either me crying, or both kids and me crying. Now that I see this in writing it seems like testing crypotheses is not ever a great idea. But, strangely, it always feels like the right decision.

My final word today is more of a concept. I found myself

wondering this morning whether there is a term for what I am: highly dysfunctional doesn't quite capture it. *Dysductive*? See, I'm somewhat dysfunctional. But also highly productive. I can get a s**t ton of stuff done in a day, it just isn't usually the stuff that I'm "supposed" to get done. My sister-in-law told me once, when I asked her how she was so productive and on top of her game, that she often takes time when she's in the shower to think through the big plays of the day and make sure the food for dinner is defrosting, that she has everything in order to go to work, take care of her kids, sew a new costume, make a five-course dinner, make homemade candy, redecorate her house, train a dog, raise money for charity, translate Greek poetry, and look great. When I'm in the shower, I'm usually thinking about awesome words like crypothesis or just wondering where the last ten minutes went.

This blog is a great example. I'm moving this Friday to a new house. All of the (too many) objects in my house of four people have to be boxed and moved and unboxed. Plus all of the utilities changed, plus the new house is a fixer-upper so the deceased vermin have to be removed from under the stove (etc.). And yet I found time last week to start a blog, post almost daily, sign up for guitar lessons, and record a YouTube video.

Who do I think I am? My daughter still has not been to the dentist (ever). I pulled a dirty shirt out of the hamper this morning to wear to work. I've been dehydrated for a whole week. I can't even provide myself with enough water.

I guess I feel like if I stop now, maybe the Jenaissance will lose momentum. And I just can't risk it. I'm sorry family. I love you guys and I promise I will figure out a way to pack and unpack those boxes. The vermin will be gone. I will deep clean the cabinets. I will figure out what to do about the poison ivy. I will schedule the flu shot. They are baby teeth, so can we let that one slide? No? Okay. I will cook the Thanksgiving turkey. I will make the Christmas list. I will be thoughtful. I will reach out to friends. I will brush my teeth (note to self, as soon as you finish writing this remember to brush your teeth).

But it's taken me twelve years to start this and I don't want to stop.

Return of the Jenaissance

November 19

Yesterday I sat in my car and googled "manic depression." I wasn't sure exactly what that term means, and I had a small, secret fear that maybe it has something to do with me. With the fact that I started a blog the week before I moved to a new house with two kids under four. That I not only started the blog, but posted daily, signed up for (and subsequently discontinued) guitar lessons, recorded a YouTube video, and felt *alive*.

I started the *Jenaissance* blog on November 4th, decided to take the plunge on November 10th and share with my Facebook friends, including friends from elementary school, relatives between the ages of fifteen and eighty, friends of my mom, my friends' parents, my children's friends' parents, who are also my friends (it gets complicated). I started getting likes and comments from people in all of these categories. And that felt amazing. People signed up to be notified of new posts. People I haven't been in touch with in twenty years.

And then I tried to think of what to write next. I kept thinking of the individuals who were lovely enough to subscribe to my blog, and what they would think about this idea or that idea. Would they be horrified? Is that not what they are expecting? And I froze. I'm still slightly frozen, but that could be because I am subsisting on a diet of tea and ham crusts.

Then I went into full move mode. It was hard. It was dirty. It was freezing cold. We should have had more stuff in the new house taken care of before moving in. The previous occupant owned between six and seventy cats over the thirty years she lived here and was apparently somewhat laissez faire in her ideas about cleanliness. So we had the air ducts cleaned the day before moving in (note to millennials: this was not good timing) resulting in a thick layer of sticky gray dust on every surface house-wide owing to the fact that the duct guy didn't cover the vents before sending pressurized air through all the duct work, stirring up 30 years of accumulated cat.

The furnace was also venting improperly so the majority of exhaust (carbon monoxide in particular) was escaping into the walls of the house. No biggie though because the house is so poorly insulated that there is *plenty* of fresh air getting in all the time. Four days and thousands of dollars later we may have hot water, carbon-monoxide-free air, and a functioning furnace at the end of today (recognizing there are billions of people on earth who don't have these things, I'm fortunate to have had to wait only four days).

So everything is sheer madness. It is unseasonably twenty degrees Fahrenheit and my daughter goes to a Waldorf school where they play outside NO MATTER WHAT and we can't find the mittens (that's what I told the teacher but the truth is that I don't think we own any mittens. We've lost all of the mittens we've bought and I've been too busy blogging to purchase additional seasonally appropriate clothing for my child). Then, two nights ago, I went out to dinner with a friend and had a (one) margarita. I came home from dinner, went to bed on the late side feeling like we'll never have enough money to make this house functional / safe / clean / warm / non-toxic. I woke up the next morning feeling overwhelmed, tired, ate my normal breakfast of ham crusts and tea, didn't shower, brought daughter to school without mittens, went to work, left work to get daughter, and sat in car googling about being bipolar. And I'm not saying this lightly—I was concerned.

I'm less concerned today. I went to bed early last night. I didn't have anything to drink (no alcohol, that is, and practically no water either since we're talking liquids). I haven't eaten well today but I did brush my teeth and shower. I think there may be toxic fumes affecting my ability to think clearly, and I'm not sure I'm going to post this, but it is definitely a phase in the Jenaissance so maybe I will. I don't know.

I have this cautious voice asking me, why would you post something like this on The Internet for everyone you know and their parents to read? What about future employers? What if they know that I don't have it all together? That I write blogs in my car and don't brush my teeth and get overwhelmed and feel guilty that I have so much and I'm not appreciative all the time even though I really, really should be?

When writing a blog, you can just barf whatever is in your mind down on a computer, hit publish, and then people somewhere might read it. And you might feel embarrassed about that when you see them at the pool next summer while you're home visiting your parents. Luckily, by then you will have forgotten everything that has happened in 2014 so it's probably cool. Also, there are *lots* of other things to feel embarrassed about when you go to the pool, so this blog will probably be pretty far down on that list.

Idea for my next post: living in a house without mirrors has an unexpected bonus of making you feel much more attractive.

I might write a book

November 21

Packing for our move involved, as may be expected, multiple existential crises. Example: About two days before the move basically nothing in the old house was packed and we were planning to do all of the packing ourselves (well, I *had* sorted through two bookshelves and given away seven books after two weeks of agonized soul searching). I had a box full of cooking magazines from 2005–2006. Old *Gourmets*, *Saveurs*, a couple *Art of Eatings*. Good stuff. My plan was, at some point, to flip through each magazine and tear out the best recipes, then recycle the magazines thus taking up less storage space but not losing the wealth of amazing cooking experiences just waiting for me in the pages.

It is important that you also know about my stack of recipes, torn out of magazines over the past ten years and probably seven inches high. I can measure the stack when I find the box in which the ruler is packed. I have probably leafed through some portion of the seven-inch recipe stack one time since its inception and maybe cooked something—once—from one of the pages. Other than that I cook the same few recipes from the same two books. Or occasionally I look something up online.

In considering my plan to peruse each intact magazine to tear more recipes out to add to this seven-inch stack, it occured to me that this might constitute a form of hoarding. At this moment of startling lucidity I decided I should definitely recycle or donate all of the remaining magazines. But, just in case, I browsed through the pile. *But I really want to learn The Secrets of Mexican Cooking. And they don't print Gourmet anymore, how can I get rid of this vintage treasure?*

No, you are not keeping these.

Wait, how old are these?

Given the publication dates, a quick trip down memory lane revealed that I must have packed and moved each of these magazines six times, and this would be seven.

No. No way. You have a problem.

Then it hit me—I CAN BLOG ABOUT THIS! I decided to keep all of the magazines as a reminder that I want to write about keeping them (yes, I see the circularity). But to show myself that I was definitely not attached to them anymore, I decided to look through the stack—again—and choose a few to recycle immediately. *No, no, not that one, okay here's one with vegetables on the cover* (gone). Twenty minutes later I had finally made the decision about what to do with this stack of magazines. I put them back into a box, I labelled the box, and I recycled two magazines.

So not only have I been moving, I'm also waging existential battles with myself about hoarding and accumulation, about over-consumption and materialism, about choices and time management and dreams and plans and making space for the new by getting rid of the old but also not being totally comfortable with the modern ethos of just getting rid of what you don't want so you can buy more of exactly what you do want.

I have an idea about a book that has something to do with this. My other big project ideas at the moment: rock opera, posting my YouTube video on the blog (?!?), thinking of a way to "blog for good," and a couple of others that don't sound very appealing in print but could be fun so we'll see where to next.

Aerobox

November 24
OH-MY-GOD youguys. I have discovered like the best new workout. EVER. You know how I'm always going into my closet in the morning (or, you know, whenever pj time is over, if for some reason it has to end that day), on the mornings when I don't just put yesterday's clothes back on, and looking around and kind of shoving stuff from side to side and then I throw myself down on the bed and say I don't have anything to wear even though by some mirage it looks like there are numerous articles of clothing hanging in a reasonably organized fashion right there like three feet away from me?

You are gonna freak out. Totally. I have INVENTED a new thing. Aerobox (pronounced [ai-roh-boks] (like aerobics but "box" at the end instead). A complete cardio workout with built-in strength training and you don't need any fancy equipment or embarrassing yoga pants. Here's what you do: Pack like everything you own which should include tons and tons of stuff you never use but might someday into a bunch of boxes. Label some of the boxes but not others and then unpack some of them and repack them with different stuff that is totally dissimilar and then don't rewrite a new label on the box. Extra credit if you reuse old boxes with labels from the past and then don't cross out the old label so you aren't totally sure which of the two descriptions is correct. Extra extra credit if, since you're finally moving to your own house, you ask your parents to bring up all of the stuff that has been stored in their house for about twenty years (so clearly stuff you are gonna use, like, today) and make sure those boxes are also not labelled or maybe just have the word "Jen" on each one. There should be at least twelve of these but probably more like 30.

Okay, ohmygosh I'm so excited. So then you move all of those boxes to a new house. Make sure not to indicate to the movers what goes where (except by using like bright pink stickers that clearly indicate which room each box belongs in) and try not to be present when they are asking questions about anything. Again, extra credit if you are having plumbing or other work done in most storage spaces in the house so that all boxes must be deposited wherever the heck someone felt like putting them at that moment.

Here's where it gets good. Now try to function! I promise you: you will lose weight, you will get in shape, and you will look great doing it! And since you don't have mirrors, no way to know otherwise. A total win-win! The great thing about this is you can just keep moving those boxes from one place to another for days in a row. Upstairs, downstairs. You can put them in one place so that you can clean another place, then move them back.

And, youguys, my pants buttoned this morning. That one pair of pants that I have for going to work that I'm starting to suspect my colleagues might know is my only pair of pants—they buttoned. And I can still breathe! I did it—after just one week of aerobox, coupled with surviving on ham crusts and whatever is left on my children's plates, I can button my one pair of pants! I'm, like, totally taking a selfie and posting it on Facebook.

IN WHICH SHE LEAVES HER JOB

Note: At this point in the blog, I shared a video of myself sitting in my (messy) kitchen singing a song that I had written 20 years prior. As of today, the video is still available on YouTube. It's called Pageant Song. Not my finest performance, but very authentic.

Like pulling off a band-aid

December 1, 2014

Thanksgiving is over. It's been almost a week since I've written a new post. I had a late night with an old friend and I have work to do for my real job today. What's a girl to do?

Oh, oh—I know! I will post that YouTube video for the world to see. Details pertaining to myself and the judges are factual. I fictionalized several (all) points in relation to the pageant winner using a bit of artistic license.

I'm sure there are excellent reasons not to post this video but without further ado...

(Lyrics below, for readers who are not planning to rush to the computer to search for this video.)

I'd been to watch the high school girls when I was just a kid
I knew when I was older I would sing just like they did
The years went by and I practiced my showtunes every day
Even bought a push-up bra so that the judges might look my way
After years of waiting, my turn finally came
I imagined the spotlight as I walked forward to say my name
Hi, I'm Jennifer and I'm a senior

Hi, my name's Jennifer and I'm a senior
Good evening and welcome, ladies and gentlemen,
*   my name's Jennifer and I'm a senior*
I'd surveyed the competition, thought my chances looked okay
But I knew to win that crown I'd have to practice every day

It's been seven years since it happened
And I know I need to give myself time
But maybe if I'd done some things differently
That swell bouquet could have been mine
Sure days go by, sometimes I forget
The hollowness and the pain
But I'd trade all I've done since for one chance to try again

The big day came, the interview, the judges were sitting in line
They asked me lots of questions, it seemed to be going fine
Then the scariest one of them looked at me, made me feel like crying
Asked if I knew Andrew Lloyd Weber's "Requiem," I said yes
I was lying
Time to sing, the song I chose a Barbra Streisand hit
And maybe I lost because of those few notes that I missed
In my evening gown I was a bright blue sequined vision
And then we all lined up to hear the local celebrity judges' decision
They called the top ten finalists in a random order
And I started growing nervous as the number left grew shorter
How could it be they forgot me my dreams are crushed
It's over

It's been several years since it happened
And I know I need to give myself time
But maybe if I'd done some things differently
That rhinestone crown could have been mine
Sure days go by, sometimes I forget
The hollowness and the pain
But I'd trade all I've done since for one chance to try again

When I think back on the pageant I wonder why God punished me
I usually decide it was because of the lie or maybe my own vanity
But now I know I've got to make it
to show those bimbo judges they were wrong
And to let that tramp who beat me know
it was just because she picked a better song
Anyway I hear she's really ugly now
and that she's had her boobs done
Probably would have been better off if she had lost and
I had won

It's been (twenty) years since it happened
And I know I need to give myself time
But maybe if I'd done some things differently
That title would have been mine
Sure days go by, sometimes I forget
The hollowness and the pain
But I'd trade all I've done since for one chance to try again
I wouldn't trade all I've done since but I'd like to try again
I wouldn't trade any of this
but sometimes at night I still have dreams, literal dreams,
of trying again

A brief explanation of the Jenaissance

December 5

I am deeply embarrassed by the blog name, *Jenaissance*. I am also aware that blogs with photos, or some attempt at decent layout and organization, are likely more enjoyable for everyone involved. I think/hope that one day I will change all of this about my blog, or whatever it turns into.

But this is what I know/knew when I started the *Jenaissance*: Sometime between 1997 and 2014 I turned into this really serious person. There were all of these things that I worried about, I was afraid of making mistakes and doing the wrong things, of messing up my kids, of being a bad wife, of not having enough money for something unknown that might happen or be needed in the future. There were all of these rules about what goes up on walls or doesn't, what kinds of foods to eat or not, what kind of music we admit to liking, what percentage of body fat is okay.

Also—and I guess this is a crucial part of the story—I have spent a fair amount of time living in other countries (like India, Mexico, Guinea, Ghana) where I was more than a tourist and got to see up close how people in these countries live and how the choices people make in other places (e.g., America) have a strong impact around the globe. Those experiences really impacted me and I felt this RESPONSIBILITY that can feel pretty heavy to a girl. I don't want those kids to be hungry, I don't want those people to lose their homes, I don't want that mountaintop removed. *I have a responsibility to live my life in a way that fixes those problems.*

That's something of an unconscious mantra that's been underneath so many choices since then. I want to help. I want to be good.

But I want happiness too. I want joy and silliness and lightness. I didn't realize how much the silliness and lightness had disappeared until I spent some quality time in the wilderness with two old friends (*they* aren't old, but I've known them since I was seventeen) who hadn't seen me in a while and helped me to remember who I was before I "lost my innocence." And the contrast between me at twenty and me in October was stark—where had I gone?

I came back from being with my friends and felt pretty blue. And then I had an idea, or more a question, a train of thought that I wanted to follow. So I wrote a few paragraphs. And the next day I wrote a few more. I wanted the writing to have somewhere to live so I decided to see how hard it was to set up a blog. I was driving in my car that morning and had the thought: *I'm having a Jenaissance*, a private joke. So when the webhosting service asked me to select a URL name I chose Jenaissance, partly as a temporary placeholder—and partly because I wasn't planning to share this thing publicly. But writing that one post, the one about my pants, and the next one about fear—and sharing them—felt so good. It felt so much like *me* that the next thing I knew I had recorded a song I wrote twenty years ago and posted it to YouTube. I had hemmed and hawed about doing that for a while, not sure how to do it, who could film me, where I would sit, could I still play the guitar. Then one day I just did it. All by myself. In my kitchen. With my kids in the next room. And I loved it. I am so happy I made that video. If I never make another one I'm glad that one exists in the world.

I guess what I'm saying is that these efforts, these experiments, are me trying to bring that part of myself back to life. And I suppose it is self-centered and I'm not sure what it is that makes me want to share it, but sharing it is also part of what I've been missing. I feel some inner turmoil about the fact that this blogging isn't helping solve anyone else's problems, isn't addressing some global imbalance, not righting any wrongs, not standing up for anything. It's just me talking about myself. Sometimes it's funny and sometimes it's like this.

I'm trying not to listen to my inner critic. I feel like this is what I need. Like this is good for me. And that to make my best contribution to any of that other stuff, I ought to bring the full me to the table. So, right now, the Jenaissance is about being silly. And light. And also like this. Just genuine I guess.

Walk of shame

December 11
Yesterday I attended my fourth (I believe, but who can keep count?) Blue Mercury holiday "party." In case you are lucky enough to not know, Blue Mercury is a retail store that carries a variety of high-end beauty brands: La Mer, Trish, Laura Mercier (something

about writing this particular list, knowing these particular words and what they mean, makes me feel ridiculous).

Those of you who know me may be surprised to hear that I (that would be capitalized for emphasis but you see my problem…), yes I, have heard of and even set foot in a Blue Mercury shop. I know I don't look like someone who bathes daily or ever gets a haircut or owns contacts. And usually I'm wearing yesterday's clothes with my hair pulled back in a sloppy bun and my six-year-old glasses with who-knows-what prescription.

But once a year I forget about this version of me and, for a brief moment in time, I imagine another me who is groomed, pretty even. (What, who wrote that?) Okay, it's true. I would like to look in the mirror in the morning when I'm on my way to wherever and think: *I look good. I look clean and my skin looks nice and my hair is shiny and I have a "glow"*—not necessarily a youthful glow but a nice middle-aged glow with as few lines and dark circles as is naturally possible (and by naturally I include whatever I can buy in a bottle but doesn't require surgery or injections).

Each year, Blue Mercury has a holiday party where you get 10–20% off of everything in the store depending on how much you spend on products that, in general, never go on sale. So each year I remember right around this time that there's a huge sale on this very expensive stuff that can make me "beautiful" (if I just knew how to use whatever it is) and I look it up online, find the date, and go.

I went last year. My son was nine months old. He was a preemie and had been permanently attached to a monitor at home for the first four-plus months of his life and we had had a tough year. I had just left my job of almost ten years and was no longer earning a paycheck. As a physical specimen I was close to my nadir, sleep-deprived, exhausted, having lost none of the babyweight. My mom was in town for the week. What else should I do with my one free hour but go to the Blue Mercury holiday party?

At this party they provide free champagne and have magicians, professionally trained wizards, who use products in ways you never, ever could at home. They take forty-two different things and make you look like you just woke up from a week alone at a yoga smoothie reiki sweat lodge spa. Who is that 25-year-old vision of loveliness? I'll take it. Whasever you did (hiccup), I want to do that at home.

So I'm standing at the register and the woman gives me my total. (Wait, you must also know that, on my way to the register, basket swinging in hand, my mom had called with an "emergency" situation and I had to head home immediately. There are two kids screaming in the background, I don't know what the situation is but a) I'm gorgeous and b) I have to get home now.) NINE HUNDRED WHAT????? Okay, don't panic. The contents of this basket weigh six ounces. How is this possible? Definitely don't vomit here in the middle of Blue Mercury with all of the beautiful people in black. I'm just going to take it home, pick two things to keep and return the rest (because that's clearly the rational choice here, right? Otherwise, how will I know if that was "radiant poverty" or "peony youth" that he used to line the middle underside of my left, um, I don't remember what).

Get to the car. Look at receipt. "Returns for store credit only." I'm crying on the way home. I do not have a job. I don't even need to go anywhere. I can use Oil of Olay or just some olive oil from my kitchen. What is in this stuff? It is magic, yes. I have the eyes of my two-year-old daughter right now. But this is totally unsustainable. And not necessary. I'm happy. I feel pretty good most days in my glasses and dirty hair. People like me or I tell myself that. Heck, I like me (except not right now when I feel vain, ridiculous, stupid, gullible, selfish, idiotic, wasteful…and should I even be driving? I didn't expect to be drinking at 2 PM at a cosmetics store…).

My sweet mother goes through the entire bag with me (after

I come clean about how horribly embarrassed I am about what I've done). She'll buy x as a gift for y. I can exchange z and buy her fifteen jars of moisturizer to use over the next ten years. She'll give me z2 (ran out of letters) for Christmas. We figure out how to cover about $200 in this way. I'm totally screwed. And terribly embarrassed. And sober again. *This stuff has to go back.*

I look in the mirror. It does look pretty good. But not really like me. And for goodness sake, if I'll just wash my face every morning and buy some dry shampoo for the days I don't shower, that would be a pretty good start. And maybe some mascara. I could do that. (And toothbrushing, as I believe I've mentioned before.)

So, in the rain, I drive back to the store the next day. Wearing no makeup, my fifteen-year-old raincoat and memory fails but I'm guessing my maternity jeans. And as I'm walking into the store I feel pretty good, proud of myself. Like me. I walk in the front door with my bag of beauty products. I say I need to return some things. I make a joke about a walk of shame and the gal at the counter doesn't bat an eyelash or offer a tiny hint of a smile. I don't know if she sees this all the time or if I'm an anomaly.

I got all of the money back. I didn't ask how. I did keep one little thing and now I'm emotionally dependent on this tiny jar so I went back to the party this year because how can I not get that amazing discount? WHEN WILL I LEARN? DO NOT GO TO PARTIES WITH ALCOHOL WHERE THERE ARE MAGICAL BEAUTY PRODUCTS ON SALE.

Luckily, I made sure to go first thing in the morning when there was no booze, and they didn't have what I was looking for anyway (so next time you see me I *may* look a little less radiant than when you saw me last or maybe I'll just do a few jumping jacks and look exactly the same).

What's next

December 15

Today is my last day of formal employment with a company I've worked for since 2002. There have been brief pauses in that employment, but no other employers in the meantime. It's a pretty big deal for me and, contrary to my usual blabiness, I'm going to keep my feelings about it to myself. As with any job, there are great people and there are struggles. There is also a balance to strike between the things in life you need to do and the things you want to do—and hopefully with some luck and hard work the line between those two can be thinner and thinner. Or at least you feel peaceful and grateful about what needs to be done in your life.

So today = last day. Tomorrow = first day of the rest of my life.

There's a lot going on at this time of the year—family visiting, moving houses, feeling guilty for not shopping, feeling guilty for shopping, feeling guilty for feeding my kids like they are on the South Beach diet while I secretly eat a bag of Golden Flake Cheese Curls (think Cheetos but made in heaven).

Next time I write I will be self-employed (for some reason I keep thinking of Laraine Newman "I'm an artist and an entertainer"). I'm excited about the next chapter. Really excited. Just not exactly sure what I'm doing.

The first day of the rest of my life

December 18

Monday was my last day at my job. Gone are the office, the company laptop, the work email, the pending discussions and decisions and negotiations and frustrations. No more office gossip. I went to sleep Monday night, exhausted, but happy and hopeful and feeling that there might just be possibilities around the corner.

I awoke the next morning to vomit. Lots of it. All over the place. My poor, sweet second child was lying in his bed covered in the stuff. So, when I posed the theoretical question, *what's next for me?*, the initial answer is upchuck.

I still feel sure there are possibilities around the corner. Just not the next corner—there are going to be a few blocks to walk before I find the corner with the possibilities. And some of those blocks are going to be a bit mucky.

IN WHICH THE INITIAL EUPHORIA
WEARS OFF

2014 in review: the year of Hans

January 5, 2015

Note: I had intended to share the following post just before Christmas. This was before I, along with my husband, sister, mom, dad, aunt, cousin, and possibly hundreds of innocent patrons of Cracker Barrels along I-81, contracted the dread vomits mentioned in my previous post. Rather than updating the text to reflect the fact that it is being posted in 2015, I am choosing to write this explanation in italics.

The end of the year, I've been told, is a good time to review what's going well and what could be improved in one's life situation. To set goals for the next year (goals being much more en vogue than resolutions these days). If you're serious about this, and have some spare time on your hands, I recommend Chris Guillebeau's blog post on annual reviews and goal setting.

As I was looking at his excellent suggestions, itching to make a detailed spreadsheet of three to five goals in ten or so different categories of life as I have done in years gone by, I decided that I should probably focus on, say, one goal in each of the ten categories. I may then have a chance of being successful in accomplishing two to three things over the course of the next year other than what I'm doing today which is whatever I possibly can to avoid having more vomit spilled on the various surfaces of my person, my older child's person, and, in particular, any non-launderable fabrics or upholstery in my home (you'll note the vomit has transferred from child two to child one).

I thought for a while about what would signify a good year to me. What could happen in 2015 that would make me feel like I had really accomplished something? And, bingo, I got it.

You may have heard of a little film called *Frozen*. In my home, this is not so much a film as a way of life. It is starting to abate, slightly, from the frenzy of last winter, but is still a frequent theme of most days. I like the movie (enough), thank goodness, because I have seen or heard it at least a hundred times, and that is not an exaggeration because it takes five back-to-back viewings to drive from DC to Birmingham and then you have to drive back again.

Here's the thing about *Frozen*. In my house there is a very predictable and stable casting: Maggie is Anna (never Elsa). She is also the permanent casting director. Daddy is Kristoff (always). Sam is Olaf (usually) and Deedee (my mother) is Sven. So who am I? The one who grew you, nursed you, is cleaning your puke off my sweater? I'm Hans. I'm always Hans. I just don't get it. Partly, I think it's because she doesn't fully understand the story.

I *think* she thinks that Hans is the romantic lead. But she doesn't get that dreamy look in her eyes and giggle about Hans the same way she does about Kristoff so…I think she's confused about Hans and what he's all about. I just want to be Olaf or Sven. NO WAY she'd ever let me be Elsa. Anytime I even imagine that I'm belting out "Let It Go" in the kitchen, I get a polite and immediate shutdown. *Mommy, please don't sing.* Unless it is the Anna and Hans duet—then I am invited, nay compelled, to sing and dance all of the moves including the two sets of hands making the heart.

Hold the press. Newsflash to myself (turns out blogging is a pretty good way to work through the deepest issues in one's life). First, some additional background: We decided to branch out and try a new princess movie and I, mistakenly, thought *The Little*

Mermaid could be an acceptable alternative. Good music, terrible plot, too much talk about kissing, and way too much flesh. And ever since then she wants me to be Ursula. What the?? And after she heard the story of Cinderella she always wanted me to be the stepsisters, never the fairy godmother.

Reading books and talking to friends before I had kids, no one ever told me I was destined to be cast as the bad guys. Is this a thing? Or am I doing something wrong?

I'm realizing that "figure out a way to be cast as a good guy" probably isn't a great goal for 2015. I was hoping for Olaf, the feel good, warm-hearted friend you can't help but love. I'd be fine with Flounder—that annoying sidekick who doesn't help much but has your best interests at heart. But I'm guessing there is value in working out what "bad" is in a safe space, and seeing your mom behave like a naughty character is probably far more satisfying than seeing her just be nice and supportive like she wishes she could be more of the time.

So it's back to the goal-drawing board. I'm thinking: 1) something about eating more vegetables, 2) something about getting more sleep and in the earlier part of the night, 3) something about spending more time with friends. Those sound more like resolutions, so clearly I have work to do before January 1st.

In which a snow day makes a mockery of my one resolution for 2015

January 7
I have spent a fair amount of time thinking about some actionable goals to work towards in 2015. New year, new you and all of that. I have three in mind that are still pretty amorphous: 1) write something, 2) earn some money (not necessarily in relation to #1), and 3) something about some kind of life routine. More work is

required to develop these to the point where I would have any idea of what success looks like. Have I already succeeded with #1 because I am writing this post? For #2, does returning a Christmas gift count?

But while waiting to develop the perfect goals with 3–5 clear outcomes and daily/weekly action points, I decided I could at least get started with one element: to wash my face every morning. There are going to be days without showers. And days in yesterday's clothes. But it shouldn't be too terribly difficult to wash my face each day.

I told myself on New Year's Eve: you don't have any clear goals yet for the year, but do the face washing thing for now. Just wash your face every morning until it becomes routine, just like you always wash your face at night. Pretty easy win, really. Genius. Okay, January 1st—done. Face washed right after breakfast. January 2nd, took a shower when I woke up. Check. January 3rd, remembered around 10 AM. That still counts as morning, still safe, three for three. January 4th is the day I decided the goal was to wash my face before noon. As long as it was before noon then I was okay. January 5th I took a shower in the morning—that was a good day. Back to school, normal routine, all is well.

I am writing this on January 7th and the fact that there is a gap in my reporting should alert you to something. Cue ominous music. January 6th arrived, bright—very bright in fact because it was a (duh duh duh) SNOW DAY. Not the kind of snow day where you pile back in bed and cuddle with your precious cherubs while getting extra sleep because there's nowhere to go. And then bundle up in your perfectly organized and easy-to-find snow attire which fits correctly and is all gender appropriate. Where you play in the snow for hours, building forts and cheeky snowmen and then come inside to drink hot chocolate while daddy warms up the creamy tomato soup that you made in the summer from those homegrown tomatoes that the squirrels did not take a bite out of (every single one) before using as stools for their giant scrotums.

No, yesterday was the kind of snow day where snow has accumulated on the ground, it is still snowing, it is predicted to keep snowing and, for some reason, the powers that be decide not to call it a snow day. You feel confused. You don't have a four-wheel-drive vehicle and you live on top of a Dr. Seuss hill, ridiculously steep by both approaches. But school is on so it must not be as bad as you feel like it looks like it will be. You go about your day as normal except that you have to find snow clothes for everyone, including yourself. Okay, breakfast consumed, lunch prepared, children and parents bundled, few minutes of play outside, car scraped of snow and ice, let the games begin.

The roads were very quiet. This confused me. School is on. Work is not cancelled. Where are all the people? What do they know that I don't know? While the car did slip around, and we saw a few stuck cars and buses, eventually we got Maggie to school. Then Sam and I, as planned, were heading to my sister's house where he was to spend a few hours with a sitter who was still on her way because my sister's work was also not cancelled. I remembered that I had not packed spare diapers or any food. Hmmm... let hungry child squirm in dirty diaper or risk going back up and down hill?? This (obviously shouldn't have been but) was a tough call.

The car slipped slightly on our way back home, but we made it. Located diapers and food, drove down the hill to my sister's. The sitter arrived after two hours in transit. At this point I decided it was ridiculous to drive back up the hill to go home and then come back down the hill to get Sam and then go back up the hill to bring him home for a nap and then back down to get Maggie and then back up to bring her home. So I gave up on having my now two hours of time alone (the first two hours in twenty months that I would have been in my own home alone. I was kind of looking forward to it). So Sam and I headed towards home, up the big, blind curve on the big hill at the same time as another car was driving down. We didn't know another car was driving down until mid-curve, when both cars had to shift from the clearer center of the road towards the edge where we slipped all over the place. And then we were stuck. Eventually I reversed down to level ground and tried one more time. We made it home but the car was now facing the even steeper hill with no way to turn around (we have street parking on a narrow street). The temperature was in the low 20s, there was no grit, no salt, and our street goes nowhere. It should be the last street plowed or gritted in the whole city.

Then I got a call that they were closing school early. I guess I'm the dummy and I should have just stayed home with the soup and the grilled cheese (or the toast and Cheese Curls which is closer to reality). I called a friend with four-wheel drive. She offered to pick Maggie up, along with her own daughter. They came by for lunch. It was delightful. The kids and I fell asleep after lunch for a late nap and woke up at 4:30 PM. I think I realized around that time that I hadn't washed my face yet. And that changing the goal to washing my face each day by 5 PM was possibly just a bit of a stretch from the original intent. It turned out to be a pretty good day though. And I don't think I lost a friend for lack of cleanliness.

My face is washed today. I'm not giving up because of one snow day. So now I'm 6/7. Still working on developing the other goals. But washing my face (most days) in the meantime.

1975

January 26

I turn 40 this year. Turns out a lot of people I know do too (also a lot of people I don't know). Yesterday, I read an article on *Medium* by Amanda Clayman, a Brooklyn woman turning 40, "Age 40: Ain't nobody got time for that."

I really understood the perspective, and celebrated it, as I've been having conversations with a number of girlfriends who are also approaching this milestone and it feels like we're all in a similar place—learning to understand what we choose or choose not to accept in our lives, asking for what we need (and not always in the most gentle or understated ways), putting aside the long lists of to-dos, even if very sporadically, to carve out a bit of space for our own flickering little lights to shine (those lights that may have been hiding under a bushel and oxygen-starved for what feels like a long time).

But the article also made me feel something else. The author sounds like she's so together. She's got this thing down. She's 40, she knows what she likes and what she doesn't and she's willing to ask for the former. She's set her life up so well, she's successful, she's not worrying about a few extra pounds or dwelling on mistakes or trying so very much to please everyone all the time, or comparing herself to everyone else or judging the choices of others.

I love that. And the mindset, I get it and appreciate it. But for me the logistics of it all are still, well, impossible. In approaching 40 I feel some clarity on the what, but a whole hell of a lot of frustration in the how. Of course, I'm not *quite* 40. I have over six months to go. So I'm going to keep giving that little light periodic bouts of oxygen (as I'm doing right this very minute), I'm going to clear some clutter (physical, mental, and to-do list clutter), I'm going to figure out a workable childcare situation that supports my kids' and my needs, I'm going to make a space in my home where I can be productive and creative instead of always needing to be in a café or my car to think clearly, and, for now, I'm going to leave the towels hanging as curtains in my bedroom windows, I'm going to appreciate that I have a kitchen with running hot water and a gas stove instead of worrying about the horses on the tiles.

And who knows, maybe by the magical day when I enter my fifth decade I, too, will have caught my stride.

Lemon vs. Knope: a response

February 13

I haven't written a new post since reading another article from *Medium*: "A Leslie Knope In a World Full of Liz Lemons: Liz Lemon is who the world wants you to be. Leslie Knope is who you should aim to be" by Hanna Brooks Olsen. There are a few parts that really resonated with me. One example:

Identifying with Liz means not only embracing our flaws, but investing in them, highlighting them, and touting them as our most memorable, interesting qualities.

Check. Done that.

I have been thinking about this article since reading it (a week ago) and have decided that, as much as I love Liz Lemon, I don't want to be her. And I don't want to feel like I have to apologize for myself, or focus on the things that I'm not good at, or never talk about the things that are going well.

And as funny as it is to write about all of the struggles, and to see the humor in them, it seems like it might be too easy to fall into a pattern of emphasizing what is bad and what is wrong, what I'm not good at, what's messed up, what about life isn't what I expected.

So I'm thinking about channeling my inner Leslie Knope. It's hard to write that because who in her right mind wants to be Leslie—right? But I think I used to want to be Leslie and then I found out that people find her annoying and abrasive and so I learned how to be more of a Liz. Maybe a lot of us did. So I'm thinking about celebrating what's good. When I do well. Looking for solutions to problems. Kicking ass.

It's just a thought…

(If you have no idea what I'm talking about, you should probably set aside a week or so to binge-watch all fourteen seasons of *Parks and Recreation* and *30 Rock*. Then come back and read this.)

Update to my readers

March 9

I trust that most of the regular readers I had developed over the first couple of months of relatively regular posting (the ten of you) will have abandoned me by now as I have pretty much stopped posting except for the occasional shared article with brief commentary. (Number one rule of success as a blogger is, apparently, consistency.)

I am not sure of the future of the *Jenaissance*. I don't love blogging. The act of writing I love. And having people read and sometimes comment is very satisfying. But the requisite onlineness and more regular contact with The Internet (a deep, deep hole that can pull me in and, truth be told, really wreck my day) is something that I have serious trouble balancing. A day on The Internet is a day with tears. I went online today and—voila!—I cried. Children with sick mothers, sick children, soldiers and candles, animals befriending one another or saving people from fires. I should be more selective, and I have gotten much, much better about clickbait (unless it is about Taylor Swift, who knew she was such an adorable toddler?). But, for me, resistance seems futile if I allow myself to step into the world of Facebook, Twitter, Medium (which inevitably lead me to HuffPost, the NYT, Upworthy). I want connection and inspiration, but I mostly end up slightly depressed from my expeditions into the online world and drained of motivation to do the things I believe will move my life in a positive direction.

I have lots of ideas to write about, but in addition to the problem of going online, I don't love what happens to me when trying to build a blog. Checking stats, looking at traffic numbers, I get a little, obsessive?

Here I return to the thought experiment where you have a pail and a beach covered with stones and there's a limit to what fits in the bucket. So you have to choose carefully. Writing is one of the stones for me. And I think writing songs is another. And spending time with my kids while they are little. And having time to be outside. Cooking. Reading books. Singing with old friends in the middle of nowhere, dressed in the same wet clothes you've been wearing for days, with cactuses in the background and warm, squishy mud underfoot.

Dear reader, I may spend a few weeks writing stream of consciousness and putting it out into the universe. I've embarked on a journey that I'm calling project:defrag and I think allowing myself to be authentic could be helpful.

Lots of love to you, whoever you are, if you find yourself here. I believe that we can be part of creating and recognizing beauty in the world and I'm exploring what can make that possible in my life.

IN WHICH SHE GETS SELF-HELPY

Note: Hi. 2019 version of me here. The time period of April to October 2015 is tricky to deal with for the purposes of this book. For reference, I was home with the two kids, trying to find contract work to pay for the childcare that I had prearranged in order to be able to do contract work. Please pardon me for not knowing how to explain what comes next. I write briefly and with little detail about a star chart that I developed (like a sticker chart for kids but mine was for my husband and me) and shared with some friends, some of whom found it helpful, which was never completed, mostly abandoned, and never mentioned again.

I then describe a "mom opera" that I wrote by changing the lyrics to excerpts from a range of popular songs (from Temple of the Dog and Aerosmith to Judy Garland). I recorded myself, wearing a wig, singing it in my kitchen. My best friend told me that when she saw it she wondered if I had had a nervous breakdown. I changed almost all of the words, but there was a Marvin Gaye part and I've since become aware of the litigious complexities of making art based on other art (although almost all art, or in fact all art, responds to the work of the artists that came before). I was planning to leave the video on YouTube, in case you wanted to see it while I don't yet feel too embarrassed, but I don't know the laws and it costs money to obtain guidance in this matter. So I may have to take it down.

I find this section aggravating, but maybe you won't. Also, I promised to share the annoying parts, since that's part of the journey. I think it gets better again around page 65.

Mid-life makeover (or nine things that can change your life)

April 2, 2015

About 1.5 years ago I stopped working to stay home with my two kids. I did this right before winter came with its usual phlegm, vomit, and school cancellations and found that staying home with two very small children, no local extended family, a relatively weak community social network (the kind where you interact in person with living people), and little cash is a seriously tough gig. So after about five months at home, I took an offer to go back to my previous employer on a part-time, flexible basis, primarily so that I could afford to pay someone else to spend some time with my children.

I started working again (in February 2014) and within two months my outlook on life had turned rather black. I was mad at my husband, impatient with my kids, gaining weight, not exercising (this was not a change from the status quo), experiencing road rage, eating too much mac and cheese. Possibly one could say I was depressed. Maybe that's not the right word, but my best friend, on one of our infrequent phone calls, sounded the alarm bell and suggested I talk to someone. This isn't the kind of thing she normally recommends, so I paid attention. I knew something had to change, I just didn't know what could change. I guess, more than anything, I felt trapped.

So I did very little research, found a therapist who took my insurance, and started going to talk to her. I have talked to therapists before. It can be very valuable. But I didn't want to talk about my grandparents or how I got to be where I am. I wanted to make a plan, to make some changes, to spend time imagining what could be.

In lieu of therapy, I've tried a number of things over the past nine months that have contributed to the Jenaissance. In chronological order of when I tried them, rather than order of importance, they include:

1) *Hypnotherapy.* I had one session with a hypnotherapist that seemed to clear some old cobwebs. I've been trying to get an A+ from someone else for most of my life and the hypnotherapist helped me try to listen to my own inner voice. Incidentally, I made an offer to buy a house three days after my session. I had not been looking for a house. As I did not think I could afford a house, I did not have an agent. I had wanted to buy a house but there were so many reasons not to. Then I got hypnotized and now I love my house.[2]

2) *Coaching.* One reason I had not gone the coaching route initially was because therapy was covered by insurance, coaching was not. But since I was working again, and it seemed likely that I would continue to work into the future, I decided a reasonable use of some of the earnings was to figure out what I was doing and where I might want to be going. I worked with a career coach to put together a "strategic life plan" (similar to a business plan, but for your life).

3) *Reading.* I started reading blogs by James Altucher, Seth Godin, and Danielle LaPorte (among others). James A. wrote a book called *Choose Yourself* that was helpful for me. I also read *The Art of Non-Conformity* (blog by Chris Guillebeau) and a few other self-helpy / nonfictional books: *Working Identity, The Four-Hour Work Week, The Gift.* (I also started reading *War and Peace* and finished it two days ago.)

4) *Kayaking in Baja.* Here's where you roll your eyes. Who does this with two small kids, little disposable income, and a once-a-year exercise habit? My friend was turning 40. She organized a NOLS course to sea kayak in Baja, Mexico. I felt crazy and scared but I also felt a strong pull to go. This used to be me—someone

---

2 Truthfully, I have mixed feelings about my house.

who loved to be outside, who loved to be in wilderness getting dirty and eating slop that you've carted around on your own back (or in your own boat) for days. This trip was where the Jenaissance originated. I came back and knew I had to be creative, I had to be outside, I had to be myself, alive, again. I must interject, even though I mostly refrain from writing about him, that my husband has been incredibly supportive all this time and it surely hasn't been easy. Especially when I came back from Baja pronouncing that the "me" he had known for ten years wasn't the real me. Who did he marry then??

5) *Starting to blog and posting my pageant song* (also writing a story for children and starting a novel). Finding time to be creative has been hugely challenging, especially after I stopped earning a paycheck again in December (2014) and have had the responsibility of the two rugrats and the age-old restricted cash flow what with the new house, vermin, erosion, carbon monoxide, and all. That said, writing, making music, putting the pen on the paper or the words on the screen instead of just thinking about it has been hugely satisfying and I want to find more time to make all kinds of things.

6) *The Life-changing Magic of Tidying Up*. Marie Kondo's book began a shift for me that has made life feel better—it is the origin of what I've been referring to as project:defrag.

7) *Green smoothies*. I've started drinking green smoothies for breakfast, another major change. Fact is, sometimes when you feel depressed you're actually constipated. We sit at desks, we eat sugar and flour and meat and a little lettuce on the side and nothing can flow. Not ideas or the music of our souls, or poop. I'm not saying green smoothies will change this for you. But when I'm getting two cups of greens *at breakfast*, the day is just better. I feel a lot better.

8) *Exercise*. I'm walking about twice a week for thirty minutes and doing lots of yardwork and housework. That's a significant improvement, and it feels good. It's not extreme, it doesn't take a

lot of time, it could be better. But it's made a difference. If I find myself with the mean reds or if I start thinking of escape plans, a thirty-minute, child-free walk can reset the day/week for me. It needs to be outside if possible as breeze is an added benefit, and sunshine.

9) *Star Chart.* I developed a grown-up star chart for two. I'll write more to explain but I will say my husband LOVES[3] our star chart. It has made a difference in how we interact, how we spend our time, and how we feel about how we spend our time. I started it because I just wanted a star chart (I like to get stars) but this chart has strengthened our relationship, improved our lives, and been a lot of fun.

So there you have it, a list of what I've tried in the past nine months of my mid-life makeover. More details on project:defrag and the star chart to come.

Help me help you

April 7

About three months ago, I inadvertently developed a star chart for myself that has turned out to have made a fundamental difference in how I am living my life, and a few folks have indicated that they would like a star chart of their own. So I'm in the process of writing a guide to developing your own chart and I'm looking for a few volunteers to participate in a pilot group.

I haven't described much about the chart, mostly because my mom has been watching Shark Tank and I don't have this thing licensed yet. I can tell you what it is not. You won't get stars (stickers) for every tedious and oppressive to-do on your current list. You probably won't get stars for doing the dishes or laundry.

---

3 When he read this he noted that he "appreciated" the chart. "Loved" he said was perhaps too strong a word for his feelings. He was a very good sport.

You might get stars for buying new underwear, fixing a bicycle, or having dinner with friends. Nobody's star chart will look like anyone else's. The idea is that the chart can make life feel more fun, more directed, more action-oriented, and more of a team sport. It can help you have more of what you want in your life and help you figure out what that might be. And it turns out that when you spend more time doing what you *do* want, you spend less time doing what you don't want. While it's a game for two, it is not a competition. It's for learning about yourself, learning about your partner, supporting each other to have what matters to you both, celebrating progress, taking small steps, and, of course, getting lots and lots of stars.

I'm really excited about this and am looking forward to sharing and refining with some of you. And for everyone else, stay tuned for the rollout of the official (and definitely to be renamed) "Make your own grown-up star chart" in a few months'[4] time.

---

4   years. Still not available, but not abandoned.

IN WHICH SHE AGES WITH GRACE AND DIGNITY

What I did on my summer vacation

July 22, 2015 unpublished [5]
My kids have been at camp for the past few mornings leaving me, for the first time in living memory (which, as I've noted, dates back five hours from whatever time it is), in my own house, alone. Today is Wednesday. The plumber was here Monday and Tuesday fixing the bathroom sink, which has been draining into a bucket for six weeks, and also removing a live wire from the kitchen wall. But today, for about four hours, I was in my house *alone*. I accidentally locked myself out of the house and forgot to bring my kids' lunches to camp, and I had work-related calls for an hour and a half, but I had *at least* forty-five minutes of unscheduled, child-free time.

I have been waiting and preparing for these two weeks, thinking of this time as my mommy summer camp—I can do *whatever I want*. I made a giant list: clean out the basement, sign up for ebill for the utilities, go to the doctor, plant those dying azaleas, rebalance my 401k, you know—CAMP!

Then I had the 45-minute chunk of time this morning and I said *f*** it. F*** ebills and the f***ing basement. I'm making a video.* (That's how I said it in retrospect. In real time it was more like:

---

5   This is the first of several pieces that I drafted for the blog and never posted. The date represents the day I started drafting the piece. All "unpublished" entries have been edited from their original version for inclusion in the book

Hmmm…it could be fun to NOT do those other things and make a video instead. But make sure the curtains are closed so the neighbors can't see you wearing that wig.)

I've been working on this project for a few months. I write lyrics down when I think of them and a few times I've recorded it, made some changes, tried again. It's been "ready" for a couple of months but the stars never aligned. Here are the stars that have to align:

1. Kids out of house
2. Clean mommy
3. No military planes overhead, no sirens
4. Refrigerator not making that really loud sound
5. Storage available on my phone

There never seemed to be a time when all criteria were met. Introduce wig. With the wig in hand, #2 can easily be removed (and besides #1, this was always the killer).

Today all criteria were met. I recorded the video. I liked it. I was ready to publish and I hesitated. It was the pervert factor (partly)—fear that perverts are going to see this and?? Write gross comments? A brief visit to YouTube led quickly to the observation that most perverts would likely choose any number of other videos over watching an almost forty-year-old woman impersonating a singing Julia Childs in her kitchen. My husband shared my impression that a pervert would have to be into *really* weird stuff to choose this particular video out of all that is available in Interspace.

I am not sure why I am compelled to do these things. But I think, well, if I die tomorrow will I be happy that I did this? And the answer is yes. If I *do* die tomorrow, know that I had a really fun time making this. Thus, without further ado, I present the second video of the Jenaissance: Mom (Primarily Rock) Opera #1…[6]

---

6 There was further ado. I did not publish this post and I didn't share the rock opera for another five weeks.

40-til-40 countdown: mom opera

August 28

Yesterday, or possibly this morning, I had the idea for a birthday countdown where I make a list of forty things to accomplish before turning 40. I counted the days until my birthday and it turns out there are forty days—from today—until the auspicious date. As with many things in my life, I wasn't quite ready to get started. I need time to think of parameters: countdown objective, components (and so forth). In case you haven't noticed, I have the tendency to come up with lots of ideas and lists and to-dos and get a bit (ahem) overwhelmed and not always follow through.

You may also have noticed a lapse in my blogging activity of late. The star chart has taken on a life of its own, requiring a significant portion of my minimal discretionary time. The remainder of my discretionary time has gone into making another YouTube video. It's me in a wig (and wearing makeup which apparently was more surprising to some folks) singing popular songs with the lyrics changed about the trials of motherhood. I *loved* making this video.

Since finishing the opera, I'm searching (that's the positive way to put it) for a direction to my "professional" life that combines humor, performing, song lyrics, making the world nicer for more people (and also for other beings who aren't people), and writing about how we choose to spend time and what we value.

No answers are readily apparent. So for now I'm going to work on my 40-til-40 countdown. The idea is to write daily and to accomplish the forty tasks on the list (or to have fun trying). Number one was to post my mom opera on the blog. So here goes...[7]

---

7   At this point I did, in fact, post the video.

39 til 40: 85 billion bugs

August 30

Today I worked on sorting my large inbox of random pieces of paper that remind me of various things that I've been meaning to do for long periods of time (Item: clear inbox before 40).

I vacuumed every room in my house (Item: have a clean house before 40). I also changed all of the sheets and put all of the various hand-knit baby blankets in the laundry basket.

I tested a paint color in my kitchen (Item: paint kitchen wall).

I left voicemails for two long-lost friends (Item: get in touch with people who have been important to me in my first 40 years).

I bought some stuff at Whole Foods that is supposed to make your house smell better (Item: have a house that smells good by 40). It did not work well. Any pointers on good-smelling houses welcome.

I decided that some things that have been sitting around my house as to-dos are never getting done — ever — so I discarded whatever was reminding me that they were not done.

And I finished item 2, day 39 (counting backwards): buy a probiotic. I've heard lots of good things about probiotics and cultured foods and have been meaning to add something to my life: unsweetened yogurt, kombucha, sauerkraut, miso. I'm going to look into these in the future, but figured I'd like to cross into 40 with a few extra gut microflora. So hooray. Done!

38 til 40: learning experiences

August 31

Word to the wise: do not take your two small kids to Next Day Blinds when you have never in your life bought a single window treatment and it is ten minutes to closing. Because you are going to make some bad decisions, this stuff is custom made, and who knew that blinds could cost so much more from one place than from another. I thought there could be a 50% difference, for example. And unfortunately, because there was a diaper incident, I was not accessible when the bill was presented and my husband assumed that I had at least asked how much the blinds cost before charging ahead and selecting colors and giving measurements. I knew they were more expensive than blinds from Lowe's. But we've been living in this house for months with an old sarong as our bathroom curtain and a now ruined pillow sham taped over one of the windows in my son's room, and even with the ruined sham in place he wakes up at what seems like 4:30 every morning as soon as the tiniest sliver of light falls on his face (I think his superpower may be SensitivetoLight Man), so we felt that solving the window treatment problem was a high priority for overall family well-being. And I guess I felt that, at the age of nearly 40, I should not be too afraid of my inexperience to try to figure out what to do about these situations. In my bedroom there are two seven-year-old Ikea curtains from my apartment three homes ago that are at least two feet too long for the room (I'm told the puddled look is the most formal and elegant). I don't know how to go about figuring out what to put on a window—I've only rented before and there have always been shades and that's been just fine with me. I did purchase the Ikea curtains, but the investment there was so minor and the service performed (complete and total light blockage) so worthwhile and obvious.

So shades were purchased and the bill was very upsetting and unexpected and when I called back to cancel the shop was closed and it very clearly states on the receipt that, as these are custom blinds, you can't cancel your order. And it makes sense that to be *next day* blinds they would have to get to work making something pretty quickly so I guess the damage is done.

This is possibly why I seldom buy anything. I cannot deal with buyer's remorse. I think of how many hours I will need to work to pay for those blinds. Or of the other things I need or would love to have that I could have purchased with the same money.

So I'm trying to figure out what lessons I can learn. And I'm trying to figure out lots of them to make the cost worthwhile.

#1 Don't take your kids with you to buy blinds. Maybe window-shop for blinds with your kids, get ideas. Don't buy anything.

#2 Um, ask the price of something at the beginning of the conversation.

#3 To assume makes an ASS out of U and ME. How many freaking times do I have to learn this lesson? Don't assume these blinds are "a little more" expensive.

#4 It's great to try to get a lot of stuff done, but don't let it push you to make bad decisions. I don't know how this is going to work as a lesson, because the other side is to be paralyzed and never make any decisions or move forward because you are terrified of making bad decisions which is something I struggle with a little bit.[8]

That's not nearly enough lessons, by the way, to cover the cost of these blinds.

On the bright side, it will be nice when my neighbors cannot see just my bottom half (the top half is covered by the sarong curtain) when I'm in the bathroom. And if Sam sleeps for fifteen extra minutes each morning then it may well be worth it. Except that I probably could have achieved the same result by taping a garbage bag to his window which I only thought of this very minute. Oh well.[9]

---

8   more than a little bit.

9   I'm glad I didn't think of the garbage bag solution and bought the blinds. Home ownership has come with a number of unexpected expenses, but the blinds turned out to be a reasonable, functional solution. By bringing the kids to the shop we avoided months of heehawing around trying to figure out how to save some money. Hindsight says: don't make cheap the enemy of done.

37 til 40: old friend

September 1

When you are feeling blue, have a case of the mean reds, don't know what you're doing with your life, or can't quite figure out the next step you should take; If you have been eating chocolates and frostbitten ice cream sandwiches while drinking old wine straight from the bottle; If you are sitting in a cafe trying to work (because you can't work at home since your kids are there) but every song you hear makes you want to cry because how can they express life with such depth of emotion and you are once again working on another Excel spreadsheet; If you feel like you keep trying and trying to figure out the secret key, the one more thing you can do or not do to all of the sudden feel that lightness and rightness of life that you are sure is right around the corner... there's really only one antidote.

Call your friend. The one who knows the good and the bad. The one who has always been honest with you, even when it might have been something you didn't want to hear. The one who has supported you, who believes you can write a novel, or run a marathon, or take a musical theater comedy class.

When you get off the phone, nothing will be different. The dinner won't be made. The house will be a mess. One child will probably be throwing something at another. You probably won't know what the next step is. You may still have work to do on that Excel spreadsheet. Heaven knows your house will probably still smell bad, the backyard will still be eroding at a frightening rate, you will still not have discovered a magic pot of money, you will not know what you want to be when you grow up, and you will not know how you are going to do a good job helping two little kids figure out how to grow up.

But it's okay. Somebody really knows you. And after all this time, she still likes you and you still like her. Magical. After a talk like that, it's easier to take care of yourself, to be patient, to not eat those ice cream sandwiches. You need some of those talks. At least I do.

As I get older I have started to think of my oldest friends as the family that I've gotten to choose. It's a whole different category of relationship. And as part of the 40-til-40 countdown, I intend to reconnect with some folks who were highlights of the first 40 years and who I really hope will be part of my next 40.

36 til 40: finishing

September 2
A number of items on my 40-til-40 list are things that have been on my various to-do lists for months or years (finish my wedding album, for example. I've been married eight years). What's been great about this whole countdown exercise is that it's helped me get perspective and has made it easier to finish stuff. I've had a piece of paper reminding me to think about joining the North Ridge Citizens Association that has sat in a stack for over six months and I look at it every week and put it back in the stack. Ugh. So today I joined. It took less than five minutes and now I never have to look at that piece of paper again.

My secret formula is this: when something pops into my head or I see one of those "reminders" lying around (a broken appliance that I keep meaning to call about the warranty), I think *do I want to still be dealing with this when I'm 40?* If I don't then I either put it in the giveaway pile, recycle it, or DO IT. (Or I add it to the growing "Sell on Ebay" pile which has become a bit overwhelming itself and will probably be sorted pre-40 with most of it going to the donation pile because I am not going to look at that Lenox Holiday Covered Warmer (with rack) for another eight years. (Further note: I would never put a broken appliance in the giveaway pile. But I'm not sure where I would put it which is probably why I still have these broken appliances.)

There is so much unfinished business around here and not enough time in one life to finish it all. So I'm making some choices. It's good. But not always easy.

The countdown item finished today was a contract I was working on that is now complete. It feels good to finish things. Now time for sleep.

32 til 40: class

September 5

It seems like every time I post something light or funny on Facebook, or anywhere, something tragic is happening somewhere in the world that makes me feel like a total jerk for having been happy or silly that day. One of the points of starting this blog was to reconnect with my silly side and not be so heavy about everything all the time. But hells bells that is not easy in this world. At least not for me.

I have my list of forty things to do before turning 40, but when I look at the state of the world and the situations that many people are facing all of the items seem so preposterous. Which reminds me of something I've been thinking about.

I'm a recent first-time homeowner having bought a fixer-upper a little under a year ago. Since moving in lots of things have had to be fixed, lots of time has been spent figuring out how to keep the house from washing away. I sometimes walk around my new neighborhood in the early mornings and while walking I look at other homes for ideas about what we could do with our yard, what grows here, what people have done with similar houses on similar lots (our house is on a significant slope that backs up to a steep, wooded ravine).

I also have spent a bit of time in the DIY blogosphere, choosing paint colors, figuring out why it is important to get your A/C unit serviced (this is the first time I've had central A/C in years) (my A/C broke yesterday) (it is fixed now).

So here's what I've been pondering on my morning walks: Each of these families has their own little castle with their own little yard and each family works to make it look just so and spends all of this time—hours, years, lifetimes—learning how to DIY, buying furniture, choosing fabrics, colors, objects. I love being in a cheery room. I love a functional kitchen where food is cooked and people share it together. I love a beautiful garden growing sweet-smelling flowers and rosemary and all that good stuff. But we do all of this work, or pay for all of this work to be done, for one family's use. I am happy to shovel dirt, paint walls, cook food, watch kids, think creatively, whatever. I think people like to work if the purpose is clear and the work is possible and well organized. Especially if they can work together.

It feels like an awful lot of life energy goes to getting things just so for one individual family and I guess I wish that my work to build a garden was for more than just me. I think about all of the creative energy people have for decorating, redecorating, renovating their homes and wonder if some of that could be used to fix some of the myriad other problems in all of our communities, countries, continents, planets. And not in a somber way exactly, harnessing that creativity that people so clearly want to use for something other than our individual abodes.

It doesn't seem possible for me to do all that feels required as a homeowner by myself and still have any time to do anything else in the world. One question I've been asking myself is what *feels* required and what *is* required? Does my daughter need a new bed or is there a catalog picture in my head telling me that? It is pretty tough to break the programming that tells me that things need to look a certain way to show that…something. That we are good people? That we love each other? That we care about the world and other people?

In other news, and totally changing the subject, I'm behind on the countdown but have completed #5: Sign up for a class (I chose musical theater comedy). Hooray!

29 til 40: new friends

September 8

This past weekend was an extra-long, long weekend. Our A/C broke on Friday night. We had 14 cubic feet? meters? (a mountain) of dirt dumped in our front yard on Saturday morning (to fill a retaining wall we built in the backyard, down, way down, hill from the dumped pile, the plan being to, by any means possible, move the dirt from the pile to the backyard). The weekend's agenda included a wedding rehearsal dinner, a child's birthday party, and a wedding, among other items. Dave hurt his back in the midst of this and there are torrential rains predicted for thirty hours from now (I mention this because of possible implications of precipitation and gravity on dirt mountain).

Altogether, it was a great weekend. And helped me to recognize or remember a few things.

While it is important to be grateful for old friends and to appreciate the people who have known you when you were making lots and lots of mistakes earlier in life, it is also important to recognize the beauty of new friends. It can be hard for me to put energy into making new friends. I'm not in regular contact with many people who I love. Which in some ways makes putting effort into new relationships feel like a betrayal of old friends who I'm not calling, who I would love to hear from, who I would love to see.

But new friends are people who are drawn to who you are today, people who are some part of whatever circumstances you are experiencing in your life now. New friends don't love you because you've been through so much together, but because they see the person you are right now and feel like that is a person they connect with. New friends can help you become who you want to become because there is no one you have to be with a new friend but whoever you are. There are not the same expectations to live up to.

On the other hand, old friends can help remind you of the parts of yourself that you loved so much but haven't seen in a long time (old friends being the impetus for this Jenaissance in the first place). I think I've been so loyal inside myself to old friends that it has been difficult to see how necessary, how life-giving, it is to make new friends.

My thoughts about friends may not be that different to my thoughts about my things. I have all of this unfinished business hanging around my house and it's hard to begin or focus on the projects I want to do until I tidy up all of the to-dos sitting in different piles. I feel like I can't do anything new until I've dealt with the old, until there is order and all boxes have been appropriately checked. I think it is the same with friends. When there has been "disorder" or lack of contact (which there is in my case with pretty much every friend) then it feels like why make a new friend? I have all of these great shirts that I'm not wearing so why would I get a new shirt? But maybe what I really need now is a painter's smock. And those blue t-shirts are so comfortable, and I will never give most of them away, but is it possible that one or two no longer fit?

Another thought from the weekend: A good thing you can do for your marriage is to have a big dirt pile delivered to your front yard that needs to be moved to the back and to have no plan for how this is to happen other than one wheelbarrow at a time by some family member (yes, Maggie does have a wheelbarrow). Doing hard physical labor together with your partner feels nice. Even if your face gets super red from overheating. Even if at multiple times during the weekend you feel "moderately" frustrated because just what was he thinking? And also, is now really the best time to be putting together a cart, maybe better to do that, you know, before the soil came? But I appreciated the things he could do that I could not, and he appreciated that I was out there with him working my a** off. I felt like part of a team that I wanted to be on. And there's something else that's harder to put into words. I felt like I could look at myself and say "He's thinking that I'm a hard worker and he respects that and it makes him feel proud of me." He maybe didn't think those things. But I thought those things and it made me feel strong and happy. And the dirt pile got smaller. And someday we will have a small flat spot in our backyard where we can sit together and smile contentedly[10] and remember all that dirt we shoveled in wheelbarrows to make something for our kids and ourselves. It was good.

Now on to countdown items:

6) Sing with other people (I sang in a group for the recessional at my friend's wedding. It feels *great* to sing with other people (this is a scientific fact) and I rarely get the chance these days).

7) Go dancing. Also at the wedding. And my husband danced with me, even with his bad back, until I managed to join a roving band of loosely acquainted women whose partners were also for one reason or another less inclined to dance to every song. I had a blast.

8) Plant something. Yesterday I took a break from shoveling to plant a (tiny) tree in my front yard.

Also making progress on some other items: paper inbox almost completely dealt with, art almost all hung. Today I'm thinking of re-evaluating the list and making some adjustments as I am now under 30 away from 40... onwards!

---

10   contented smiling on backyard flat space still pending.

26 til 40: borrow

September 11

Dave and I were talking about Syria last weekend—talking about what we could do to take better care of the world, to make it a better place for as many beings as possible. We had a bunch of soil in our front yard that needed (needs) to be moved to the backyard and were discussing the possibility of buying a new cart with which to move the soil. Dave said he didn't want to buy the cart because it was just another eventual piece of trash to be thrown somewhere to pollute some place near where someone lives (even if the someone isn't a person). This was tied in his mind to taking more responsibility and thinking through the impacts of our actions. I agreed with the sentiment but wasn't so sure the cart was the best place to start making changes. He said you can always put off taking responsibility or making changes every day until you have lived your whole life in a bubble. Well, he said something similar to that. I respected his point. A lot. But we needed to move that dirt.

I said in my perspective the most responsible approach would be to find someone—a neighbor—from whom we could borrow a cart. My theory was/is that borrowing something weaves a small thread between you and someone else that might grow over time. And maybe someone else comes to you in the future for the proverbial cup of sugar, or maybe stevia or coconut water these days. And then you have a relationship and a community and connectedness and caring. Problem is, Dave and I are just about the last two people on earth to walk up to someone we don't know and ask to borrow something. How does that conversation start? "Hi, we're your neighbors, you may have noticed the giant pile of dirt that we've placed on our communal street. Is there any chance you have an implement that we might borrow with which to move it? We are very responsible regardless of the fact that you have seen our stroller parked on our front lawn for almost a year in all weather conditions." Doesn't sound so bad actually. I think this may be how the world works. But we just don't know how to do it.

Dave does not buy the cart. The dirt stays in the pile.

Next morning, cart is bought. Turns out it is not the right tool for the job, but the kids love riding in it and pretending it is a ship. Great tires apparently.

Two days later, a neighbor drives by with her window down. We start talking. I mention the forecast of rain. She mentions that she has some giant tarps we can borrow to cover the pile so it does not cause flooding or other catastrophes. I smile and she drives on. I'm not sure which house she lives in or what her name is. So it is pretty much guaranteed I will not be borrowing the tarps which have now been offered and are desperately needed.

NO. We will not need those tarps. We will move this soil before the rain comes As God Is My Witness. So then, um, ithrewmybackout (imagine that is typed so tiny you can't see it, I'm trying to say it fast so you don't hear me). Yep, my back is gone, I'm on the floor for the rest of the day. The soil does not get moved because now Dave has to take care of me, make the dinner, put the kids to bed, do the laundry (and whatever else it is that I do all day) and the rain is coming.

So the next day I look down the street. I see the tarp neighbor taking out her trash. I grab both kids by the hands, hobble very slowly and uncomfortably down to her house. She is inside by the time I get there and she sees me through the window and waves. I motion to her in some way to indicate that I'm there to see her. She comes out, I say something like "The dirt is still there, do you think we could possibly take you up on your offer?" She invites us in to meet her pets, she gets the tarps, puts them in a wagon, walks me home with the tarps, tells me about when she got soil delivered and how they used the tarps to make the job easier.

The rain came. The soil is still all in place and well protected except for maybe three-fourths of a cupful that washed down the hill in front of the house. There was no flooding. My back is on the mend. And I feel a little more at home on my street and in the world. It is good to let people help you and good to help people.

So #9 is a retroactive achievement: borrow something from a neighbor.

And even though this is already a lot of words today I'll report on #10: finish my wedding scrapbook. I decided I could either never do it or do it quickly so I opted for quickly since all of the materials have been sitting half-finished somewhere for almost eight years. So in about an hour yesterday and an hour today (nap time), I finished making a wedding scrapbook which will now go straight back into storage but I'm sure I will enjoy looking at it during my 50-til-50 countdown. It was a beautiful wedding and fun to spend a few minutes enjoying all of the details again.

20 til 40: moving targets

September 17
Today is the halfway point of my 40-til-40 countdown. Twenty days down, twenty to go. I have completed eleven items on the list and many more are in progress. What I've been finding is that I have time either to get stuff done or to write about getting stuff done but not both.

2 til 40: a brief and hasty reckoning

October 6
I haven't provided an update in two weeks and only hours remain until my fifth decade on earth begins. How is this possible? I remember turning 20 (somewhat hazily), but I remember lots of other stuff that happened when I was 20 like it was pretty recent

history. I don't want the next 20 years to go as quickly as the last 20 have! PLEASE SLOW DOWN!! I can't quite believe that tomorrow is the last day of my thirties. Where did that decade go? I guess I got a Masters degree, got married, changed jobs (or at least positions within the same company), bought a piano, bought a car (a VW diesel, I'm saving that for the first few raging posts of my forties), had two kids, left my job, went back to my job, bought a house, left my job again, started a blog, posted songs on YouTube, started my star chart, became an aunt (six times), lost two grandparents who both lived into their late 90s, lost my dog/soul mate, purged a significant amount of "clutter" from my life, gained weight, lost weight, laughed, cried, read *War and Peace,* watched *Arrested Development, 30 Rock, Parks and Rec, Battlestar Gallactica,* and *The Office* in their entirety, visited a bunch of different countries (the UK, France, South Africa, Spain, Poland, Germany, Denmark, Sweden, Costa Rica, Japan, Mexico, Brazil, LA), met new friends, saw old friends, cooked some new things, grew some flowers and put them in vases. I guess when I look at it this way it's been a pretty great decade. I will take some time tomorrow morning to give a full update on the countdown but never fear, progress continues (and time marches on!).

40+1 (part one): the last day of my thirties

October 8

Well, I made it here to the other side. Here's what I'd like to share: the last day of my thirties, the final 40-til-40 list, thoughts on the fifth decade. I'll start with the last day of my thirties.

I woke up, went for a walk outside and felt the wind on my skin. My skin liked it. I wished I were stronger. I thought about how much my body loves to be outside. And how I wished I had spent more of my thirties outside instead of inside, sitting, in recirculated air that rarely caresses you or whispers to you that you are alive.

I ate breakfast. I don't always do this because there are so many things to do in the morning to get everyone ready but I made the decision that for the last day of my thirties I should take care of myself. So I wasn't hungry all morning, I was patient, and I felt like someone had taken good care of me. She had, it was me.

I called my dad. At first I was going to call my mom but decided that for the last day of my thirties I would call my dad. He answered, we talked, I felt happy.

I went to the Goodwill. Trip #6 (or so) of this year full of decluttering. I hate to even write this because I know my mom will read it and she will feel like I felt. I donated some stuffed animals. Someday I will post a photo of the unreasonable number of stuffed animals that have been cohabitating with my family. We had a day during the 40-til-40 where the kids and I decided which (fewer than required but it's a first step) should go to new homes. One pair we gave away was a mother monkey with a baby and they sit together and can attach by velcro. I watched the man at the Goodwill empty the bag of animals into a giant crate and saw the two monkeys separate and I guess they will never be together again. Someone will always wonder what the velcro was for on each monkey, and why the mother monkey has a big space in her arms but nothing to hold. I don't know when I got those monkeys but I don't remember not having them. I felt that chest-tugging feeling watching them separate and wished they were still here, collecting dust together. It made me want to buy less and less because figuring out how to dispose of things that you don't need is complex and has taken up too much of my life already. I also felt a feeling about the fact that I was there discarding more bags of stuff and a man was there dealing with my stuff and I thought about the lottery of life that made me the one with so much to donate and him the one sorting through other people's clutter and it… felt.

I bought a dress for my daughter. I saw it there, hanging outside of the consignment shop. It was brocade. Real, beautiful fabric. It was a costume for an eight-year-old (she's four). There was no picture of a Disney princess on it. I walked away once but I wanted it so much for her, and probably for me, so I bought it for us for my birthday. I thought about clutter, about budgets, about materialism. I remembered the hundreds of hours I spent playing in my mother's and grandmothers' beautiful old clothes and I bought it. The lady at the store gave me $10 off, just because. Happy Birthday to me.

Then I went to the vintage clothing store where I have frequently window-shopped but never entered. I decided that, for the last day of my thirties, I'd like to play dress-up too. I tried on a dress from the forties, one from the fifties, two from the sixties—dresses made for women's bodies. Not for girls' bodies and not for hungry people. I felt feminine and sexy in those dresses and I bought three for about $100. I may never buy another non-vintage dress again.

I had a BLT for lunch on the last day of my thirties. It was incredibly satisfying. I am trying to eat less meat, and to eat meat only from sources that I know are humane and sustainable, but that BLT made my heart sing. Food is delicious when you pay attention.

I sat outside on my deck for the first time ever (I have lived in this house for almost a year now) and drank a cup of tea. It was peaceful and beautiful. I wrote an email to my first "true love." Writing to him had been a to-do in the back of my mind since he wrote to me, six years ago, after my dog/soul mate went to doggie heaven. Writing the email took five minutes. Again, I felt, not sure what but definitely something.

I took my daughter to ballet. She is still learning to listen[11] and I struggled a bit with my response to her behavior. I felt frustrated

---

11   as am I.

and angry and knew that I shouldn't. I was tired and hungry and thirsty. We went to the grocery store. I tried to get back into a good frame of mind. It was challenging.

We came home and made tacos. I had never made tacos in my own home as an adult. We had an amazing dinner. The kids loved putting their own toppings on, we had great conversation, everyone was hungry and happy and then we had my favorite ice cream (hubby bought it as a birthday treat and suggested we have it early).

I cleaned the toilets, changed all the sheets (as a birthday present to myself), baked a birthday cake (chocolate soufflé cake), finished the last items of my paper inbox, and crashed in bed around 11.

When I woke up I was 40.

40+1 (part two): the final list

October 8
Here's what I completed in my 40-til-40 countdown, in order of accomplishment so you can see the ones I crammed in at the end:

1. share mom opera
2. buy a probiotic
3. call Sarah
4. finish contract
5. sign up for a class (musical theater comedy)
6. go dancing
7. sing with other people
8. plant something
9. borrow something
10. finish wedding scrapbook
11. visit with Claire
12. send birthday invitation
13. remove tree stump from front yard, make garden bed

14. make dinner reservation—Inn at Little Washington
15. buy a new bra, dispose of old nursing bra
16. responsibly dispose of all poison we inherited when we bought this house
17. dinner with Becky
18. discard shirts with holes (refined to be more than one hole in a noticeable place) (some of these had already been mended, blog about featherweight cotton in a future post)
19. hang all art (Dave did most of this, but I instigated)
20. paint kitchen wall
21. go to the dentist
22. get a facial
23. go to high tea
24. book a ticket to celebrate 40s with college roomies
25. wash sofa slipcovers
26. make chocolate soufflé
27. buy new socks (super easy, makes a huge difference)
28. drink tea on my deck in the sunshine
29. buy a Barbra Streisand cd (*On a Clear Day* soundtrack). Why have I spent so much of my adult life without show tunes?
30. plan and shop for birthday dinner
31. listen to all voicemail
32. buy an old/new dress; play dress-up
33. email first love
34. clean toilets
35. change all sheets
36. clean out paper inbox of to-dos that have been accumulating for years. (Note: Inbox zero is an *amazing* feeling. I keep being surprised when I look at that space and there are no unmade decisions staring back at me.)

There were more than 40 items on the list because I wasn't sure what would/could get done. The ones that remain that I'd like to complete in the first 40 days of 40 are:

37. photo book of Sawyer (golden retriever soul mate who went to doggie heaven the year before Maggie was born)

38. frame katydid picture (I have a species of katydid named for me (!), *Brachyamytta mccolloughae,* and I've wanted a framed picture in my home since it was named in 2008).
39. buy tickets to see a show (I have a plan)
40. buy an outside compost bin (Dave gave me the kitchen compost bucket for my birthday, just need the outside bin)
41. plant a camellia
42. list remaining items on eBay (not much to go)[12]
44. buy new underwear
45. plan summer road trip

So that's it! I will share some thoughts on the whole exercise next[13] but my kids will definitely be awake soon.

The Jenaissance turns one

November 4

Somehow the universe sent me a message tonight to check the date of the first blog post of the *Jenaissance* and — what do you know — TODAY is one year exactly from the birth of this blog. I, of course, feel this needs to be marked by at least a tiny post acknowledging the fact and reflecting, just a bit, on what has changed over the course of the year.

Has the blog been a good thing? Have I learned anything? Had fun? Lost friends? Damaged my reputation? Made bad decisions? Embarrassed anyone (other than myself)? Been destroyed by online criticism? Been stalked by perverts?

Will I continue blogging? Why?

Hmmm… (thinking, thinking, I have to write this quickly and there is a certain urgency that it be posted today as the date is rather critical to the nature of the post). YES. That is the answer

---

12   still working on this.

13   Never wrote out the thoughts on the whole exercise. The only notes I have are these five words in a draft post that was meant to come next: Outside, Music, Tasting Food, Body. Wish I had a few more words to go on.

to the question about whether the blog is a good thing. The blog helped me to leave a job that I needed to leave. The blog helped me to record a song and post the video on YouTube. The blog gave me an outlet of expression. The blog drove the creation of my 40-til-40 countdown.

Learned anything? Trickier question. I've learned that I can't write for my Facebook friends. And that if I don't share posts to Facebook that I can be more authentic. If I have in mind that I'm writing for that audience, or if I think about who might be reading, I get all locked up and can't hear my own thoughts. But if I think of one good friend who loves me, or just listen closely and write what feels true at the moment, I am happy when I read the post later. Sometimes. And sometimes I read later and wish I had edited more closely, or not said that in that way. But mostly when I read what I wrote I feel like I can hear myself (better than I can during the rush of most days) and that I—gasp—like myself. I can recognize who I am and I'm okay with who she is. When I'm surrounded by all of the rush and busy and undones and measuring, I can feel like I'm not enough. But when I read what I wrote a year ago, I'm okay with me. I like that girl.

Had fun. Yes. The mom opera was the best part. I've loved some of the sillier posts and I want to write more like that. But I have to feel it and I have to be connected with a particular muse and most days have more of the trudge elements. It's a challenge to keep the silly spark lit. But I really want to.

Lost friends. None that I can directly attribute to blogging, but it's not unfathomable. It's possible that there are people who would have invited me to their birthday party one year ago when I had not publicly exposed myself as whatever it is that I am. I don't mean any disrespect to whoever disapproves or thinks I'm weird/self-centered/a bad mom/whatever it is, but I'm okay if we aren't friends. I don't know who you are and I'm guessing you aren't reading this because you disapprove. I wish you all the best and I hope you have a lovely birthday party. But I think blogging helped me decide that I need to be me and stop trying quite so hard to be what I'm guessing everyone else expects of me.

Guess that's tied in to reputation—I'm not sure what my "reputation" would have been. Hard-working, serious person who cares about the world and does what is expected. I can accept a and c but I needed to change b and d. I'm not saying I have to do what is unexpected, or that I can't be serious, but (see paragraph above).

Bad decisions. Paying $15 to get those jeans patched a second time may not have been a great decision (time will tell). Also, I've mentioned the expensive blinds. We bought the house BB (before blogging) so that is not under consideration here. Otherwise, I'm sure there have been choices that, with perfect information, I would have made differently. But I can't really think of any regrets specifically related to the blog, or really regrets about anything important since I started blogging.

Embarrassed anyone? The only possibility—I think—would be my husband but he's been pretty supportive. My kids can't read yet, nor can their friends. I am sure they will be embarrassed in the future, but that's a given no matter what I do, right?

Online criticism? Well, first of all people have to read your work to criticize, so I'm relatively protected there. Most of my comments come, I believe, from people paid to leave comments on blogs. I haven't figured out who these people are, or who is paying them, but pretty much every comment I receive, unless it is from a relative or close friend, I assume is coming from someone who is being paid to surf blogs and leave comments. This is primarily because the username is something like *RayBan Outlet: I love your blog* or *FastAbsNow: I looking for many times at good content of yours. This for my report helps* or *Online SEO: Hi. Your site could get a lot more traffic if you follow this one tip…* So, if you're curious, I haven't had any slanderous comments yet. I guess we build to that.

Perverts? None that I know of. But I was pulled over today by a policeman for a moving violation, which I did, in fact, commit. (I saw that it was a turn lane, but it looked like there was a police car parked to the right so I couldn't figure out where the straightahead lane was and I was busy singing *Wicked* at the top of my lungs. Turns out the police car wasn't parked there. He was in the straightahead lane.)

Why mention this with perverts? Well, after he didn't give me a ticket he asked for my number. And he also wrote it on a separate piece of paper, like a blank piece in a little notebook from his pocket. Not the same notebook he had been using to write all of the other information. But I clearly had on a wedding ring and had two car seats in the back of my VW. I'm sure he needed the number for an official reason. Or maybe he thought I was driving my sister's car? (This just occurred to me, I had mentioned I was on the way to pick up my sister's child.) And wearing my sister's ring? No, he needed the number for an official reason and is not going to turn Ray Liotta on me (note to millennials—this is a reference to the film *Unlawful Entry*). Otherwise, that is including today's episode, no perverts noted. (He was a very nice, respectful policeman. I'm just unclear about the number is all.)

Yes, I will continue blogging. When or why? Don't know. I'm kind of enjoying just writing when life allows and when I am moved to do so. I'm not writing to make money. I'm not building a list or going in any particular direction. I don't know exactly what "happy" is but I'm more comfortable in my own skin, more at peace than I was one year ago and that feels like a good thing.

So Happy Birthday *Jenaissance*. Thank you.

jenny rising

IN WHICH SHE CASTS ABOUT FOR MEANING

A somewhat incoherent letter to the universe, and Leigh

April 14, 2016

Hi there. Me again. It's been a while. Once you've stopped doing something on a semi-regular basis and the gap in time starts to grow, it feels like you have to do something great if you want to start again. Make some huge commitment or declaration. It starts off as pressure to write something a little clever, clever grows into meaningful, which turns into spectacular eventually. Or at least coherent, with a clear narrative and direction. *I have to tell them what the plan is—and it needs to be good.*

The question that I ask myself next is: *who is this THEM*, this imagined audience to whom I write? At first I thought (a few minutes ago), just write to the universe. Tell the universe what you're thinking, what might be next. Then I reminded myself that at least one friend has added the blog to her RSS feed. So hi Leigh, I'm either writing this for you, or for the universe.

So Leigh and universe, since we haven't had many chances to talk recently, here's what's up. I'm planning to start blogging again. I'm actually planning to start some kind of business. Here's the thing: I have ideas (lots of ideas) about things to write, things to learn, stuff to discover, tools to develop and share. I think some of these things would be interesting and helpful to other people. I want to do the work. I love doing work, truth be told. I like connecting with other people. I see a huge need in the world (who doesn't!) and I'd like to contribute my tiny spark. And in some way help other people contribute their tiny sparks too. The question I keep running up against is in what way is this a business?

I'm not going to put advertising on a blog. I get really annoyed every time some giant ad from a website I was just visiting pops up when I'm trying to figure out how to get my sink to drain or read about what lice look like (coast is clear). Yes, it is a company I purchase from, I will come to you when I need something, please don't put your ads on every page I visit, particularly if you sell lingerie.

Here's my reality: I need to earn some money during the time I spend not taking care of my kids. And the even shorter-term reality is that I have to get my kids in thirty minutes (from now). So I would like to figure out a way to create a business and "do what I love," but I love a lot of things, some are more useful to other people than others, and I haven't quite figured it out.

I'm going to start writing again. Initially on the *Jenaissance* blog but the larger plan is to start something new, with some particular direction and clarity. I have some ideas involving heroes and villains, board games, star charts, checklists, tools, upcycling, philosophy, books, money, clutter, America, the world. Among others. Maybe music and video too.

Now I'm going to throw something out there that is not well developed but is a tiny seed. I've had in my mind something that I read in an essay, "On Freedom," by Einstein. He writes of two goals that he thinks most people would agree on, the second being:

2. The satisfaction of physical needs is indeed the indispensable precondition of a satisfactory existence, but in itself it is not enough. In order to be content men must also have the possibility of developing their intellectual and artistic powers to whatever extent accord with their personal characteristics and abilities.

I read this at the beginning of winter, soon after the experience of the 40-til-40 countdown. It has been whispering to me since then. When I read it, I wondered what is it that gets in the way of developing intellectual and artistic powers? I presumably have my essential physical needs met, so where are the barriers for me? Where are the barriers for my neighbors? And where are the cultural barriers to figuring out systems that meet both the first and the second type of needs for more people?

I'm not being clear about this here, but I wanted to put it out there to you, vast universe, and you too Leigh, and to work and wait and watch and listen and cook and plant and clean and practice patience and show love (I'm practicing showing love) and keep putting words down and looking for teachers and learning new things and nursing the spark and hoping that you are nursing your spark too.

Jane Goodall's advice: How to raise curious children

April 25

I'm not sure whether or not Jane Goodall has ever explicitly provided parenting advice. However, her remarks during a recent talk at a high school here in Alexandria suggest that she feels she was well parented and that this had something to do with what she was able to do in life. I was not in attendance (I was not invited nor did I know she was going to be in town) (I have never met her, but I did once take a picture of myself with her in the background, it was kind of a big deal for me) but I happened to read the front page of the local newspaper, the *Alexandria Times*, which provided a brief review of Dr. Goodall's remarks. I kept thinking of her words as I sat over the course of about an hour, rocking my three-year-old son in a desperate bid to get him to nap, while he stuck his fingers in my nose, among other incivilities.

The article's author Chris Teale writes:

> *Goodall recalled how, at just one-and-a-half years old, she collected*

a handful of earthworms and soil and took them with her to bed. In
an indication of her mother's support that would last throughout
her life, Goodall said she was not disciplined at all. 'Instead of
getting mad at me, she said, "Jane, I think they'll die; they need
to go back into the garden"' Goodall said. 'So we carried them
carefully back.'

(Brief aside: I've been parenting on the assumption that specific memories don't kick in until around age four. I was not aware of the fact that my actual words would be quoted back to me in this manner. Though Jane Goodall is presumably smarter than the average chimp (groan) so maybe not representative of most kids and maybe the dates here are being generalized to mean, say, younger than four.)

Later in the article, Teale writes

She shared how at the age of four, she stayed with her grandmother
for a time and tried to observe hens laying eggs to understand
where they came from. For four hours, she sat silently and watched,
having learned that disturbing the hens would scare them away.
'Isn't that the making of a little scientist?' she asked. 'Curiosity,
asking questions, not getting a right answer, deciding to find
out for yourself, making a mistake, not giving up and learning
patience. It was all there in that little four-and-a-half-year-old
child, and a different kind of mother might have crushed that
scientific curiosity and I might not be standing here now.'

So, I think what Jane is saying is that when my son has a toy and he takes it apart, instead of putting it on the NO shelf (usually reserved for toys that are used to hit his sister), I should sit down with him and ask him to show me what he's learned? Or when my daughter shouts "There's a rainbow on the ceiling!" I should say "Wow, I wonder how that got there? What do you think?," instead of explaining that light is a wave and when it hits a new medium the speed of the wave changes and the light is bent (that is me quoting another grown-up who lives in my house, I cannot explain the rainbow but I usually try).

During my pre-nap rocking extravaganza, I tried to think of a few principles of parenting based on these two little snippets from Jane's life and my several years' experience raising two kids in America. These are in no way endorsed by Dr. Goodall. And my oldest child is five, so what do I know? But here's a stab:

Don't answer all of a child's questions. Show interest, and ask questions back. And give her some independence and latitude to discover things on her own. A child should be allowed to make mistakes and to not know.

Let kids make a mess. My kids have somewhere picked up the idea that they are not allowed to make a mess. Why is that this great fear? You can clean up a mess but if you are too afraid of spilling, of going outside the lines, of breaking anything, how can you create anything or learn anything? Speaking of breaking anything, we (I'm talking about Americans here) have these houses filled with all of this s**t and if one headphone on a talking car breaks off the child is chastised: Johnny (not his real name), what were you thinking? We have seven million objects in this house all crammed into a variety of organizational systems and you dared to try to see if those headphones could come off of one. Don't you know it is supposed to look just like it looked when we took it out of the box, forever! To the dungeon! How could you disrespect this tiny piece of crap? I will crush your spirit. (2a. Let them clean up their own mess. Not based on Jane. Just if they are going to make a mess, they should also learn to clean up that mess. In a nice way.)

Leave time for boredom. I'm guessing that if little Jane had owned an iPad then she wouldn't have been watching those chickens. Or if she had needed to get to soccer practice that morning. Boredom is a wonderful invitation to explore or create something new and most kids I know are being taught that it is somebody or something else's responsibility to find a "cure" for their boredom. My mom always said *boredom is a lack of using your own imagination.*

Maybe that's an old-fashioned way of shaming a kid for saying she's bored, but it sure worked. I would NEVER have admitted to being bored, it was like acknowledging that I was not very imaginative. I hear kids (mine included) saying they are bored like it is someone else's problem or fault. Let them be bored and then see the first two points above.

Teach kids to be thoughtful and kind by being thoughtful and kind. Jane's mom could have said something like this: *Valerie Jane Morris-Goodall, how could you bring all of that dirt into this house? And into your bed? Disgusting. Now your sheets will be all covered with slime. You take those worms and you put them in the trash right this minute.* Instead, she indicated that she cared about what happened to the worms. It was this concern for the worms that motivated her action. I'm down with that (kudos, Margaret).

At almost all times, children should be dressed in clothing that can get dirty. I heard a teacher say to a little girl who was climbing up some rocks at my son's school: *Susie* (not her real name), *get down, you'll get your clothes all dirty.* (Cue inner fury! WHAT?!) The clothes do not matter. The learning does. For the love of everything, don't tell a little girl not to climb on rocks that were put there specifically for climbing! Her body was in no danger, just the fabric meant to protect her so she was comfortable enough to learn to explore, to learn what rocks feel like under her hands. Buy children's clothing at thrift stores and let them play! They should be getting dirty! I'm not sure what this has to do with Jane except that I'm guessing nobody was stressing about her UGGs getting wet.

Love the kid you have. (I got this one from my mom earlier this week when complaining about the recent behavior of one of my children.) Maybe Jane's mom wasn't into wildlife. Maybe she wanted a little ballerina. But she let Jane play with worms and chickens because that was who Jane was. To quote Kahlil Gibran: *Your children are not your children, they are the sons and daughters of life's longing for itself.* I should probably put that on my dresser and read it every morning when I wake up. Don't worry so much about what people will think about what your kid does. Love your kid. Get to know her. See what brings him to life. See what makes her laugh. Let more of that be in your life.

Finally, I have to acknowledge that many parents may not be interested in raising little scientists. If the risk of fostering curiosity, respect, and kindness is that my kids might end up living with apes and teaching the world things about our closest relatives that we never knew before, I'm honestly a little nervous about it. Maybe it is safer to raise a little investment banker or a little reality TV star. Maybe if we protect them from curiosity and exploration then they can be as happy as we are in our 4 BR, 2.5 BA w a newly renovated kitchen.

But I think the world would be a nicer place for our little munchkins, for munchkins everywhere, if there were more people in the world like Jane Goodall. How nice to think of a world where a child is given space and time to to get to know herself, to find herself capable, and to ask questions of and interact with the world, in her own way, at her own pace. Maybe little Suzy (not her real name) might grow up to help us all to better understand the world and our place in it.

Note to self: you will never reach your potential

May 3
There is a fair amount of self-help out there detailing how one can do it all, be it all, live the life you have imagined (and so on, etc.). I respectfully disagree.

You and I will never reach our potential. What potential exactly do you have in mind? Your potential when you were five years old? Your potential today? Your potential ten years from now? The thing about potential is that it keeps changing. Let's say today I have the potential to write a song. So I write a song. Then I probably have the potential to write an album. So I write an album's worth of songs. Then I have the potential to record, go on tour. Then I could start a recording label. Then I could sign one hundred other artists to my label. Then I could fund music education for kindergarten students across the state, the country, the world. Then I could teach chimpanzees to play the flute.

As soon as you've done something, taken action and made something real, your potential expands from there. So the more you do, the more potential you have to do other things, creating a never-ending loop of needing to do even more to meet your new and improved potential. Did Einstein reach his potential? Or with each new accomplishment did he create a whole lot of untapped potential?

I'm writing this because I was feeling kind of ornery about "not reaching my potential." But in considering this I realized that I don't believe anyone who speaks to me in terminology centered around helping me to reach my potential. So I should stop feeling dreary about this abstract, limitless concept that only references what is not yet and what is always beyond reach, no matter what. There is no need, no benefit, to using imagined possibilities that are always changing, and completely theoretical, as a lash, or a yardstick to evaluate how I measure up to a myth.

Instead, I can do one of two things:

I can look at what I can do today, take some small action to grow, enjoy that action if possible, be thankful for the ability to do the action and for whoever supported me to take the action. Repeat. Don't worry so much about the potential as about the moment, the step I can take today.

Alternately I can recognize that whatever "potential" I feel I have is based in part on what I have done already. I've done some things, I can feel happy to have had those opportunities, appreciative of the people who supported me (and those who criticized me and helped me to learn). I can sit down somewhere, drink a cup of tea, take some breaths, appreciate what's happened so far and enjoy the fact that I will never reach my potential for a few minutes.

I'm not saying don't try or don't work. I'm not saying don't use your gifts. I'm not saying to whom much is given, from her little is expected. I'm removing the abstraction of potential so that my feelings are less manipulatable by eager marketers, by people trying to motivate me through the tension of feeling less than enough. I will be thankful for the work I can do. I will do my best. Don't be trash-talking me about potential. I'll let the universe decide about that.

I will never reach my potential.

I can never reach my potential.

I don't have to worry about reaching my potential.

It feels kind of liberating.

Maybe it's just me but I feel better already.

Now maybe I'll sit down and write that song.

IN WHICH HER HEAD IS BURIED
DEEP IN SAND

41 til 41: *another year older*

August 28, 2016

I'm a day late, but have decided to do another countdown this year. I debated whether to try this for 41 so I revisited the list of tasks completed for the 40-til-40 countdown last year. Most of what I feel good about accomplishing last year either happened during that countdown, or was inspired by it, so I figure it's a pretty good exercise for me.

I have no idea what the list might include this year. The idea is to accomplish 41 tasks that are related to my intentions for my 42nd year. I think about what matters and what will put my/our life in a good place for the next year and try to clear the decks and prepare and introspect (whatever the verb is for that—it isn't reflect because I'm not thinking back, I'm thinking forward/now but internally). I won't come up with the list today, and I'm a day late starting, and I've got a ton of contract work to do between now and September 15, but the will is there, so let's see what I can do.

19 til 41: *not giving up yet*

September 18

Haven't managed to make any progress on the 41-til-41 count-down. The first days of kindergarten and life in general have proved to be all I can manage in the past couple of weeks. There's been a heavy feeling in my gut every time I watch that tiny little thing walk off with her backpack all on her own, so proud and so independent. I miss her. And also thank goodness she's in school because she and her brother were about to make me lose my mind. But I really miss her.

I was thinking about how to devise a list for the countdown, what the principles could be. I wrote down what I want more of in my life and what I want less of:

More: wind, mountains, oceans, breathing, music making, writing, good smells, experiments, showing love, laughing, cleanliness, celebration, routine, family meetings, chores for kids, sunshine, movement, nurture

Less: shouting, back pain, debt, saying things I don't mean, undone (undone are things you encounter, a physical object or in your mind, that remind you of a decision that you haven't made or a thing you haven't done)

I thought about making a list of tasks to increase one group and decrease the other but haven't managed to do this yet. What have I managed to do?

1. Clear off the top of the piano
2. Plant fall lettuces
3. Unwrap wooden spoons and put in drawer for using
4. Make bouquets from yard-grown flowers
5. Go to the native plant store
6. One family meeting/family star chart
7. Try two new recipes (ham+cheese strata, apple crisp)
8. Buy new cleaning supplies

Other ideas for to-dos in the next 19 days:

· house plants
· some kind of aromatherapy diffuser or those sticks (look into healthy options)

- make apple cider vinegar toner[14]
- bath fixtures
- new sheets
- go for a walk
- backyard beds (choose plants)
- plant front yard plants
- do a tour to find undones—make a list and move the objects

So 41 - 8 = 33 and 33/19 = 1.7. Doable but the next couple of weeks are going to be pretty intense work-wise so I may have to be creative.

12 til 41: small steps

September 25

A few more items (completed) to add to the list:

9. Disassemble faded, crumbling wedding bouquet. Compost most of it. Take dried lotus pods and arrange them in vase on dresser. LOVE IT.
10. Clear planting beds in backyard of weeds/ivy
11. Wash Snoopy and clothes (mine from childhood)—now stink-free and usable
12. Dance with kids. Sam loves "So Lonely" (Maggie used to call it Salami)
13. Connect speakers to stereo (so we can listen to old records)
14. Clean grandmother's tea cart and bring up from basement (still not sure where it will live)
15. Fix: bubble shooter, fan, maraca, ladybug nightlight, toy workbench, black table knob, Miss Kitty

And a few more ideas:

- hang wind chime
- replace basement windows
- make a boat with Maggie

---

14 Note from future me: this stuff goes bad pretty quickly. White + cloudy = bad.

- clear and remove basement to-do shelf
- have a tea party with Maggie and Sam

So, current tally: 26 to go / 12 days = 2.16 per day to get to 41.

I'd like to be more thoughtful about this, but I do feel like there is good change happening at our house lately. Clearing off the top of the piano or turning the old bouquet into something that I love to see rather than something that every time I see it I wonder what I'm going to do with it—when I see these changes, every time still, I feel a good feeling, instead of a heavy feeling.[15]

I recently finished reading *Spark Joy: An Illustrated Master Class on the Art of Tidying* by Marie Kondo. It was helpful and gave me some good ideas. I've also been inspired in the past few months by *Zero Waste Home* by Bea Johnson and have been working to make some changes (more buying bulk has stuck so far).

Now to switch gears and try to finish some actual (i.e., paid) work.

---

15   I still feel this good feeling every time.

POP!

October 30, 2016 unpublished

On Thursday afternoon I was standing in my kitchen. My laptop battery was running low so the computer was plugged in while I searched on Amazon(Smile) for an aromatherapy diffuser and a small Lego City submarine, an enticement for my son to use the toilet. I had just sent my sister an email about a Christmas gift idea for our nieces and had finally made an appointment to have the tree people look at the gaping hole left in an oak in my front yard after one of its enormous limbs fell several months ago, to seek advice on the three remaining limbs that loom uncomfortably close to several homes, including my own.

I was in checkout mode on Amazon. Making sure I had two-day shipping selected because I needed that potty prize asap. My kitchen is on the back of our house. It's pretty small—you can stand in the middle of the kitchen and, if you stretch, your leg could touch the sink, the fridge, the oven, and any of the three doors (one to the basement, one to the deck just outside of the kitchen, one to the dining room). And the outlet I was using is near the sink, which looks through two windows out onto the deck, which looks out onto a bunch more oak (and tulip poplar and maple) trees in a wooded ravine, an unusual situation for a house three miles from the Pentagon. There's a family of foxes living in the ravine, box turtles, salamanders—it is actual woods.

The windows aren't covered. When we bought the house the kitchen featured horse-print curtains to match its horse-print tile. I removed the curtains, probably the first day we owned the house. I think we signed the mortgage then drove directly to the house and took those curtains down. I love(d) my kitchen windows. Our dishwasher has been broken for a month and I've spent quite a bit of time looking out at the trees and feeling like I'm in a treehouse.

The only time I don't like the windows is at night when my husband is traveling and I'm home alone with the kids. When I walk in the kitchen alone in the dark I try not to look at the windows because I've always feared that one night I'm going to see Jack Nicholson looking in with that Shining face. My heartbeat speeds up. I avert my eyes.

But this was afternoon. About 12:35. I know the time because I had a physical therapy appointment at 1:00 and I was trying to productively use the few minutes remaining before we needed to leave the house. We were also going to pick up my new contacts, so I figured we should leave by 12:45 since I had Sam with me and we'd need to find parking, negotiate hand holding, stop to look at any skeletons or giant spiders along the way. So this Amazon(Smile) purchase was my last thing.

The laptop was about 18 inches from the sink. The sink looks directly out across the deck which is reached by a steep flight of stairs. I was typing on the laptop. And there was a knock on the window. On the window on the deck at the back of my house. On Thursday at 12:35 in the afternoon. The lights were on. Our car was parked in front of the house. My three-year-old son was playing in the den. I looked up and there was a man/boy. He was wearing a hoodie sweatshirt. He was panting a bit and he walked towards the deck door that leads into the kitchen, it's top half an old, thinly paned window. Holding on to the doorknob, he told me he needed to get into the house. Something like: *I need you to open the door. I need to get inside.* Me, my mind racing to understand the situation: *I'm not going to let you into the house.* Sort of like if my daughter had asked if she could jump on my head, that same tone: *I'm not going to let you jump on my head.* He walked back towards the window (two steps). We were face to face with about 20 inches between us. About eye level.

Can you open the door? Some guys tried to jump me. I just need to get a ride home—I live over by TC Williams High School. Can you let me in? He looked at the door. At the suddenly very thin piece of wood and glass separating this breathing man/boy—much stronger than my PT-needing self and my tiny son—from the inside of my fortress. He's sweating. His story seems plausible.

I'd like to help you (I say), *but I can't let you in the house. There are some men in the house next door—a group of men* (there are workmen renovating the house next door). *Why don't you go over there—they can help you. But I can't let you in here. I'm a woman, with a child.*

I'm sorry. He said this after I mentioned being a woman with a child. I specifically remember his apologizing at that point.

Can I just sit here for a minute and call my mom?

Sure, I say, *that would be fine.*

He looks scared, or not sure what to do. I think about the guys who are chasing him and what they want or what the situation is. So then I say: *I can call the police if you want me to.*

No, he says—too quickly. And I think, well, maybe he's nervous about police. Lots of people are nervous about police. Or maybe he's selling drugs and the guys chasing him are trying to steal from him. But he looks like a kid. Like a regular, sweaty and nervous, kid.

He picks up his phone—I don't hear him talk to anyone—and then he's gone. I don't know where he went. I didn't know if I believed his story. And I didn't want this brown-skinned boy to think that I suspected him of something. I wanted him to know that any sweaty young man who had come and knocked on my deck window, at the back of my house, asking to be let in, would have been offered the same treatment. So I didn't watch where he went because I didn't want him to see me peeking through the curtains that cover the other windows of the house. Our basement door is made of rotten bark and a half millimeter of 40-year-old glass. It would take a plastic sandbox rake to break that door. I did take one tiny peek, just trees.

I was supposed to leave the house to go to my appointment. I didn't know if I should call the police. I called my husband. He said to go to the car, go to the appointment, to come get him at his office afterwards and he would check the house to make sure everything was okay.

About eight minutes had passed since the incident. I did not see the man/boy anywhere. Across from our house is a house of two sisters—both over 80. One house next to them is empty, as is the house under renovation next to me. My neighbors on the other side were in Jamaica for a wedding. Diagonally from me is another woman over 60. Hers is the only phone number I have.

I put shoes on my son. We stood at the front door: *Sam, I need you to be a good listener when we go outside. If anything happens I want you to run to Eva's house. Knock on the door and go inside.* He looked at me, somewhat solemnly, and out we went.

On the way to my appointment I thought about my neighbors. I thought, if there are bad guys chasing a man/boy and they are in my neighborhood, the police can help protect my elderly neighbors, my out-of-town neighbors. I thought: I should probably have called the police. But more as a future note to self. I still didn't call the police, didn't call a neighbor.

I heard someone honking for a long time—a held down, consistent HOOOOOOOOOOOOOOOOOONK. I realized it was the person driving directly on my tail after I had made a right-hand turn. I must have done something wrong but I'm not sure what. I was looking around at life in slow motion, seeing all of the people on their way to get a coffee, or buy some cheese or a birthday card, leaving yoga class, walking their dogs. Expecting life to keep on the way it is supposed to. Thinking about getting a new sofa, or replacing the shutters, or frustrated because their phone is running low on storage space again. Life goes on and we—some of us—

expect safety, predictability, invulnerableness. We live inside our bubble, there is a blip and we see the edge, then time passes and we securely live back inside, worrying that Maggie's Halloween costume, a tail-less dragon, will make it obvious that we didn't spend that much time being creative this year. How hard is it to figure out how to make a tail, after all?

After the appointment, during which my son was reintroduced to Elmo via my phone, much to his delight, we collected my husband from work and drove home. As we were turning the corner to our street we saw a police car and, further down the road, an officer with a dog. My husband suggested I speak with the officer so I walked over to his car and told him about my visitor. He called the sergeant and they both came to our house about ten minutes later. I tried to wash the dishes when I saw them pull up. Dishes from breakfast and lunch were lining the counter and I didn't want the policemen to come in and see how messy it was. I washed two plates before the doorbell rang. I started to tell the story again in my kitchen. The sergeant interrupted me midway to ask if I knew what had happened after 12:35. Here's what I heard him say: A block away from me one man/boy entered my neighbor's house around 2:00 in the afternoon. The neighbor, a woman, was at home, alone. Her neighbor saw someone open her back door and go inside. That, observing, neighbor called the woman at home alone. I didn't get any details after that but it seemed like the intruder had left, the woman was okay, the police were looking for the intruder and they wanted a description of the man/boy at my window to see if it was similar, which it was.

My son, at this point, was so engrossed in watching Elmo on my phone that he failed to notice the two policemen standing inside our house, talking to me in the kitchen. At any other point in time this would have been one of the highlights of his year. He was sitting on the sofa, three feet from the front door where the two policemen, in full uniform, walked into our house. He didn't look up. At no point were the real live policemen in our house more alluring than Elmo and his four ducks.

It turns out the woman intruded upon at home had not locked her door. The intruder had turned the handle and walked in. When he realized someone was there, he ran away. It has been suggested that his profuse sweating was likely related to drugs.

One part of me feels dumb for maybe believing his story and telling him *I'd like to help, but you can't come inside.* But maybe he was a kid who needed help. If he was, I wanted to help. I want to keep alive in myself the possibility of believing someone, of helping. I think about the priest in Les Miserables who gives his silver candlesticks to Jean Valjean. Just because someone has a questionable intention doesn't mean they can't be helped. I want to think that recognizing someone's humanity, that not automatically acting with suspicion and disbelief, can set in motion a virtuous cycle, a butterfly's wing that reverberates across time.

I also want my neighbors, and my children, to be safe.

My overwhelming feeling in response to this would-be invasion was a mixture of vulnerability, a reminder that real life is always just outside whether we perceive it or not, and guilt. The man/boy was a person, and I'm a person. And I was inside and he was outside. That night, I slept in a warm bedroom on an expensive mattress, maybe he did too. Maybe.

I wonder how did I get to be here? How did the girl who was in India trying to learn about how to save the world get here, with an uncomfortably large mortgage, a house full of stuff that I move from place to place every day, a stack of papers full of IMPORT-ANT things that have to be dealt with, a little bit of community, not much time with friends, and work that I don't particularly enjoy and also don't feel is helping solve problems. What am I doing? How am I helping?

Juxtaposed to all of this, it is Halloween. And my husband asks if we are going to buy some new decorations this year. Like the neighbors with their zombies and gravestones and fake bottles of blood and venom and that spiderweb stuff that I don't know what it is made of but I'm pretty sure it just goes straight in the trash on November 1. Straight into some turtle's belly in the sea.

I bought costumes on Amazon this year. Brand new, polyester, costumes. I meant to make them. Or at least shop consignment or eBay. But I bought a shark costume and a cape for a dragon. I figure the cape will be used for a long time but I felt ashamed, I guess, or unprincipled.

Then I get a bit angry. With who? I don't know. With me. With the world. What are we doing? What is Halloween about? What do I tell my kids—how do I use this day, this ritual, to teach them something of value?

Halloween comes from a Celtic celebration that marked the end of the harvest and the beginning of winter. Winter was a time that was super scary for the Celts. Lots of people died in winter—they ran out of food, got sick, froze. And they believed at this time of year that the lines between life and death were a bit blurred—they thought if they dressed as spirits that they could confuse the spirits roaming on this night and maybe outwit death. It was a recognition of mortality, a communal response to the difficulty, the uncertainty, of the coming winter.

And when the church took power and All Martyrs' Day became All Saints' Day (and All Souls' Day), this could be used to recognize that we stand on the shoulders of those who came before us. We are one link in a long chain of humanity that has enabled and supported the life we have now. We recognize those who have come before us. We are part of the human family, of the progression.

So I tell my kids: At Halloween we dress up in costumes that we just bought online. We go door to door and ask our neighbors for candy. People put skeletons and gravestones in their yard because they are spooky. We participate in this as a community and it is fun. I know I usually say candy is not very healthy for you, but tonight eat your heart out. Tomorrow we will donate the candy to people who don't need it. It is also not good for them, but I am proud of you for sharing with people who don't have any candy. By the way, there are a lot of people who have died in the past. We honor our ancestors. The tiny plastic skeletons outside of the drugstore are an homage to those who have gone before. All living things must die. You will die someday. Trick or treat!

It feels strange that my lot in life is to live in the white-picket world, in a circumstance of such abundance. Abundance that feels disconnected from meaning. Excessive. Thoughtless. I think about moving. But where? Where is not like here?

I have had advice from neighbors since Thursday. Get an alarm system. Get a dog. Get a taller fence. Put up fake cameras. Or real cameras. Don't answer the door—ever. Deadbolts. Shotguns. Foghorns. Panic buttons.

I'm a fucking dreamer, but I don't think these are the answers. We will replace the door downstairs—it is not secure. But we were already planning to do that for better insulation and because the current door has resulted in several mouse deaths due to the fact that they can squeeze in under the opening at the bottom and I feel terrible every time I see one of those tiny bodies dead in a trap.

What is unexpected is that I feel a connection to the man/boy. My conservative upbringing taught me I should hold him responsible for his choices. My experience in the world tells me that he's also a result of a system, a yin to my yang. I feel guilt in his sweaty, panting desperation and my abundance. My bubble to his need.

I don't feel angry with or threatened by him. Maybe this is some kind of self-preservation. Like if you admitted the danger it would be too difficult. I do feel vulnerable, but not to him so much as to life. It feels that life is out there, all around me—in my little routines I am sheltered from noticing it mostly, but it is there and it is close enough to touch me. No fence is tall enough. And this is a dread, a terror. But also a call, possibly an obligation. If life is out there, all around, if it can reach me, touch me, hadn't I better live in a way that loves life? That nourishes and heals? That connects and contributes? Or do I batten down the hatches, strengthen the fortress, go to the shooting range? What can I do?

Pray? I've been thinking about books I read in college where amazingly intelligent people have had these philosophical, semantic, scientific debates for centuries about whether something is or is not real. Even if there is no man with a beard throwing down thunderbolts and blessings to punish or reward us, we still need shared spiritual teachings about what we value and how we might live. Stories, discussed, interpreted, modified, according to the world we find ourselves in, help us understand how to live.

Simplify? Don't have anything for anyone to steal? I'm struggling. I'm also eating too much pimiento cheese. I have work to do—to repair the fortress, to buy the doors, to fix the gate, to plug the leaks, to fix the trees.

I don't know where else we would go. I haven't figured out how to help. How much of my life I can give to helping.

The leaves are turning, bright red, orange, yellow. They'll be gone soon.

Trick or treat? Boo.

HOLIDAY HIJINKS

November 19, 2016 unpublished

I have recently heard the suggestion that the perfect holiday gift for the Trump-supporters in one's life would be a donation, in their honor, to one of a number of organizations. Organizations working to combat issues such as climate change, racism, sexism, xenophobia, etc. I initially loved the idea, it was funny and made me laugh (which was the intention of the person I heard it from). I thought of someone, laughed gleefully, and said "sign me up."

So amongst millions and billions of tumultuous, life altering, perspective changing, soul searching, paralyzing thoughts I've had over the past two weeks, I've been considering this idea of holiday-gifting support for a climate-change organization to a number of climate-change deniers in my life.

But it has started not to taste good. If you have decided that a person's beliefs and values are so abhorrent to you that you no longer care about them or want them as a part of your life, then you are free to not give them a gift. You are not compelled to give a gift to anyone just because your TV is telling you it is the time to do so. If your spirit or soul can in no way connect to this individual, give a gift to charity in your own name or in the name of someone you are actually trying to honor.

Assuming you *do* still care about this person, that you recognize there may be one thing that connects you; assuming they are a part of your life and you have some interest in having a relationship with them, there are still ways to honor them, to respect their perspective, and show where the two of you share common ground.

For example, one Trump-supporter in my life is a climate-change denier. BUT I know that he cares about money. So I'm not giving him a gift that focuses on the climate side of the equation, I'm giving him a gift that focuses on the money side of the equation. Here is the gist of the note that will accompany the gift:

Dear Joe (not his real name),

I hope you love these felted dryer balls. I have some myself and use them all the time. The reason I thought of you when I saw these is because they cut down on drying time by 30% which can save an average family $X over a year. I know in the recent election you were very concerned about the average family's pocketbook and being able to keep more of our hard-earned money and not give it to the government. I also know that you believe in personal responsibility where individuals make informed choices, rather than in government regulation. I think you will be pleased to know that major energy companies support such efficiency measures, so they will not work to create any regulations through the new administration with regard to felted dryer balls specifically, though they may request additional government subsidies. Perhaps you will someday help me to understand how these subsidies are an acceptable part of your ideology, but this is Christmas. I apologize that this gift also makes a positive contribution towards decreasing carbon emissions into the atmosphere. I understand your position about the large number of Canadians who would appreciate a warmer climate and your concern for their well-being has always touched me. I hope you will understand that sometimes there have to be trade-offs and I thought that your interest in accumulating money would take precedence over your long-standing support for a possibly warmer Canada. You can add a few drops of essential oil to the balls to give your laundry a fresh scent, but I didn't include that here because I know your position on hippies and didn't want to upset you.

Love, Jennifer

THE END OF THE WORLD AS WE KNOW IT

Note: Do you know how sometimes, when you are preparing to do something that you feel scared about, you think maybe you should write a letter, to your parents or your spouse or your kids or posterity? So you can say those last things, in case you don't get a chance later. Not because you really think there's a strong likelihood that you won't return. You're just scared, and a letter feels appropriate.

I think about such letters sometimes. I almost never write them. I wrote this one, but I probably also had a lot of laundry to do that night or maybe I fell asleep putting a child to bed. I didn't share my best and most beautiful thoughts about life. But I thought I'd share it with you anyway, to show my frame of mind at the time. I thought about rewriting something more beautiful, or at least trying, but I decided to write these words in italics instead.

A brief letter to my children, in case I die tomorrow or soon after

January 21, 2017 unpublished
My dearest children,
Being your mom has been the greatest joy in my life. I am so sad to miss what is to come, so sorry to not be there in person for the amazing and beautiful things in your lives, and for the hard times when you will need someone to call who loves you more than anyone else. I hope you know or will know that I will always be a part of you, that I will always be with you and you can talk to me, like I sometimes talk to your grandmother or my grandmother and ask for their guidance.

I love being alive and there are so many things that I want to do with you, that I hope you do. I hope we cook together. I hope we dance in the kitchen together. I hope we see the Grand Tetons and Jackson Hole together. I hope we swim in the ocean together. I hope we snuggle many, many more times together. I hope we read *Swiss Family Robinson* together. I hope we play Fan Tan together. I hope I can help you learn to love life, I hope that we can practice loving life and the earth and the world, together.

I'm writing this because tomorrow I'm going to Washington, DC to march for women. And I'm scared. I know that everything should be fine. But I've never felt like this before. This vulnerable. And like things were so on edge. I want to stay home with you, to make sure that I won't leave you. But I also want a good, safe, beautiful world for you and I think this matters. I think that it should be safe. But what scares me almost more is that somehow I will get my name on a list as someone who is somehow a problem or a threat. I'm not anti-conservative, I call myself an independent. But I'm scared of these people and of how they work.

Please let me be okay. Let me come home and hug you and feel your soft faces and listen to Sam tell me about his bottom and to Maggie's beautiful voice singing anything at all.

I'm scared,

your mom

Note to self

January 22, unpublished

In "The Abolition of Man" C. S. Lewis wrote, "I am very doubtful whether history shows us one example of a man who, having stepped outside traditional morality and attained power, has used that power benevolently."

Note: I don't consider this my finest hour, but I'm leaving it in as a record of my mental state. I wanted to share with you what it looks like when I am in the depths of despair, diabolical rage. In the following piece, I address the deepest darkness, aka preschool snack and relevant policies, because what else, I ask you, in February of 2017, what other, more pressing topic was a mom to expound upon to vent her strong emotions?

Let them eat cake

February 5, unpublished
Warning: I am writing in bitch mode today.
I'm curious. The preschool that my children attend requires that parents provide a snack for the entire class on a rotating basis. The school has a clearly defined, relatively simple snack policy as guidance on what that snack ought to be:

> [School name] *asks you to bring in healthy and simple snacks consisting of one protein source and one source of complex carbo-hydrates, for best energy-boosting quality and brainpower…Raw, unprocessed, whole grain foods are always preferable to processed, refined ones*

(and so on and so forth). Yes, this rant makes me one of *those* moms. If "those moms" means that I understand the difference in protein and carbohydrate and that I know the difference in cake and a muffin.

Oh, you ask, what is the difference between cake and a muffin?

There is no difference. They are the same food in a different shape. Let's consult our friend *Merriam-Webster*:

Cake *noun* \'kāk\: a sweet baked food made from a mixture of flour, sugar, and other ingredients (such as eggs and butter): a mixture of food that has been shaped into a ball or a flat round shape and baked or fried

Muffin *noun* muf·fin \mə-fən\: a small bread or cake that is usually eaten at breakfast

Since that does not provide the desired clarity, let's dig further by comparing a recipe for a cake and a recipe for a muffin. For statistical validity, I chose the first, highest-rated cake on allrecipes.com that didn't come from mixing boxed mixes together.[16]

Cake—24 servings—flour, sugar (2 c.), baking powder, baking soda, salt, eggs (2), buttermilk (1 c.), vegetable oil, vanilla.

Muffins—24 servings—flour, sugar (1.5 c.), baking powder, baking soda, salt, eggs (2), milk (1 c.), butter, nutmeg, cinnamon.

I was wrong and I'm sorry for feeling angry about this after all. There *is* a difference between cake and a muffin. They have the same amount of protein (in the form of eggs and milk) but there are several tablespoons less sugar in a muffin recipe. So each muffin has only 1.5 tablespoons of sugar as opposed to 1.75. I see. How foolish of me. They obviously are right in line with school policy.

Look, yes, I am one of those parents. I'm fine with having Rice Krispie treats, cupcakes, cake, cookies, doughnuts, hell, lollipops, on a birthday. But, I will point out that I don't ever remember this happening when I was a kid, we had cake at home, not at school.[17] To be honest, I think that seventeen days out of the school year where kids have cake in school, in addition to going to the seventeen birthday parties that happen out of school, in addition to special occasions at school, or the day where Suzy comes back from vacation and brings cookies for each kid's school bag is

---

16   To clarify, there is absolutely nothing statistically valid about this exercise.

17   except at Mardi Gras. I do remember having King Cake at school. And it is a good memory.

unnecessary, unhealthy, and supports moodiness, bad behavior, and inability to concentrate or behave respectfully, all the things we hope happen during school (and all the time).

I brought apples and cheese sticks today. I was feeling rebellious so I didn't take the stems or seeds out of the apples, I just cut them in fourths and put them in the snack basket. And a number of the kids weren't hungry for snack. If five-year-olds are not hungry for an apple or string cheese, we've got a problem people.[18] It was not celery sticks or fish. It was not spicy.

Out of curiosity and slight evilness, I glanced through the list of snacks provided for the past few weeks. There were fewer than a handful of days in the past month where there was not either a muffin (at least half of the days there were muffins), a birthday treat, or something made of white flour and refined sugar.

And what's more, on the muffin days, the second food was a fruit. So I guess the fruit is the source of complex carbohydrates and the muffin is the protein source?

Yesterday for snack my daughter's class had chocolate chip muffins and fruit at 10 AM. I went to the school that day to supervise "lunch bunch" where a few kids stay after dismissal to eat lunch and play. The tiny, 35-pound, four-year-old girl who sat next to my daughter had Oreos and a chocolate chip granola bar among the seven items in her lunch box. She gave some of each to my daughter. I swear to you that when I looked at my daughter after lunch, her pupils had dilated to a larger size than her entire iris. You can watch her after she eats this stuff and know that shit is going to go down. It isn't because she isn't used to it—she eats snack in this class four days a week and attends all of the birthday parties, so even if I prohibited all sugar at home (which I don't), she's exposed to sugar all the time. But after a snack-time muffin and some smuggled lunchbox food from a friend, she's primed

---

18   no lady, maybe you're the one with the problem.

and ready for a meltdown. Which of course did happen.

Probably also because I was so mad about the bleeping muffins (not the specific instance, just the pattern). I get it. Parents are busy and figuring out a snack for seventeen kids isn't easy. Well, it can be easy: I bought six apples and three bags of string cheese. I removed the stickers from the apples and rinsed them. I cut them into fourths. I opened the bags of string cheese.

I think the barriers for parents are: muffins are easy to serve, you don't have to figure out a baggie. Hummus—how do you prepare that for seventeen kids? Maybe what parents need is examples, or help to think about how to easily serve the foods mentioned in the guidelines.[19] Because we don't have or take the time to plan something and then it is the day before and you think—a ha, a muffin, a scone, banana bread (that is also cake, by the way).[20]

It makes me feel sad and frustrated. I'd love to hear another perspective that made me feel like we are somehow doing a great service to our children by letting them eat cake at school multiple times every week, at 10 AM, between breakfast and lunch. I'm not even talking about an afternoon snack.

Or maybe I should just throw my hands up, say f**k it, and let them eat cake. Zucchini bread, anyone?

---

19 I don't agree with myself here. I still have this question about the food we give to children in communal settings, more than ever after three more years of raising children in America. Reading this piece, I feel like I need to lighten up. Geez, lady, it's just a chocolate chip muffin. Maybe you need to just eat some carbs and relax. But I have read and thought a lot about this topic in the meantime and while my tone is annoying and my indignation perhaps misplaced, I agree with the underlying questions

20 I'm so annoying, but I don't think that's what we think. I think most parents think: What does little Suzy want me to bring? What does she like and what will her friends like (and what won't she complain about). Fruity Pebbles? Chocolate donuts? Done.

IN WHICH SHE FINDS A QUARTER IN THE TRADER JOE'S PARKING LOT AND TURNS HER LIFE AROUND

25 days of good luck

April 19, 2017

I found a shiny New Hampshire quarter, minted in 2000, face up while walking in the Trader Joe's parking deck this afternoon. I felt that it was auspicious so I bent down and picked it up. The bonanza would have been an Alabama quarter minted in 1975—that would surely have been a sign from the heavens. But as state quarters were not around that long ago, and as New Hampshire was my first home away from home, and 2000 the year I settled in what I had no way of imagining would be my home for the past seventeen years, I have been able to find a way to make this quarter super meaningful (maybe I just need something to hold on to).

I've always loved found coins. Always checking the date believing that finding my birth year, or really any year to which I can attach some specific connection, bodes well for the period of time represented by the number of cents the coin is worth. Lucky penny, lucky day. Lucky nickel, a good work week. Lucky dime... you get the point. So a quarter—whoa.

Now I'm set to have twenty-five lucky days, so that means good luck through May 12th. Which doesn't mean bad luck after that, just that this is a window of opportunity for lucky things to happen. I feel determined to make good use of this window. Which is why I'm publishing a post for the first time in over six months.

I have lots of plans up my sleeves and I've been quietly working away at many of them and maybe, just maybe, I can use some of this luck to move some things forward.

Things I've resisted for too long

April 20

I meditated this morning for about eight minutes. I went to a website where Deepak Chopra offered a timed meditation on hope. I didn't think I needed more hope. That's not what I would have said had someone asked me, but upon further consideration I think I did—do—have a serious lack of hope at the moment. He told me to say the mantra: *Shivoham* (or something like that) whenever a thought arose and then started a timer and some music and I wasn't sure I would make it through the time but I did and afterwards I felt great. My body felt a different kind of energy inside it. I could literally feel something inside my body that I wasn't feeling earlier.

My doctor told me that I need to do something like meditate, mindfulness, yoga—ANYTHING—to help get my cortisol levels down. They are, apparently, off the charts. I thought I was pretty laid back but it appears that I must internalize everything and not let anyone, including myself, know how wound up I am all the time. This explains my inability to fall asleep many nights. She prescribed some form of mindfulness each day—this was back in December. I've followed her advice on this twice since then. Today made three times.

Other health advice I have received or internalized over the years and had never acted on:

· Eat vegetables every day
· Exercise regularly
· Consume fermented food each day

I'm sure there are other standard practices that we are all told to do and mostly don't do. I don't know why I have resisted these things. I eat three or more times every day so there has always been ample opportunity for eating vegetables. I just made the choice to do otherwise. I think it was some kind of arrogance—something like *look at me, not eating vegetables and still seeming like a pretty healthy person*. I can't remember why I thought that not particularly caring for vegetables was a good enough reason to not eat them.

My point here is that, for whatever reasons, which I hope to explore more over the course of my twenty-five lucky days, in the past year, and especially the past two months, I've stopped resisting. I eat serious vegetables at almost every meal including breakfast, I consume at least two tablespoons of fermented food twice a day, I am *determined* to build some kind of mindfulness practice. Exercise? Does yard work count? This is really hard for me. I'm a pretty active person, but I have no regular exercise practice. I'm doing a bit of yoga every night before bed. A little tiny bit to try to help me fall asleep because of the previously mentioned cortisol issue.

And do you know what? It makes a difference. Doing these things that I was told all along would make a difference—surprisingly makes a difference. My body feels better. My body works better. My skin feels better. My mood feels better (not always, but I like to look at the trend which is up). It turns out, no one was saying this to make money for veggie farmers or fermenters or people selling sporting equipment.

Just in case you are curious, the fermented food always seemed so unappealing and difficult. It is super easy. You can do kefir, sauerkraut, kimchi, (some) pickles, kombucha, unsweetened yogurt. I have two tablespoons of unsweetened kefir after breakfast every day and two tablespoons of red cabbage sauerkraut at lunchtime. Sometimes I have some kombucha because it is tasty and (can be) low in sugar. I will expand to kimchi in the near future because I'm learning that variety is the spice of life.

Why am I writing about this on my second day of my twenty-five lucky days? I'm determined to make these twenty-five days count—to be ready for whatever luck comes my way. But to be ready when things come my way, I can't be down. I can't be angry, scowly, overwhelmed, iPad-addicted, depressed me. It would behoove me to be my best me. And it turns out that these things I've dismissed for so long are at least part of the key to being that version of me. Another part is spending time doing things you love and being with people you love. OR, as I think I sort of learned from KonMari, figuring out how to feel love for the things you are doing and the people you are with. But I spent a lot of the past twenty years doing things and trying to convince myself that I felt love for them, so this is a fine line to walk. You have to recognize that thing that you would pay someone else to let you spend time doing and then find some way to make a tiny space in your life for that to be alive.

I recently saw (a recorded video of) Kamal Ravikant giving a talk about love and entrepreneurship and he said (my paraphrase from memory, so hopefully it resembles what he actually said) to succeed you need:

1.   To do something that is an expression of your true self
2.   To give it your all
3.   To put it out to the world
4.   To let go of the outcome

I am working on that. I don't know what "succeed" even implies. I guess for me the four steps above are just necessary for feeling that feeling of being alive. Inhabiting life.

In summary, lucky day #2 was a good one. I moved forward in tiny ways on several things that matter to me and did what I could do to be ready for luck to come my way. Onwards.

No screens after 9:30

April 21

I turn off the lights. I turn onto my left side—facing away from that pinpoint of green light shining on the other side. Every night I think about covering that little light with electrical tape and every day I forget until it is shining and I'm lying in bed in my pajamas and I don't know where the tape is. So I turn away until I can't stand it anymore then I turn in the other direction and cover my face with a blanket or pillow, or try to position myself in a way that Dave's head will block the light. I close my eyes. I'm exhausted. I try to think relaxing thoughts. I try to think about what's good in my life. Or concentrate on the sensations in my body and try to relax each body part in a mindful way until I doze off. Or go through a list of the people in my life and wish one good thing for each of them. I've recently started stretching for a few minutes before bed so that leg cramps won't keep me awake. I try to get in bed and read, but most of my reading choices seem to bring up more questions to lay awake pondering leading me to conclude that I have to find another time to read *Sapiens* or *Zealot*. So, effective today, I'm going to do my best to initiate a "no screens after 9:30" policy. The complete sleep protocol, as it currently stands:

- no caffeine later than noon
- pre-bed stretching
- no upsetting or highly engaging reading at bedtime, particularly not about current events, bloody episodes in history, mass murderers (unwittingly, I was reading *Best Essays of 2013* and one was about a psycho killer), anything about the future of the planet or our species. No good fiction because I can't put it down.
- five minutes of mindfulness at some point in the day (I'm starting small)
- lights out by 10:30 (ideally 10:00 but, again, building to that)
- no screens, including phones, after 9:30 (exception, once in

a while we watch a movie after the kids go to bed on the weekend—this is allowed)

I read Arianna Huffington's book about sleep last year which mostly led to stress about the sleep I wasn't getting without providing substantive recommendations for better sleep other than letting me know that Arianna has some PJs she loves that were a gift from a *Vogue* editor. One thing I learned was that I would highly not recommend taking sleep aids based on the data presented in the book, which has since disturbed my waking hours via my newfound awareness of the number of traffic and other accidents caused by people under the influence of chemicals related to either falling or not falling asleep.

So, in case I didn't mention it at first, I'm having a sleep problem. Probably related to my cortisol problem (my cortisol doesn't drop to the level which allows one to immediately conk off to sleep like my husband. He literally falls asleep within six seconds of lights off. Snoring and everything).

I need to add exercise to my protocol. It is the last great obstacle still to be overcome. Well, the last one that I am currently aware of. Actually, that's not true. I still have some obstacles around relationships, some conversations, asking for help (etc.). But exercise is the last great obstacle in terms of physical health. This is why I'm standing in my kitchen at 10:25 this morning trying to think clearly and write while Maggie builds a Lego dog and Sam lines up cars to the tunes of *Moana*. If I'm going to write on a computer I have to get it done before 9:30 at night. So I'm trying to find snippets of time.

I guess I can still be lucky if I'm lying awake all night, but it seems less likely. So let's try this and see what happens.

Patience, grasshopper

April 23

I'm still not sleeping well. Last night I got out of bed at 12:21 and came downstairs, made some sleepy tea in the dark, gave up, turned on the lamp, opened a notebook, planned fiendishly for about an hour, writing down the thoughts that had been running through my head while trying to sleep. Around 1:45 I went back upstairs and managed to fall quickly into a deep sleep for about five hours. Better than the no deep sleep I've had for the past few nights but way less than ideal. Today I'm making sure to exercise and then will try a warm bath, some kind of pre-bed meditation, and will stick to no screens after 9:30.

I have so much on my mind, and a lot of it I'm excited about, but I have to find a way to chill out. I'm planning to launch a new blog but first I need to figure out how to send new posts as emails. There are tons of resources to figure this out, and I could probably call my web host and ask them or hire a millennial to figure it out if I knew where to find one.

My main problem, I think, is prioritization. Then again, I'm not sure about that because priorities are a bit of a dance. You don't know what is possible tomorrow until you've finished with today. Once you make a tiny move in one direction other options open up and you don't know about those until you've gotten there. So planning is good, and making lists and saying I'm going to do this and then this to get to that. But I don't know how to do that and leave room for improvisation or opportunity—or children. And that's probably the root of it all. Who the heck knows how much time I might or might not have and under what circumstances? I might have a free hour during nap time, or I might not. I might have time tomorrow, or someone might get sick. This is the way my life is set up right now, and I had the choice to set it up differently, but couldn't or didn't or chose not to figure that out.

The things I am wanting to do (in addition to being a loving, engaged, and patient mother with a reasonable tone to her voice) (and in addition to being a—let's go for decent—wife, nice and very occasionally thoughtful)...

Let me back up a bit. My themes for 2017 are to 1) Reinvent My Source of Income and 2) Ship My Art. And I guess I feel some desperation about the former. We have set up our life in a certain way, we've made choices and have obligations. I need to earn money to balance the family budget and I'm self employed. I have dreams of earning a living in a different way. I like copyediting, and some of my work is copyediting, so I'm happy to keep that stream alive. But otherwise I'd like to be writing: blogs, novels, essays, music. And I'd like to be doing work that contributes to helping people make shifts in their lives—through gameful approaches—towards simpler, healthier, more connected, more sustainable, more joyful, more creative practices.

We need to learn to live differently on the earth—and with each other—and I think there are fun ways to learn about doing that. And funny ways to be open about things that aren't funny but that we need to talk about.

I know that to Reinvent My Source of Income I have to do some experiments, try some things, ship some art. But I also have to earn money so I have to find the time to do the current work while wanting to make progress along the lines of my dreams/vision and be a mom/wife/friend/physical being with needs to eat/sleep/digest properly/get sunshine/relax somehow. And I'm afraid—deeply afraid—that if I can't figure this out I'm going to be trapped. I don't want to sit in meetings and write reports and travel to conferences—about *anything*, saving butterflies, restoring a watershed, feeding every child in America. I want those things to happen. I want to work towards those ends. But I want to work in a different way, to make a contribution through different kinds of efforts.

I think it can happen, but not without supreme effort and I waver in feeling like that effort is possible. I thought about writing a novel, like *The Awakening*, but instead of walking into the ocean our heroine decides to take a job so she can redecorate her house (and that was the end of her…).

Maybe tomorrow I will be able to report progress on one of my creative experiments. We have managed to refinance our mortgage, get through five weeks of Dave's travel, submit an application for Sam to go to school next year, put together a melted wax collage made by twelve four-year-olds for a school auction, take both kids to the dentist, start a new health regimen (based on strong advice from a doc), complete our tax return, have two child birthdays and Easter, brainstorm a ten-year vision and eat mostly sugar-, gluten- and dairy-free—oh, and become a Beautycounter consultant, of course. Will need to explore/explain that choice in a future post. The children are stirring…[21]

I FIGURED IT OUT!!!!!!!!!!

April 27

I FIGURED OUT HOW TO SEND NEW POSTS AS EMAILS! I sent an email to the people who subscribed to my blog 2.5 years ago! I know how to split my list to allow readers to choose the frequency of hearing from me!

I have a long way to go, but I have solved some riddles that felt like major obstacles and I feel so excited I could drink a bottle of champagne except that my husband is working on a deadline and I'm on early morning duty with both kids so maybe just a glass but

---

21 May 13 discovery: It turns out there is caffeine in kombucha. As a new convert to fermented foods, one small change I had made was to start drinking a half-bottle of kombucha most days, between lunch and dinner. I can't drink de-caffeinated tea after noon and hope to fall asleep at night, so drinking kombucha at 5 PM was a definite recipe for insomnia. Turns out, it was not all of my exciting ideas keeping me up at night.

I have no champagne anyway. I'm having some mint tea instead.
   So my celebratory post will do for now. HOORAY!!!!!!!!
   If this is the only thing that moves forward during my 25 lucky days, it is enough!!! (This and no iPad game relapses.)
   Now to make the new blog a reality.

* * *

This marks the conclusion of the Jenaissance blog. Everything that follows was posted (or almost posted) on the new blog, Adventures with Jenny Goodguts. You'll see some repetition, early on, because, for the most part, no one was reading the Jenaissance posts. I was not sharing them with subscribers (of which I had around 12) or posting them to social media. I was just writing them for myself, the universe, and Leigh. From this point on, I did share, cautiously. I had a group of subscribers (all close friends and family) and every post automatically went to this group.

adventures

with

jenny goodguts

MEET JENNY

Not holding out for a hero

May 19, 2017

I have an addiction and a theme song and only one can prevail.
Right now, it's the addiction. I've been playing Farmville 2, or
Tropic Escape, or now Hay Day, on my iPad since early October
2016. I can put it away for a few days and then somehow the
iPad is in its sneaky little spot, hidden from all view except mine,
and I'm checking my crops, making a mango daiquiri or chicken
feed. When no one is looking, I'll take a quick nip, make sure I've
planted a new row of cotton, heartbeat racing as I hear feet coming
down the stairs. Quickly close out the game, press the button so
the screen goes blank, and move towards the sink so it will look
like I was washing dishes the whole time (but I'm not sure anyone
is really fooled).

My hand hurts. I have a repetitive strain injury from playing.
Those crops can't harvest themselves and how will I know what
happens when I unlock the wharf unless I make it to level 35? Oh,
all that happens is I get a new kind of star for making apple pie?
Maybe level 40 will blow my mind, let's wait and see. I steadfastly
refuse to pay a cent to play, so all I invest is time. With time, you
can achieve the same things as someone who is willing to spend
$1.99 for 100 keys/gems. So, I put in the time and play "for free."

I started playing at a time when I was having trouble dealing with my thoughts. I didn't intentionally start playing to ease
myself through an overwhelming life episode, I just happened to

be introduced to the game at a time when periodic escape from reality was welcome and seemed helpful to my continued baseline functioning. Then THE ELECTION happened. My addiction had fertile ground in which to build from one game, initially, to a new game, then to a third game, and then to all three at once.

But what, you may be wondering, about the theme song? Well, when I'm not addicted to repetitive world-building games with very little skill or thought required where I don't even engage in the social aspects (though I did accept a friend request from Ferma Maria, so now I'm crossing linguistic borders to build agrarian allies, a stranger who sometimes purchases my extra carrots), I like to make up games to play in real life. Challenges for myself and my family. If we earn 20 stars we can get ice cream, here are the criteria, GO! I'm that kid whose parents used sticker charts to get me to brush my teeth and I just never stopped wanting those shiny gold stars.

Ah, but here's the rub: for a large portion of my life, I was not in the driver's seat with respect to the aforementioned stars. I have spent almost 40 years grasping for stars that others were willing to award me for doing whatever they deemed worthy. If there was a gold star to be had, I was IN. Just tell me the criteria.

Approaching 40, I had a revelation and decided that I'm through getting my stars from other people. I'm going to spend my days, months, years, decades (whatever I'm granted) figuring out what I think has value and doggedly pursuing those stars.

Just prior to my descent into virtual pastoralism, I was starting to think about transforming myself into a superhero. Outlining missions for myself, accomplishing them, and giving myself a badge. A real, physical badge (not an icon) that I put somewhere and the wall of badges grows and grows.

Why a superhero? Well, when I think about Jennifer (that's me) never giving another cent to those jerks at [insert Big Bank name here], I'm motivated but it never seems to take priority. But if I imagine that nefarious bandit "The Usurer" and think of myself in a battle of wits and skill with this ne'er-do-well, magically I get more energy. I feel possibility and excitement.

One morning, while thinking about becoming a superhero / finally summoning up the energy / time / focus / resources / guts / willpower to do the things that I want to do to live in the world as I imagine it can be, I was driving my kids somewhere and letting them choose songs to listen to. When it was my son's turn he chose "Come With Me Now" by the Kongos and it immediately became my superhero theme song. I can't help but believe that any morning where I get out of bed, put on my sweatpants and the shirt from the day before as long as it smells okay (my usual uniform as a stay-at-home/working mom), and listen to that song, I think that would be a day for fighting crime, even if that crime is the amount of junk in my basement.

When I hear that song I want to DO SOMETHING. And by something I don't mean write a report, tweet a hashtag, or redecorate a room in the house. Break some sh*t. For good. Or at least unsubscribe from a bunch of catalogs.

I want to stop mindlessly and passively supporting bad guys. I want to do more to find and help the good guys. I want to develop my superpowers, have a super cool hideout (with appropriate superhero gear and secret weapons) where I go to make my plans.

While I sit (or usually stand, hidden in the corner of the kitchen where I have a three-second warning before being caught in the act) building my virtual farms, I often wish that I was spending that time building something real. In my real life. In the real world. And here's the thing: there are a billion things I could do today to take care of the world, my community, my family, and myself and also make life nicer all around. Some of the things are tiny and some are huge but even a huge thing is made up of lots and lots of tiny things. There are so many possibilities for taking action and making change. I love writing. I love trying new things. I love writing about trying new things. I love games. I love making up games for myself and for other people. I love thinking about how things could work and solving problems.

So here's what I propose as a means of breaking my addiction and moving in the direction of superhero, an aspiration that is questionably ever reached by a mere mortal without a secret underground lair and lacking multiple, or even a single, millions of dollars or an advanced degree in physics: I will begin my quest and share it in this blog.

I will publish, at least once a week, and share my missions and their criteria and then report on my success, including sharing the badge that I have/have not earned. If anyone reading along is interested, he/she can earn the same badges along with me or at whatever speed he/she is capable/interested in. I'll share quest-related essays, links to inspiring sites, songs I'm writing and other amateur artwork, info from books I'm reading, heck maybe I'll even put in a podcast one day.

I retain the right to change any/all terminology. I retain the right to change the entire game at any point. I retain the right to disappear and never write again if I become overwhelmed. But I will try to come back if that happens.

We make the world and we make culture. And no matter who is in the White House, there is a lot an individual can do to not empower bad guys and to support good guys. There is so much possibility and so much to be hopeful about. And so much that is utterly terrifying. So today I'm going to walk away from my iPad and, like Princess Poppy in *Trolls*, I'm going to choose hope. But just like Princess Poppy, I can't do it alone. You can help me by letting me know that you are reading this, that any of it makes sense to you, that you sometimes wish you could be a superhero too. Stay tuned, my next post will answer the question on everyone's mind… Just who is Jenny Goodguts?

Who is Jenny Goodguts?

May 24

Jenny Goodguts saved my life.

Jenny Goodguts, a doctor's appointment, and a lucky New Hampshire quarter (face up!). Saved my life may be a touch of overstatement, but I can tell you with confidence that they brought me back to life.

There is nothing Jenny told me that I hadn't been told before. Who can explain why we are finally able to do something that seemed impossible or hopelessly unappealing at one time?

Here's what I can tell you. I was reading the book *SuperBetter* by Jane McGonigal. Jane, a game developer, has researched the psychology and neuroscience of games for over 15 years. She had a traumatic brain injury and created a game to help herself recover. Her game worked so well that she shared it with others recovering from similar injuries and then even more widely. Her TED talk on SuperBetter has been viewed millions of times.

One element in the SuperBetter approach is to adopt a secret identity. Choosing a heroic nickname can help bring out your challenge-facing attributes (such as determination), while also helping you to connect with your sense of humor and take things a bit less seriously. But I couldn't think of one. I know Vera Voce was a possibility at one point. I felt a bit stuck.

At the time I was reading *SuperBetter* I was nursing an addiction to iPad games that I was desperate to stop playing. I would read a chapter. Feel excited. And then the next day I would play the game. Read a chapter. Know this time I was really going to stop playing. Massage my aching shoulder/hand. Next day play the game. Repeat.

Then I went to the doctor. She had results from some lab work that involved my toilet, a small collection dish, and some spatulas. The results were not excellent. Basically my insides are populated almost exclusively by *E. coli* bacteria and almost nothing else. I've been working to protect biodiversity in nature for 20 years and there's none left in my own body. I didn't like this. I also didn't like a couple of things she said about markers for cancer and so I bought the pills she prescribed (all over-the-counter stuff) and came home.

I looked in my kitchen cabinet at the other supplements she had suggested five months prior. The ones that I had taken occasionally on a random morning if Mercury was in retrograde or the wind was right. I knew it was important, if I wanted my body to work, if I wanted to stop being tired and depressed, if I wanted to be able to do good work in the world, take care of my family, enjoy my life, stop playing those freaking games, I knew I needed to buckle down and take care of myself.

So of course I took one of every single supplement that she had recommended from November through March and then went on with my day. I went to the grocery store and bought kefir and sauerkraut. I went to sleep.

I woke up the next morning and there she was. Sitting right next to my bed. Jenny Goodguts knew exactly what I should do. She told me to make an Excel spreadsheet (I'm pretty good at that). The spreadsheet was divided into breakfast, lunch, and dinner. There were checkboxes at the appropriate times for all of the actions required to rebuild my gut flora. I made the spreadsheet as directed, taped it to my kitchen wall, and within a week my skin felt different. My skin looked different. I was eating sauerkraut every freaking day.

But I was still playing the game. About a week after meeting Jenny, I found a 2000 New Hampshire quarter face up outside of a Trader Joe's. Once again, Jenny to the rescue! She knew, as we all do, that one cent equals one lucky day, 25 cents equals 25 lucky days. Face up, of course. I'm not sure if face down is half the number of days or just nothing, that's never been clear to me.

But 25 days of luck! Well, you don't just squander that. Jenny had me tape the quarter to a piece of paper, write 25 empty spaces underneath, and tape the paper on the kitchen wall, right next to the Excel spreadsheet. Each morning I would check off one space and she challenged me: You cannot play the game during your 25 days of luck or else no luck!

I did not play the game for 25 days. Oh buddy was I tempted. I would walk to the former scene of the crime (the corner in the kitchen with the three-second warning before detection) and I would crave that dopamine/seratonin hit. I would want something to distract me from myself, from the decisions I can't make, the work I'm not doing, the work I am doing, some of the monotony of my current life situation (laundry and dishes, anyone?). But the quarter was staring right at me from that very corner. And it worked.

Were the 25 days lucky?

For me, a 25-day (and continuing) game-free streak was all the luck I needed. I also developed this blog, from scratch, and figured out how to send posts via email, something I had been wanting to learn for over two years. I got my first non-spam blog comment from a reader I don't know. I found out that the caffeine in kombucha was responsible for my insomnia, rather than all of my good ideas keeping me awake at night. I learned about some great local places for adopting a dog. I talked to more people. I asked more questions. I reached out. I tried things. Other things happened and I might not even know yet if they are good luck.

The cool thing about the quarter experiment was living in a way that encouraged good luck to happen. When you think you are possibly in a lucky streak, and you want to make the most of it, you get off your butt and do stuff. And it turns out that is more satisfying than planting wheat on your farm to make into a loaf of bread because you need two loaves to make a hamburger.

Dear readers, please rest assured that Jenny's primary mission is not balancing gut flora. Though she can definitely come up with some pretty convincing arguments for why this is important to saving the wider world. Jenny works for good and she's got guts (and she, incidentally, does have a full complement of healthy microbes). As soon as I met her, I connected with the name and it gives me energy so there you have the full explanation of where she came from.

I have been wanting to make challenges and secret missions for myself and my friends for over a year (or maybe a decade, or four). I'm not a superhero. I often have trouble making decisions, I often have trouble following through with (all my good) ideas, I have trouble eating enough veggies even though I know it makes my life much better all around. I just ate chocolate for lunch.

But if I sit down and have a few minutes of quiet and ask Jenny what to do, she mostly knows. She can make a list and say: if you do this, if you stick with it, if you have a spreadsheet, or some stickers, you will get to the other side, you will learn, your life will be more in line with your heart, and you will feel good. And if you get other people onboard, well, watch out! It's still partially a serotonin/dopamine thing, but the good kind. So this blog is the story of my (ongoing) adventures with Jenny Goodguts including multiple Excel spreadsheets, quests, missions, banks, bicycle helmets, a songwriting teacher named Karl, resistance, and more than likely some stickers. Stay tuned for the first mission—basic training!

FRICKING CLIMATE CHANGE

Paris and Pittsburgh

June 2, 2017
(sigh.)

This is not how it was supposed to go. There's been no basic training and I'm not ready. But it looks like Jenny has a quest for me and she won't take no for an answer. I was hoping my first nemesis could be Clutterista. I knew The Usurer was too big a fish to fry without some experience and better secret weapons. But there's Loop-O, the lord of indecision, who I was excited to do battle with, and Glossy (that terrifying vixen who stares at me in her different forms when I'm at the checkout counter in the grocery store, whispering that I'm not quite enough).

But no, I am a part of this world and I live in real time and real time has its own momentum and its own needs. So here we go…

My first "real" job out of college was working as an intern at *Yes! Magazine*. They happened to be putting together an issue about climate change, a topic that I had no interest in—at all. Yuck. But okay, I took the job and did some research on carbon footprints and renewables and dusted my hands of the whole thing. This was in the era of Y2K—maybe this climate stuff was overblown and would just go away, right?

Over time, along with significant personal aversion, everywhere I went it seemed like things started revolving around climate. My Masters research was on climate. That's all anyone seemed to be talking about. Bor-ing. Eventually I started working on UN climate negotiations during my time at Conservation International. I even married someone who studies climate change. Truth is, I can't stand talking about climate change or even thinking about it because it is a) boring and b) terrifying. TERRIFYING!!!

Can't we just keep living like we are living here in America and everyone worldwide can eventually live this way and be happy and have more, more, more and God will fix the climate??

I have been looking—as hard as I can—for some (legitimate) reason to have hope that maybe climate change won't be as bad as people say. I promise you, if there were any good evidence to discredit climate change I would tape it up to my mirror and look at it every morning. I want it to be untrue. But the truth is the reason I can't get away from this dang climate change stuff is that none of us can and nothing we are working on can either until we do something about it (the Chinese did not pay me to say that).

But do I own a bike helmet? Is my house powered with renewable energy? Have I even invested in insulation? No. It costs money, it is never the priority, and it takes time to figure it out and change.

I need time to think. I feel like I understand why 22 senators wrote a letter urging Trump to get out of the Paris Agreement, there is a somewhat clear cause and effect in my mind to explain that. But what I want to understand is why my mom's friend thinks climate change isn't real, or doesn't "believe" that if you take a terrarium and fill it with carbon dioxide the temperature inside the box will increase. That's physics. You can do it yourself. And we know where carbon dioxide comes from. We can measure it, it has been measured.

Jenny Goodguts is a systems gal. She is not into politics or propaganda—on either side of the political spectrum. She knows there are people in every part of the world who are scared, disappointed, overwhelmed, angry, worried about their kids for lots of different reasons. And those same people love something and mostly work hard every day until they can't anymore and then they play iPad games, watch more CSI, get drunk or [insert additional ways to escape].

Jenny likes to think about actions and reactions, about what an individual person can do to address root causes. Making people feel bad, or feel scared, is usually not so motivating and mostly divisive and helps us to build our defenses and further congeal into sides. Those of us who "believe" in climate change (do people "believe" in physics?) are circling around our despair, disappointment, pointing fingers and sharing statistics that we all already agree with. The "others" are not reading these articles. They don't care what the MIT scientists said yesterday after the speech in the Rose Garden. Temperature reductions of 0.2 or 0.9 degrees promise seriously different futures, but the only people paying attention to the difference in those numbers already care.

We care. But please see above. Bike helmet (uncheck). Renewable power in home (uncheck). Food miles. Food waste. Quarter-pounders. Investments. Old appliances. Driving son to school (less than half mile away). Not carpooling.

So the first quest is going to be a climate quest. Part of me wishes it were something else to take my mind off of the possible ramifications of what just happened.[22] But this will be the crucible for beginning to forge my superpowers—one of which has to be a method for not slipping into despair in the face of fear.

There is good news on the climate change front. There is so much happening in business, finance, government, communities, cities, research. It is solvable (unless we've already passed a tipping point but let's not worry about that here) and there is money to be made, there are jobs to be created, songs to be sung, coral to be saved. There are things I can do this very minute (I just

---

22 Historical context: What just happened was DT announcing that the US was pulling out of the Paris Agreement meaning that the United States would no longer work with every other nation on the planet to address climate change together.

turned my thermostat up, for example. Just now).

I'm going to spend a bit of time this weekend mapping out the quest and will return first thing next week with a plan of action. Until then, just try to eat less beef, dust off your bike, and turn up your thermostat. We'll get more creative next week.

Diabolical scientists

June 2, unpublished
I've never been great at understanding physics. But I know something about biology. For instance, if you take a loaded gun, point it towards your brain and pull the trigger, your body will not survive. There are causes and effects. Actions and reactions.

And while I am not a physics genius, or chemistry, or biology, there is one route I suspect would provide me with the most logical, most probable answer to any question of a scientific nature. My idea: I will consult the opinions of thousands of the most prominent scientists on earth.

Let me tell you something about scientists, because this is a subject I know well. I am married to a scientist. I know a lot of scientists. Scientists are not in it for the money. Scientists are not in league with the Chinese. They aren't going to listen to you or to me, they are super—super!—aggravating in that they want *evidence*. That's all they ever talk about and it can be totally aggravating. If scientists cared about money, they probably would have gone into finance or tech. They understand numbers and statistics so they could have made way more money doing something else, I promise you.

They go into science because they are curious about something. They have questions and want to understand more. They are not always right, but asking a question and getting an answer and asking more questions about that answer, that's how we have antibiotics and walked on the moon.

Feelings, something more than feelings

June 3, unpublished

I get it. You're feeling a lot of feelings. The President of the United States of America, a position you once imagined you would hold when you were an eleven-year-old girl with a crush on Woodrow Wilson (or was that just me?), stood in the Rose Garden and told a select group of VIPs—and the rest of the world:

> *As someone who cares deeply about the environment, which I do…*
> *the United States will cease all implementation of the non-binding*
> *Paris Accord and the draconian financial and economic burdens*
> *the agreement imposes on our country. This includes ending the*
> *implementation of the Nationally Determined Contribution and,*
> *very importantly, the Green Climate Fund which is costing the*
> *United States a vast fortune.*

So you go on Facebook or Twitter to commiserate. Why was this a terrible decision? Which facts did he cite that were wrong? What is Bloomberg doing? (Hooray for Bloomberg!) How is the rest of the world reacting? Lots of coverage, great information, thoughtful. Lots to be angry about. Lots to be hopeful about. You share a few articles, "like" many more, put up an angry face or two, and feel really depressed. Anxious. Angry. You read a Paul Krugman article about how the Republicans are doing all of this out of spite. And based on some of your relatives you think he's at least mostly right.

And then there are the comments that go along with that article talking about the rise of the neo-Nazis in the US, how Europe and China are going to bypass this country in terms of developing alternatives. How the US worker will suffer—how the folks who voted for Trump are being used by a handful of people who are rolling in money from coal, oil, and gas and that none of these policy changes are going to do anything other than make the situation for most Trump supporters even worse than it was. And what does that America look like, you wonder? If THIS is possible now, what else will be imaginable then?

Then there's a terrorist attack in London. Another one. And you go back to your newsfeeds and the focus has changed. Maybe there's a climate-related link here or there but the cycle has moved on and we're back to the same smorgasbord of Trump bashing, friends' vacations and children, and witty one-liners about anything.

Maybe you get upset about the newest Presidential indignities, maybe you get mad at the liberal elite.

I'm tired. Deep in my soul. Tired of the cycle. Tired of feeling all the feelings and then the next day more feelings about something else. And all of us getting so upset and feeling so justified and so right. And I think that "Basputin" (my editor/mom has advised me not to use real names) knows about these feelings. He uses these feelings, knowing that when we are in this state of feeling that we are paralyzed, that we are immobilized. Not to say that we have been immobile. I am so thankful and so appreciative of all the people and all of their phone calls and marches and meetings.

But if I keep feeling all of the feelings I will sink, down, down, down. And that won't help anybody. It is a waste of a day, a waste of an opportunity, and a waste of a life. To stop all the feelings I have two choices: 1) escape, pass time (via iPad games, material-ism, obsession with my children and their activities, moving my clutter around, celebrity gossip) or 2) do something. I have been focusing more on the escape route for the past several months and have committed to the universe to move to the second option. Though I'll admit to being sorely tempted by the first on a daily basis.

First mission is coming soon

June 7

I am excited to report that in two weeks the Jenny Goodguts blog has passed the total number of subscribers from the Jenaissance blog! I will report back when we pass one hundred and when the first person subscribes who I do not personally know.[23]

The first mission will be out *any day now*. I'm struggling a bit because while I thrive on complexity and lists (that look like tax forms, as Dave put it when reviewing the mission last night), I think most people are likely to be overwhelmed with the "game" in its current format.

The "healthy atmosphere/healthy wallet/support innovation/ market-driven/creating jobs/longer life/personal responsibility/ loving God's creation/green earth" challenge (or something like that) is going to be fun, but is a more difficult mission than I had imagined beginning with. It just seemed like the time was right and I've been waiting to do some of these things for too long.

There are many ways to play and there is a large menu of actions. Each action is worth a certain number of points. You can play on your own and set a target for the number of points you want to earn to get either a gold, silver, or bronze badge. You can get a group together and set a target number of points and when the group as a whole reaches that number you do something (have a potluck, have a party, go on a picnic, donate to charity—you can be creative). The other option is to divide into two teams to challenge each other and the team that scores the most points wins something (party provided by other team, etc.)—this would work well in a workplace, that's my vision.

So that's what I have in mind. Now I just have to take this tax form and make it look more like a game.

---

23 still waiting.

The happy atmosphere challenge

June 14

I have been hating climate change for over two decades. Willing it to be untrue. Sure that the scientists were missing something, that our beautiful, resilient planet would have some trick up its sleeve.

Reading about it, I shut down. I'm either hopelessly bored by all of the jargon or what I hear is all the things I do that are bad. Invisible gases will doom the earth and humanity and all I need to do is stop using electricity and driving. It's that simple.

It is not on one's bucket list to be a "greedy American." You don't want to doom the planet or for little kids growing up on islands to be afraid they won't have a home, say, next year. But your house was built in 1940, your job is ten miles away, and you can't afford a Tesla.

Plus, it seems like your feeble efforts to use 2% less fuel by taking heavy items out of your trunk is a teardrop in the ocean of climate change and you know your neighbor doesn't give a flip about the climate. You notice her sprinkler watering the street every morning, see her back door open all day in 95-degree heat, smell her grilling those juicy feedlot ribeyes.

Better hope that a widdly-wee machine is invented to fix the problem, if it actually turns out to be as bad as (more and more) people say it might be. It's too big for one gal.

In the midst of this hopelessness, or denial, you might receive emails from well-meaning NGOs about what you need to do. Call X to "demand" action (though I am not sure, in a democracy, that one ought to demand). Reject the big bad oil or coal companies that we oppose (yet depend on to get to work each day or to run hospital equipment). Divest—do not give your money to the bad guys. Telling stories designed to make you feel—thinking this feeling will prompt action.

But this fear and anger, guilt and sadness—these are paralyzing. I say this because I have spent many more hours than I would have preferred reading the science, seeking to (mostly) understand it, and recognizing it is dangerous and unfair in its potential impacts. And in all this time (I wrote my first article about climate change in 1999) I have taken few steps in my personal life to decrease my carbon footprint.

I might go on Facebook and feel upset about Paris, or any other thing, might sign a petition or make a phone call. But hell's teeth my house gets a slight bit less comfortable if I turn the thermostat up by two degrees. What we need is a global agreement, not my messing around with my thermostat or declining a trip to Mexico! (The answer is too big for one gal. Of course. That's why all of the governments on the planet have been working for 24 years to come up with a solution that they could work towards together. An approach recognizing that the wealthiest countries got to where they are in part from burning stuff and sticking gas in the air (unknowingly at first) and wanting to make sure countries that have burned less don't remain impoverished but also don't burn the same amount of stuff we did to get where we are.)

But back to my inaction: If I were to use one of the available "carbon calculators," a tool to help me understand the volume of invisible gases that my family creates through different activities (driving, heating, etc.), I can come up with a number, say, 50 tons each year. Then I can take steps, large and small, to decrease this number. Maybe I work really hard and cut it in half—in half! That's not an easy feat, but do-able. But after all that work, and expense, I am still generating 25 tons of emissions each year. After all that effort I am doing less bad. But still bad. Focusing on that number, and on decreasing it, in the end still draws my attention to what I don't want to be doing.

It is difficult to summon the energy, the spirit, the will to act from hate, or from fear, or against something. There is a power-ful surge of emotion but those emotions drive me straight into the arms of my beloved world-building, pastoral iPad games—a world of no feelings and cheap, endless serotonin and dopamine. But what I know about myself is this—that I miraculously somehow seem to find the energy to act from love, from optimism, and for something. I have not managed, in twenty years, to take substantial action to do less bad. But I have a hunch that I could take a lot of action to do more good.

So in this spirit I have come up with a challenge for myself—and for anyone else who might also be motivated by doing more good. A moderately epic battle to support good guys everywhere. And when I finish the challenge, I will decrease my energy bills, improve my health, breathe cleaner air, have less road rage (this would be a pretty big win), support job growth, support local farmers, waste less food, educate girls (which is good for girls and boys), increase carbon in soil and forests (where we like it), drive innovation in energy, batteries, lighting, appliances, and transit, and send fewer invisible gases to the sky.

The challenge is meant to be played as a game—on your own, as a family, with a friend, a group, or a virtual community.

I take on this challenge accepting that doing something, taking some concrete action, may not fix the problem. Doesn't change anyone's mind, might not change the world, takes time to figure out, and can cost money (and save money!). But doing something—in this spirit—is good for me. It directs my thought towards what is possible, what is feasible, what I can support. For me, it's the only option.

The challenge is a work in progress that will be updated as I go. I'll share further thoughts and resources under the Happy Atmosphere Challenge on the blog.

I am hopeful. Hopeful that there is something we don't yet understand that will mean that all of the models run by all of the scientists don't come to pass. Hopeful that the pace of innovation is breathtaking and people are working—this very minute—on solutions that, given our investment and support, could store carbon back in the earth by 2050 (more about the book *Drawdown* edited by Paul Hawken in future posts). And hopeful that—one month from today—I'll (finally) be able to report on the multiple steps forward—towards the good—that have eluded me for too long.[24]

Why did I start a blog?

June 30
I don't know what I want.

I kind of know what I want—I have a ten-year vision written down and it sounds nice. I want to be healthy, for my kids to be healthy, for everyone I love to be healthy, for everyone on earth to be healthy. To walk outside and feel the sunshine and the breeze, to breathe clean air, to drink clean water. To sit by the ocean and hear the waves and smell the salt air. For there not to be tons of plastic microbeads in the ocean being eaten by fish being eaten by me.

I'd like to be more patient. I'd like to exercise—but not in a gym because I cannot stand the smell or the feel or the screens or the machines. I'd like to have a comfortable sofa to sit on with a friend.

So, in the broader sense, I know what I want, or I have an idea of a life arrangement that I imagine would be very nice. I have a pretty nice life arrangement as it is—maybe that is why it is hard to be clear about what I want. Because, in truth, I don't really want for anything. I have a sofa. It is hideously uncomfortable. But I have friends who are kind and will use extra pillows and seem to like me enough to deal with the lack of seating and still want to come be with me. I think that's pretty lucky.

I am fortunate enough to have all of the essentials. I can afford

---

24 The full Happy Atmosphere Challenge is available at www.jenniferhole.com.

healthy food, security, shelter. I have loving relationships and good physical health.

So what is this feeling in my chest? Why, this morning, when my kids were sitting at the breakfast table, bright, shining, bursting with life and happiness, did I command silence and that they quickly finish their food because we might be five minutes late for summer camp? Why didn't I wrap them in my arms, hold their joyfulness close to me, let it fill all the cracks, kiss them, put on their backpacks, walk peacefully to the car and deliver them to camp—to camp—possibly a few minutes late?

My husband asked me why I wanted to start a (nother) blog. He wasn't being unsupportive, just trying to help me think about what I should spend my time doing. In the past 15 months, I have taken a musical theater class, worked on a novel, intermittently blogged on another blog, started songwriting lessons, written essays that I want to try to get published but have not submitted, written children's stories that are not age appropriate, read tons of nonfiction, been addicted to iPad games, played my guitar and piano sporadically, bought a (still unused) ukulele, quit and rejoined Facebook, read way more news than in the previous 10 years combined. (I have also taken on a reasonable amount of contract work, primarily copyediting technical documents related to sustainable development, and I started selling beauty products.)

I told my husband I was starting the blog because I would enjoy it—for fun. (I think I am remembering correctly.) I like to write, I like to read what I wrote last week. I like to come up with "programs" for myself and try them out and report on the results. So I think that originally the way I convinced myself to get started with this blog was that it would be enjoyable.

But in addition to that, I will tell you this. After my first several posts on this blog were published I felt some relief. Because there is a need inside me to make sure, if I die tomorrow, that there is a letter somewhere telling my kids who I am, what I love, what

I think matters, some advice that they probably won't take now but might value later. There have been two days in my life when I've actually sat down and started writing this letter to them (both nights before setting out to do something I was scared of doing). But after I started writing this blog, I felt better. I felt like some of what was inside was now written down somewhere that they could find it. And that is a comfort to me.

But where does that need come from? Surely if I am living my values, living in a way that shows what I love, what matters, they can just read my life and know what I would tell them. Yes, precisely, which is why I need it written down somewhere, because I have not yet figured out how to arrange the clues of my lived life to truly demonstrate what matters most.

Another thing: When I started my last blog, I posted a video of myself singing a song I had written. A friend of mine, later that week, sent me a recording of herself that she had just made, singing a song she had written 15 years ago. She thanked me for inspiring her to sit down, in her den, and record it. Another friend wrote that she had started working on a song of her own.

Google's Larry Page has said that Alphabet is looking to work on "billion-people problems"—how to build solutions, like self-driving cars, that can help a billion people. I guess I work on one-person problems.

I made a star chart for myself and my husband. It was really good for me, and he was a good sport. It improved our life or our feelings about our life. I shared it with a few friends. Some of them really enjoyed it and it improved their lives (or their feelings about their life).

So, in addition to wanting to write things down so they exist somewhere, I also think that sometimes I have ideas that are interesting and helpful to other people. I don't exactly know what I might share that is helpful, so I err on the side of sharing more than less. I don't know if this is the right approach, I guess I'm experimenting.

So, my faithful readers, this is all to say that I'm working it out. Am I writing to build a platform for my ideas? Am I writing to help others? Am I writing to figure myself out? Am I writing to practice? Am I writing to have fun? Am I writing to laugh or to help others laugh?

I don't know.

I write. I share. I think of each of you who has subscribed. Am I going to offend anyone I love? Are you going to lose faith in me? Am I going to be able to be authentic, am I going to lapse into someone else's voice?

My other blog was easier because I didn't share on social media and I'm pretty sure I only had one "regular" reader. So I didn't have all of this conflict when thinking about what to write—I just wrote—but then I didn't have the energy that comes from knowing that people are reading.

So I get stuck. I have to decide what I'm doing. I also have to have some time to think. I also need to get an ergonomically appropriate writing situation. I also need to exercise. But there will be quests and challenges soon to help with these things. I have not played iPad games since starting the blog, and that alone is a victory.

Have a beautiful day. I hope you feel some sun and some wind on your face today. I will.

IN WHICH SHE PREPARES FOR THE REVOLUTION

Remembering to breathe

July 7, 2017

Hungry this afternoon and browsing the refrigerator for options, I found a leftover Independence Day hamburger, some whipped cream (should I?), and a jar of pickles. And what have we here in the opaque silicone pot? Half of a raw onion. Resigned to a few minutes of labor in exchange for sustenance, I took out a carton of eggs and a frying pan. I rinsed one day's collected drawer dust out of the pan (longish story) and cracked an egg directly in. Remembering the pan was cold, and unlubricated, and that I was planning to scramble the eggs, I then poured the raw egg from the pan into a bowl, rinsed, then dried, the pan again. Cracked two more eggs into the bowl, melted an unmeasured chunk of butter in the pan. Poured eggs in pan. Added salt. Fiddled with the gas on the stove—hotter, colder, hotter until the eggs were satisfactorily fluffy, salty, and warm. Peppered.

Reached blindly into the drawer and pulled a spoon from the bin allocated to forks. Returned wayward cutlery to quadrant assigned to teaspoons. Selected a salad fork (as shorter forks are both less menacing and more appropriate for non-dinner purposes). Sat down at the table, next to the open laptop. Put one warm bite into my mouth and began to read email. Didn't taste the eggs. Shortly realized that the plate was empty. Sat more quickly than is usual to attention. What is this sudden and unwelcome sensation running in a wave from my stomach through my throat? Am I about to vomit? No? Maybe? Walked as fast as I could to the toilet. Crouched down. Burped. Spat. Waited. Three eggs remained on trajectory towards stomach, crisis averted.

Barring an intervention from the magical postman in the sky, I'm not pregnant. My son was sick with a virus last week, so that is the obvious explanation. Clearly, I have the same virus, a week later, and am feeling a bit sick to my stomach. That, or *Salmonella*— though I'm guessing introduced bacteria would take longer to percolate and would more likely result in realized regurgitation rather than continued low-level nausea.

But I'm suspicious. I wonder. I'm having trouble sleeping again and this time it is not due to my ignorance of the caffeine in kombucha. I'm caffeine-free and exhausted. My eyes are carefully guarded from blue lights and screens during the twilight hours. And for the past few nights, I turn off the lamp and I'm lying there, mind traveling haphazardly down one path, jumping quickly to another, with no theme or connection other than willing some divine intervention to give me answers, to guide me to a path.

How is all of this related to the phone call that immediatly preceded my three-egg feast wherein two non-technical, creative types discussed the future of humanity considering advances in artificial intelligence? Or to the essay I read last night by E.B. White, "Freedom," from his (very highly recommended) book of essays *One Man's Meat*? White writes, in 1940, in the midst of the Second World War:

> *The United States, almost alone today, offers the liberties and the privileges and the tools of freedom. In this land the citizens are still invited to write plays and books, to paint their pictures, to meet for discussion, to dissent as well as to agree, to mount soapboxes in the public square, to enjoy education in all subjects without censorship, to hold court and judge one another, to compose music, to talk politics with their neighbors without wondering whether*

the secret police are listening, to exchange ideas as well as goods,
to kid the government when it needs kidding, and to read real news
of real events instead of phony news manufactured by a paid agent
of the state. This is a fact and should give every person pause.

I am not here to offer unsettling opinions or doom and gloom, but I am unsure how to arrange my life, what choices to make, how to be prepared for what is next in this world.

Reading good old E.B., I am not sure of his politics (a refreshing change from most of what one reads today which so very clearly promotes one dogmatic perspective or the other). He questions too much government interference, but is concerned about the well-being of other people. He fiercely loves and defends liberty and individual freedom, which in his case includes accepting and thoroughly enjoying diversity. When did the divorce of these things occur?

I feel this divide around me. I hear people—very close to me— saying that there will be two sides and I will have to choose one. Saying they can imagine a future when women have lost the rights we enjoy today, that strong forces exist with the intent of moving humanity in this direction.

And then there is AI (artificial intelligence, that is). Industries will be disrupted. Jobs will be lost. People will be desperate. There will be a revolution. The one percent versus everyone else.

I'm not sure it will go down like that. What I do know is that I will not be among those escaping to Mars. I'll be here—on my beautiful planet. Living whatever life there is to live. With my last ounce of strength, or courage, or just a very strong will, loving my kids. Loving my friends.

In the face of all of this, and to keep from upchucking one's eggs, so to speak, what can one do? Perhaps salvation, or at least moderate happiness, lies in defining a set of principles and devising an action plan. So towards those ends, a starting point:

Take care of my physical health.

Be a friend. Help people.

Learn new things. Read.

Stop accumulating.

Manage my (neuro)chemicals.

Do more good.

Hug.

Breathe.

In a brave, new world I would feel better having a body that can get me where I need to go. I realize this won't always be the case, but it can be the case now. The better a friend I am, the more likely there will be someone I can live with when the robots take my job, the more likely we can put our (non-mechanical) heads together to figure out how to solve whatever problems we face, the more likely I will have someone to laugh or cry with. If I figure out how to help people, I can probably scrape together a living in some way. Also, the world will just be nicer. As the world changes, I do not *have* to learn how to navigate Tumblr or read more on CNN or finish watching *Game of Thrones*. But if I keep learning how to be healthy, how to be a good friend, and how to help people, I'll either be okay, or I won't. But I will feel better. Reading (fiction, essays, poetry) helps me connect with human beings outside of this moment in time with other concerns, other fears. I can see which of their worries came true and which didn't. I can feel how humanity has been good at heart for so very long, restoring my faith that goodness does seem to prevail, even if one is unfortunate enough to live through a dark period of history (of which there are many). Moreover, reading (and I'm not talking about news or Facebook) helps to remind me that people are people. They want things and they fear things and they do things but they are usually more like me than I expect, and even if they don't see things my way, they aren't as ignorant, or as selfish, as I might imagine. They are in their situation, doing their best with what they've been taught. Regarding material possessions, I have no need for a collection of My Precious Love-ems figurines, or of perfect shoes for any occasion (though I would be sad to part with my Paragon tea cups with matching saucers). These will all be lost or broken in the revolution. Move my body. Eat vegetables. Be a good friend. Help. Learn. Read. Stuff is not life. Understand how marketers use my chemicals and stop giving my power away. Stop letting them buy my attention, my ability to focus, my precious time/life for so little! DO GOOD!

Support people working towards my vision of a secure and healthy world. Hug as many people as will let me. Breathe.

Breathe. (I never remember to do this. I'm working on it.)

In.

Out.

Breathe. (Probably it is just a virus, but I will keep breathing, just in case.)

Grains of rice challenge

July 14

About thirteen ounces of tahini, some possibly expired cottage cheese, a year-old (?) bag of frozen plantains, a jar of what I now believe is blackstrap molasses, some fruity bars my children refuse to eat, half a bagful of giant marshmallows, and, I imagine, a few boxes and cans that I can't see or have stashed somewhere out of the ordinary (example, the tonic water that I am now remembering in the basement). Food that has languished, uneaten, in our kitchen.

When I was studying in India (over 20 short years ago), one morning our class was visited by an orange-robed sadhu (a Hindu monk). In early childhood, he told us, he was taught that each grain of rice is sacred. In his home, they would make sure to pick up spare grains that had strayed because to waste them would be to dishonor god (the Hindu religion is rather complex, I thought it correct to use the lowercase "g" in this case, but will stand corrected).

I remember writing a letter home from India—a letter my mom saved that is doubtlessly cuddled in my basement with hundreds of its friends, awaiting rediscovery—suggesting to my family that when they give thanks for dinner each night that they consider thanking not just God, but the members of his orchestra: the soil, the plants, the animals, the farmers, the bakers, the Earth, the sun, the rain, the universe. I think it was a lovely blessing. I know I said it for a while and I believe my family, without me, did for a time as well. Then life moved on. I got busy and food lost some of its sanctity.

I guess I've been busy for 20 years now. Too busy to be as thankful as I want to be. Too busy to be as mindful, or live as simply, as that, too easily ignored, still and quiet voice guides me to. Too busy to breathe before meals, to taste a large portion of my food, to say thanks, each time, for the bounty of life-giving, healthy food available to me and to my family.

And our approach to eating, while it has shifted significantly along the spectrum of healthiness over the past few years (towards the good end), has not made significant strides towards the mindfulness end. We don't eat in the car (my old boss was French and alerted me to the savagery of such a practice), and we sit down to dinner as a family every night, at a table, without a screen in sight. Which seems normal to me as this is how I grew up but I understand this is no longer standard practice. We say a blessing when we remember. We talk about where food comes from, what each type of food is good for. Our categories are muscles (protein), energy (good carbs), tummy (veggies), vitamins/eyes/skin (fruit), brain (nuts, fats).

What hasn't shifted much at all is how we purchase food. How we make decisions about what to cook, how much effort we put in to using the food we've bought, how much food we buy on impulse. Uneaten food is just another kind of garbage, something to be taken "away."

I remember the waffle fries my daughter was not hungry for on Saturday that are on their way to the landfill. The leftover chicken that we forgot to finish before it went bad. The moldy (not in the good way) cheese I found in the drawer.

According to ReFed.com, "American consumers, businesses, and farms spend $218 billion a year, or 1.3% of GDP, growing, processing, transporting, and disposing food that is never eaten. That's 52 million tons of food sent to landfill annually, plus another 10 million tons that is discarded or left unharvested on farms. Meanwhile, one in seven Americans is food insecure."

If you looked at the Happy Atmosphere Challenge, you'll remember that food waste is also a not-insignificant contributor to climate change. Uneaten food contributes about 8 percent of global greenhouse gas emissions each year.

There are several drivers in our household food wastage. I'd like to say the children are the #1 (and 2) suspects, lunch boxes where half-finished juice pouches have soaked a bagel remnant and half of an uneaten apple, dinners where there is no room left in their "soup tummies."

Another of the biggest factors in our family, and I would guess in others in my demographic, is what I (from now on will) call over-diverse chefery. This is where you try some tasty Lebanese food somewhere and decide that, this Thursday, you're going to try to make some yourself. So you buy all of the various ingredients, make the dish once, and are left with the various spices, sauces, etc. until you go through your annual fridge check for expired food and, what do you know, that tahini is still there, all 13 ounces of it. A month from Thursday, when you have the time and are again feeling adventurous you will try a completely different cuisine with a whole new group of requisite spices and sauces, and so on and so forth.

Or you go to the grocery store and your kids sample some of the rice from the very nice lady and you feel like you need to buy a box, even though you never actually cook boxed rice and your kids not-secretly did not eat the rice and said it smelled funny.

Or something just looks tasty and you are tired, hungry, restless, upset, distracted and for whatever reason you think buying another box of tea or a different kind of cheese, even though you have three kinds already and you've been avoiding dairy for the past month, is going to make life feel somehow more complete.

I've been thinking about food waste for about a year (having read ReFed's excellent report last summer, as well as *Zero Waste Home* around the same time) and have made shifts in our purchasing. I try to buy fewer impulse purchases. I've paid more attention to portion sizes in lunch boxes and overall. I've gotten better about lovingly reminding myself to eat the leftover Independence Day hamburger (I've been especially mindful of wasted meat). But I still have more than a few stubborn holdovers. Old quinoa, and spelt purchased accidentally because I didn't know it from sorghum.

So I thought it would be an interesting and informative (and, for me, fun) challenge to empty the refrigerator, freezer, and all cabinets and try not to discard anything in the process. I am packing up the whole kitchen in preparation for some work to be done on it in August and am hoping that a challenge like this will help me to pay attention to what we are buying and to be more mindful of using what we have.

Update (I started this post several days ago and progress has been made): I tried to use up the second half of a bag of giant marshmallows by making microwave smores for the kids last night after dinner. One giant marshmallow each. My son was literally crazed. He did not know what to do with his body—I've never experienced speed, but I think I now know what it looks like. My kids eat some sugar, but mostly not so concentrated.

The marshmallows had to go. I also had to throw away an entire shrink-wrapped baguette, bought months ago to make garlic bread (why did I buy shrink-wrapped bread?). I had stored it where I couldn't see it and now it is trash. I am trickling the remaining "junk food" (animal crackers, Cheese Curls (Alabama cheetos)) into my kids via their lunch boxes.

I did, however, salvage some shrunken blueberries and mildly moldy nectarines/peaches/pineapple into my morning smoothie. I composted all traces of mold, in case you were wondering. Dinner last night was lima beans (previously frozen), almost overripe corn, an old box of black beans and brown rice (too spicy for the kids but I will finish today for lunch), and two hot dogs (also from the freezer). It takes more work to not waste food. This morning I took the remnants of a roast chicken and am simmering it in a gallon of water with that half-onion I mentioned last week, some just-past-the-date carrots, a wilting celery stalk, some garlic, salt, pepper, thyme, and parsley (under fifteen minutes prep, four hours on the stove). It will be delicious and bone broth is the new kale, apparently.

I want to make sure that the challenge doesn't turn into another stress point, another to-do, and a one-time flash in the pan (get it? flash in the...?). I would very much like to change my relationship with food, to eat once again with more reverence, more calm, more joy, more celebration, more presence, more breathing, more tasting, more laughing, more community, fewer threats, less negotiation, possibly less diversity, but more seasonality.

So that's what I'm working on.

To provide a quick update on past posts: The Happy Atmosphere Challenge is on hold. I am planning to send a note to friends/readers who have expressed interest and willingness and see about doing it together, but the timing for doing that is not great for me right now (husband gone for three weeks, amongst other semi-relevant excuses) so I'm in a holding pattern. I have been running the dishwasher at night without the heat-dry cycle, I've been paying attention to eco-driving, and I signed up for some of our home's energy to be renewable. I am hoping to start the challenge in September—there never really seems to be a good time though because I have other things I'd like to start in September!

So many other things that I want to write about, in particular my recent thoughts on restlessness, recognizing the things I do to try to avoid restlessness and the things I might do instead. So that might be the next post. In the meantime, I have to figure out what to do with all of this tahini.

Small talk

July 22

I'm looking out the upstairs window. Across the street is the white-haired man who walks past my house every day, usually more than once, with his small, curly-haired grey dog. A little thing, maybe eight pounds of dog in all. I have been trying to smile at this man for months but he won't look at me. I can't get him to look at me so that I can smile at him so I have assumed there's something he's inferred about me or my life choices from something about the exterior of my house (the toys littered across the lawn or disrepaired shutters, perhaps?) that puts me into some group of people he does not approve of. I have some vegetables (not very successfully) growing in a raised bed near the street, so maybe he thinks I'm a dirty hippie.

This morning I see him out of my window with his little dog. At first I think about it being a good plan to get a little dog if you are getting older—we are thinking about getting a big dog and I recognize that it takes much less man (or woman) power to manage eight pounds of dog versus eighty.

Then I see another neighbor, a lady who lives across the street from me. She's outside of her house with her dog, a yellow lab named Rosie. My neighbor is smiling, as she almost always does, and approaching the gentleman. And I see him stop, his dog approaching the lab, and the white-haired man leans towards Rosie and puts his hand on the top of her head. She's wagging ferociously and looking up at him. He puts his hand under her chin, scratches. He's looking straight at the dog's face and rubbing, scratching, petting. My neighbor is smiling and I see her mouth moving and moving and the white-haired man keeps petting the dog, contentedly. He pauses and seems to listen to my neighbor. I don't see his mouth move but he stands there. And then Rosie moves towards him again and they are back where they started, petting, wagging, scratching and my neighbor smiling and talking all the while.

And then I start to feel that I am just like this man. That I am looking at myself, as I feel underneath my skin, underneath my face and my clothes and deep inside even under my bones, most of the time.

There is a block party at the end of my street once each month, weather permitting. Neighbors come with booze and snacks and popsicles and kids ride their bikes dangerously close to seventy-year-old women (my son in particular) and they always laugh it off but I am pretty sure one day I am going to turn around to see a sprawling neighbor knocked to the ground by one of the many two-year-olds zooming precariously on their scooters.

My kids love this party so we amble (or ride) down to the circle one Friday each month during the sociable and non-freezing months. People are standing around. Kids are shouting. People's faces smile at each other and they are divided into little two-, three-, and foursomes laughing or deep in discussion, though for the most part we all steer well away from politics unless it is very clear on which end of the spectrum your conversation partner is encamped.

We have lived in this neighborhood for about three years. Maybe been to these parties about twelve times. Terror may be too strong a word, but each time I'm approaching the gathered throng I'm generating as many options as possible of what I can do once I get there. Head to the drink table, sort out my children in some way, put a bag somewhere—I need a plan for what to do until I find someone to talk to.

And then comes the hard part. I'm standing next to someone and they say something and I have to say things back, preferably pleasant or interesting things. And when the sound starts to die down and it looks like the line of conversation is about to finish, I panic. What next? How does this either keep going or how does it stop—I don't know. There sometimes seems to be a very organic pattern. Other times it is like a ride at an amusement park, jolty and bumpy, sometimes sailing downhill and other times, on the way up to the next downhill, you feel a bit sick to your stomach and it's jolting you around and you wonder if the ride is well constructed or if it is about to tumble to the ground and you wonder what that would be like, hope you don't find out, and then the other person starts to tell you a story about when she had surgery and couldn't move for six weeks and that's how she got a new dog, and you are safe for a while. Usually, after an event such as this, I come home and think seriously about taking a vow of silence. I don't feel good about myself or about the random conversation I was able to make, or rather the words that I heard come from my own mouth, mostly unbidden.

True story: At the end of this school year, I was responsible for organizing the teacher gift for my son's class and also helped him make a card for each of his teachers. In the card, he had dictated some lovely things about his teachers and I had written them down for him so the words were his own. After the gifts and cards were bestowed, his two teachers approached me during a farewell celebration and thanked me for the thoughtful gifts.

One teacher remarked that she had particularly enjoyed my son's remark "I hope you don't get burned by lava" (they had been studying volcanoes, so this was relatively appropriate).

So, just for emphasis, let me restate: teachers approach me, smiling, say thank you for something nice, we liked the sweet cards. I panic. What do I say to these people? These nice ladies who have cared for my son all year?

I wanted the cards and the gifts to do the talking for me, truth be told. I put a lot of time into thinking about what would have meaning for the teachers, what would show that we appreciated and loved them. But now there are people, live people, here next to me saying words through their faces and looking at me and I'm supposed to say words back.

You should have heard the gruesome things he said that DIDN'T make the card. Smile. (Backtracking) *Not that gruesome, something about the ocean, but they, I'm so glad, you are teachers and you, my son. Thank you.* And they smile back, but their eyes…

How about: *I'm so glad you liked them.* Something, you know, traditional like that.

I feel like a good 70% of the time when confronted by the need to make conversation with someone I just take a group of words from some panicked region of my brain and throw them all together and I'm hearing it come out of my mouth and I don't even know what it means. I know that I can think clearly, I can write, I have vocabulary, and empathy, and I feel warmth for people. And one-on-one, sitting with a friend, I'm usually pretty good with words. With hearing and responding in a caring and thoughtful way.

There was a block party last night. I went late and mostly listened. I asked some questions about gardening and the amount of water large trees need in the summer heat. It made me feel lonely though. I wished I could feel comfortable. I wished I didn't feel like I'm thinking about different things from everybody else.

So this morning I see the white-haired man with the little gray dog. I see his joy of connecting with Rosie—his pleasure in the wag of her tail. He doesn't look at my neighbor's face, though I do, twice, see his mouth move in response to something she has said, his eyes still down. He says so little, but he doesn't feel so little. He's just not comfortable with small talk. And he doesn't force himself to be. Maybe he's just lived long enough to let himself be who he is.

IN WHICH SHE VISITS DIXIE

I may be right, I may be crazy

August 13, 2017

ME: They might not like it.

ME: If they don't like it, they can unsubscribe.

ME: But I personally know every subscriber, maybe they don't want to hurt my feelings.

ME: People keep reading it. They could just let it go to their inboxes and never open the message. But they don't.

ME: Maybe they are worried about me and they read to make sure I am okay. I don't want to write things that will make people feel down.

ME: But you also don't want to write things that are not real, and sometimes real is down. Or at least real is not always falsely positive and upbeat.

ME: Isn't it a little self-centered to write so much about myself? My own thoughts, my own experience, how I feel about every little thing?

ME: Maybe being real can help people feel less alone. So much of what you see on TV, online, in magazines doesn't seem like your life at all, or doesn't reflect what really matters to you. Writing what is real for you has helped you. Maybe it helps other people too.

ME: So is that the plan then, publish an online diary?

ME: Ideally no, that wasn't the plan. And it isn't the plan. But you are being transparent. You had an idea, you started something, it is evolving and that takes time. And you are keeping people (who love you and are supportive of you) informed and involved as you learn and develop.

ME: I'm afraid that if I just keep writing whatever pops into my head once a week that...

ME: That...?

ME: You know I'm a people pleaser.

ME: Yes.

ME: I am not sure that blogging is the right outlet for me. When I read my own posts on my phone I wish I were sitting down in a comfy chair with the words printed out, instead of rushing to read it quickly on a tiny screen.

ME: You changed the subject.

ME: I don't know what I'm afraid of. Can we move on?

ME: You like to blog. You are a people pleaser. You love these people and you want to do something that is helpful, is honest, is enjoyable on both sides, doesn't make anyone feel upset, keeps everyone happy. All you can do is be real. And try to be healthy. And share what you are learning. You can't keep everyone happy. And if you try to you won't be able to write what is inside you.

ME: Maybe it is arrogant to think it matters—what is inside you.

ME: (*singing softly*)
This little light of mine, I'm gonna let it shine
This little light of mine, I'm gonna let it shine
This little light of mine, I'm gonna let it shine

ME: (*even softer*)
　　Let it shine, let it shine, let it shine (*a little choked up*)
　　That was a low blow.
ME: What else are you going to do? Play iPad games, eat Justin's dark chocolate peanut butter cups, and binge-read the news?

ME: I could get a job cleaning up a river. Someone could tell me to do something and I could do it. I could do a good job. They would tell me I was doing a good job. Sometimes.
ME: And your music?

ME: I could do that sometime. Some other time.
ME: And your light?

ME: I care about rivers.
ME: And your light?

ME:
ME: Your little light?

ME: Maybe I can't do it.
ME: Maybe you can.

ME: (*in such a quiet whisper, maybe no one will hear*)
　　I hope I can.

Piggly Wiggly

August 30, unpublished

Standing at the Piggly Wiggly deli counter, looking at the remaining pieces of chicken, the three breasts, two wings, and eight hundred thighs of fried meat that no one else wanted to buy, I feel overcome, overwhelmed, and desperately like crying. I can't decide what to do. I came, specifically, for an eight-piece bucket and an extra breast. My mom said they make the best chicken, not over-crusted like at Publix, but I needed to act fast because the chicken sells out. Apparently, I was not fast enough for a drumstick, which is Maggie's favorite. She swallowed a bone around Christmas, so we cut her meat off the bone these days—probably she won't notice.

As I walked into the store, just five minutes prior to my visit to the chicken counter, I felt apprehensive about bringing my own shopping bags. At home, in Alexandria, this is *de rigueur* but here, in Birmingham, Alabama, I felt nervous that wearing my Chaco sandals and yoga sweatpants (please don't misunderstand, said pants are worn for sheer comfort rather than activities of an athletic nature), but particularly carrying my brightly colored reusable bags, was a sure beacon to all around me that I'm one-a-them liberal elites. It crossed my mind to wonder if someone might "accidentally" run into me in the parking lot. I don't know if that is insensitive to say, but it did cross my mind and it made me feel a) sad that it crossed my mind and b) nervous/weird and I went into the store, head down, to do my business and get home to safety and other (whisper it…) liberals pronto.

I'm standing, looking at the chicken remnants. A woman comes to the counter to ask how she can help me. She's soon joined by another woman, around twenty years old maybe. The first, older, woman has skin the color of café au lait, the second more like a Hershey's bar. The younger woman looks at me with bright, kind eyes and with her white, smiling teeth she says "Hard to choose, huh." In the nicest way. I smile back. And this wave of sorrow washes over me. I remember what I have been reading in the *Birmingham News* this weekend. Opinion pieces about Charlottesville and statues and history. Neo-Nazis and Confederate soldiers and flags and stereotypes. I think of the women, the three black women who cared for my grandfather as he was dying. Who bathed him, sat with him, listened to his shrinking repertoire of stories over and over, so gently and warmly. The black woman who sat with my grandmother as she took her last breath. The people who have served me dinner at white-only clubs.

I grew up in a town that desegregation forgot about. If you made paint of the skin colors in my high school, it would be slightly whiter than I am (who has a bit of olive in my skin either from 2% of Greek or Spanish DNA way back somewhere). There was no color in my school, or in my neighbors. But it was certainly all around me—in house cleaners (we called them maids), yard men, caddies. Benjamin, Lily, Evelyn, Katie. I never once had a feeling that there was any resentment, any feeling of injustice. I felt nothing but warmth and kindness, at least in my particular circumstance.

I get that same feeling from the girl at the chicken counter. She is warm and smiling and she understands how tough it is for me to be standing here and there are no drumsticks. What will I do when faced with such a predicament? Her smile and her eyes let me know that I am understood, that I am perfectly in the right to feel however I feel at the moment. We are a team, and she will help me get that chicken.

I feel guilty, helpless, ashamed. I feel like I want to show her I'm not like the people I've read about in the newspaper, that I understand her circumstance, recognize that we are sisters in one human family and then I imagine how tiring it must be to interact with people being extra nice to you as you scoop their chicken into a box, trying to prove that they care about justice or your humanity for the five seconds before they move on to look for Stouffer's mac and cheese family size and other, more pressing, concerns.

Walking through the store, I recognize that my anxiety about my shopping bags, my fear of retribution for stepping out of the accepted bounds in this place, at this time, are a drop in the bucket to the life she has lived keeping within the accepted boundaries set by her history and color.

And then I think about the relationships I've had, the people I have felt love for and who, I felt, loved me. I wonder, if your survival depends on smiling while you put my chicken in a box, are any of the smiles real? I think they were. Then I think about my smiles, my love. Real love takes an interest, seeks to understand, gets its hands dirty, goes to work. That's what real love would do.

I'm scared to write this. Scared to offend. Scared to enter a dialogue that is two hundred plus years in the making. This is something I've sought to understand, academically, in school and through studying literature (the way I've sought to understand many things). But I don't know the intricacies. I don't know the words to use.

In the store, I wished that I was just a girl, standing in front of a girl, asking her to help me get some chicken. I felt sad, I questioned my assumptions, my relationships, my history. And then I drove up the hill to my parent's house where I felt safe and comfortable and I ate some chicken.

Lessons from an American girl

August 30, unpublished
My daughter wants an American Girl doll. She has become obsessed with Maryellen Larkin, with her "heart full of high-flying hopes and a head full of pie-in-the-sky ideas." Maryellen knows that if she stays true to who she is and what she believes, the sky is the limit. Without any previously expressed interest, my daughter now *must* have this $115 doll.

> MAGGIE (at bedtime): Mommy, do wishes *ever* come magically true? I mean, without someone having to do something with their own hands like plant a garden. I mean, really magical?
>
> ME: Um, yyyyess. They can but not usually overnight. Usually you want something and you wish for it and someday, in a way you weren't expecting, the thing you wished for can

sometimes come true.

MAGGIE: But is there magic? Other than Santa Claus? I wished that I would wake up and Maryellen would be here in my arms. Can that kind of wish come true?

ME: I guess it could, but I wouldn't count on it (big hug, kiss).

Next morning

MAGGIE: Mommy, I am going to work all day long. I am going to do work for ten hours today and I am going to earn $115 and buy Maryellen this week. (It has been suggested that she can ask for Maryellen for Christmas but four months feels too long to be apart from her heart's desire.)

ME: It will take longer than a week, but we can definitely find some jobs for you to do to earn money and save for Maryellen. I have one job you can help me with right now.

MAGGIE: How much will you pay me?

ME: We can go outside and pull weeds together and when you fill a basket you can earn $3.

MAGGIE: I am going to work all day. I am going to earn $115 and buy Maryellen this week. I am going to work for ten hours.

ME: Great. Let's go outside and do some weeding.

MAGGIE: Are there any other jobs? Not a small job like pulling weeds, but a job where I can work for ten hours and earn enough money to buy Maryellen?

ME: I don't know of any jobs like that, but I do know of one job you can do right now and earn $3. And then we can see if there are any other jobs to do.

MAGGIE: I would rather not do that job. I will ask Deedee if she has any jobs. (Deedee does have a job. Maggie is also not interested in earning that dollar.)

Why am I writing this? Well, I think my beautiful daughter has just helped shed some light on a number of my challenges. We'll call the phenomenon "All or Nothing." I'm either going to become a superhero or it isn't worth it. I'm either going to start a full-on exercise routine, say train for a marathon, or forget it, I'm either going to have a clear path, a set of goals, and know that I'm on the road to success or putting my shoes on and taking that one walk, what's the point? Maybe a better approach would be to pull one basket of weeds and take it from there.

FYI

August 30, unpublished
I'm feeling a bit hopeless. Megastorms and statues and propaganda and missile testing and worrying about people I love and watching bad television...

BASIC TRAINING: EXCEL TO THE RESCUE

September 13, 2017

After an unplanned and too long hiatus, I am dipping my toe back into the waters of oversharing and underdelivering to provide you with an outline of the long promised, never before explained Jenny Goodguts Basic Training Program (take 1). Using this kind of spreadsheet has changed my life. My life then reverted back to how it was before, somewhat, but I'm trusting that reinstituting the spreadsheet will once again change my life.

And don't take it from me, I have one reverberating testimonial:

Thanks for telling me about your spreadsheet. I made one too. It was helpful (paraphrase) — Angie

The spreadsheet is a printed piece of paper listing a number of small daily actions that are slotted into a timezone (breakfast, lunch, dinner). The sheet is taped to the wall in my kitchen. At the assigned time of day, I look at the sheet and try to make sure all relevant tasks are complete.

Originally, this spreadsheet was mostly used to help me remember to take certain supplements, breathe before eating, and consume cultured foods so it was a perfect system for those tasks. I (almost) didn't miss checking a box for eight weeks.

The tasks in Basic Training don't fit as easily into the original timezones, and are not as simple to complete, so I'm experimenting with a new spreadsheet and will modify.

Basic Training lasts four weeks and focuses on preparing the individual to be stronger, healthier, and more resilient so that we can get to the superhero stuff down the road. It follows the Jenny Goodguts principle: Do More Good. That means it does not focus on things you shouldn't do or on what you might be doing that is "bad" for you. It focuses on adding good things to your life, on ways to spend time and energy that support your vision of what you want to be instead of focusing on what you don't want to be.

I'm sharing the actions that are part of my own spreadsheet as an example but you can adjust any way you like. I'm in desperate need of it myself, as well as of some accountability, which public blogging provides, so I'm rolling it out barebones to start with.

Basic Training includes five aspects: Nutrition / Energy, Movement / Strength, Clarity, Spirit / Soul, Rest / Restoration where spirit = what is bigger than me? and soul = what am I?

The Basic Training (take 1) components are:

EAT MORE SUNSHINE: Drink a green smoothie every day

GOOD GUTS: Eat two tablespoons of cultured food, two times a day

MOVE: Dance to three songs every day

MOVE: Attend one exercise class every week

CLARITY: Meditate for ten minutes each day

SPIRIT: Spend ten minutes outside every day

SOUL: Play a musical instrument for ten minutes every day

SOUL: Write for ten minutes every day

REST: Out of bed by 6:30 AM every weekday

RESTORE: Enjoy screen-free activities after 9 PM

My rules are that I can get the tasks done at any time during the day, the timezones are just useful guidelines of when something might fit. I predict that rest/restore will be the most consistently challenging element, but making time to play music will be a close second.

I pulled out my old 45 records over the weekend and danced to "Vienna Calling" by Falco. You probably have no idea what I'm talking about, but it was pretty amazing to be transported back to 1985. I could almost remember feeling ten years old again.

HOW TO FIND YOUR LIFE PURPOSE

September 18, 2017

My kids are back to school. Both of them there for seven hours each day. Four-year-old Sam, who weighs so very much when hanging off my neck as if I were a tree, wearing his too-big backpack, his little legs moving quickly to keep up with his big sis, to grow up and learn the ways of the world.

For the first time in over six years, I have a day at home, alone, with no sounds but some cicadas, a few unidentified birds, my A/C, the helicopters flying towards the Pentagon, a neighbor's yard service, and acorns falling from the massive oak trees overhead, plummeting to the ground. They want to be the massive oaks of one hundred years from now, but most of them will be raked up, an inconvenience for the manicured lawns, sent away with the leaves to be made into mulch for tidy gardens in the spring. Sitting outside (for my ten minutes of sunshine a day), I hope none of them hit me square on the head. I try to remember physics: I know the mass of an acorn is small, and force = mass x velocity? I'm not sure that's right. But they have that sharp little point at the end. I consider getting a hat or helmet. I decide to risk it.

Elsewhere, the world is on fire. The world is under water. But here it is blue-skied and mild. Elsewhere people with very slightly different DNA to mine, DNA that dictates that their skin has slightly more melanin, people whose ancestors primarily lived in South America, Africa, Asia, human beings whose kids have also just started school, they struggle with different fears, and then again probably a lot of the same fears, as me.

I am lost. I don't know what to do with myself. I have financial obligations, and once the obligations are met, I have a wish list. The uncomfortable sofa. I feel guilty wanting a comfortable sofa. I think about the people with the different DNA, mothers and fathers with different circumstances. I think about the families I lived with in India who have no sofa.

But I had friends to my house yesterday and didn't ask them to sit on the sofa. They weren't my best friends, who know to get a pillow to prop you up and then it is okay. So we sat at the table and had a nice time. If I earned a bunch of money, I could have a different sofa, maybe I would ask more people over. Maybe I would feel different.

I used to travel to places like Rio, and Kyoto, and Poznan (no offense Poland, but that was not as exciting as some of the other trips). I sat in meetings in beautiful places all over the world. Back then, people asked me what I did and I told them "I'm important" (paraphrase). "This company and this title validates that I'm something."

Someone assigned me something to do. I did it. Then they said my name during a meeting with more people and mentioned that I was very useful. I blushed. That moment was over and I remembered the hundreds of hours of my life I had traded for it. Sometimes it felt worth it. Usually it felt a little bit less worth it than I thought it would.

Once I sat across a table from Harrison Ford and explained to him what my team was hoping to accomplish to save the world. He nodded. Once I drank tea with the Queen of Bhutan. We took a photo together. Once I sat with a group of older men in a West African village and explained why a group of people (mostly other older men, with very slightly different DNA from the villagers) were going to look at insects and birds in their forest. They nodded. But one of them said "This is why we should send our daughters to school." That moment felt worth it. Another time, I cried in a hotel because I was scared to sleep in a tent in the middle of Africa for a month. My friends were comfortable on mattresses on another continent, they were not listening to convoys of Liberian militants drive by them in the night.

And here I am now. No fancy job. No fancy title. No paycheck. Two kids whose little legs will get longer and longer until they are long enough to carry them to Africa, or Poland. I will be here to help those legs get longer and stronger and to hopefully point them in a good direction. But they will have less and less need for me.

So what will fill these long days? I think my sister thinks I should get another job. I think that because when I was telling her that I wanted to clear yet more of the clutter out of my house she said something like "Maybe it isn't the clutter that is bothering you. Maybe it is that you need to get out of your house and maybe get another job" (paraphrase). I think what her loving, beautiful heart was saying was that she thinks I need something to do. Some structured something that I apply my mind towards.

So, I decided to start selling cosmetics and skin care. The *clear* solution to this dilemma.

I have to back up here, to when I was about four years old. Or maybe five. You start kindergarten. Someone tells you where to sit and what the rules are. And when you sit where they told you, and you demonstrate that you are willing and excited to follow the rules, they give you a certificate. I know this because I have at least 300 such certificates in my basement at this very moment. Little photocopied slips of paper—and when you do something they want you to do, they take out one of these little slips and put a star on it and your heart soars just a tiny bit and you take it home and your mom puts it in a box and saves it for you until you are 40.

I was very good at collecting certificates. My "personality type" (according to a test I took over the weekend at the recommendation of the beauty products company that I represent) is to be a "Helper." When I carefully read the report about my type it explains that as a Type 2 (Helper) I believe that "I must be helpful and caring to survive." Not, I enjoy being helpful, I feel value when I'm helpful. *To survive.*

I'm pretty sure that selling cosmetics is not my purpose. There are some benefits to doing this at this point in time, and perhaps I will explain it in the future and perhaps I will just know that I have my reasons and be okay with that.

That said, I know there is other work for me to do. But I can't quite figure out exactly what it is. So at night, after a day of selling cosmetics, after feeding the kids and washing the dishes, I spend my screen-free time soul searching.

To more precisely locate and connect with my "soul," I am reading a book by Danielle LaPorte called *The Firestarter Sessions*. It contains about 20 different sessions where you think about your strengths, interests, allies (I can't give you the full list, I'm still on the first session). To be honest, I'm a bit stuck on session 1. There is a list of questions to think about and answer and I don't know the answers.

Can you remember who you were before the world told you who you should be?

What I mostly remember is listening to the radio, to Casey Kasem's American Top 40, making up stories when no one was around, dancing with my mom to Diana Ross and the Supremes, watching rain fall off the roof with my brother and watching the pine bark floating, making mud pies (more specifically, they were beignets), and studying my giant-sized map of Disney's Magic Kingdom. I remember liking to play dress-up, but that may not be as separate from the world's influence on me as all the others.

I'm not sure how these memories point me in a direction.

What activities cause you to feel useful, vital, better than before?

I'm a Helper, so I can't really focus on useful. It makes me feel useful to clean the toilet or to do whatever somebody asks me to do. I don't think that's what we're looking for.

So *vital*.

Singing.

Making a bouquet of flowers.

Dancing.

Reading?

Organizing stuff?

I love to organize stuff. But that might just be self preservation in this overstuffed world.

I don't know.

I don't know.

I know that there are dishes when I wake up and more dishes when I go to sleep (duh, if you leave dishes when you go to sleep, they are going to be there when you wake up. That's a lesson we all learned in *Frog and Toad*). I know there is dust on most everything and I haven't changed the sheets in too long. I know there are dirty rivers and plastic in the ocean. I know there is a scourge of dehumanization in the ether and it needs fixing. I know the atmosphere cannot manage all of this extra heat energy in a way that is acceptable for human life.

I like to sing. My body feels good when I am making music. When I am moving.

I have financial obligations. And I would love a new sofa.

My kids just started school. I am selling cosmetics.

And I don't know who I am apart from all of the certificates.

I like frogs. The tiny little tree frogs.

Now I'm going to go pick up my children and hug them as tightly as they will let me. Except that they will probably argue the whole way home so maybe I'll just threaten to send them to their rooms.

I can hear the cicadas. The wind is blowing. I'm alive. I'm confused. I'm okay.

BASIC TRAINING: WEEK ONE UPDATE

September 22, 2017

One week into Basic Training and here is my report:

Waking up at 6:30 is (I think) helping me fall asleep more easily and makes the morning smoother. The problem is, if I stay in bed until 7:00 the kids do too but if I wake up, so do they (we are in close, squeaky quarters). So getting up earlier isn't buying me extra child-free time. And they are exhausted so I'd prefer they get the extra sleep as we transition back to school. I think the solution is to push my wake-up time earlier (6:00 is the eventual goal). I feel good about the progress made so far, even though I have missed 6:30 for the past three days in a row (by 15 minutes).

Meditation. As a beginner, I need an empty house to meditate. If I wait until after the kids are asleep at night, Dave will be running water, tapping at a keyboard, breathing, and I can't yet still my mind in the face of such obstacles. I'm enjoying Headspace (I'm still in the free trial) but I remember one guided meditation I did over the summer where you repeat a mantra in your mind and I actually felt a change in my body, like a different frequency, during that meditation. So I will continue with Headspace (good for learning how to meditate) and then look for some more mantras to chant.

Writing. Crossed this off the list. The first time I sat down to write as a 10-minute task I cried. I wasn't sure what the point was, or how writing for 10 minutes was supposed to connect me to my soul. I want to develop a more structured writing practice, but it is no longer one of my Basic Training tasks. I still track days that I write because it makes me feel good to see the checks accumulating.

Smoothie. Every morning. One of the most fundamental changes (practice-wise) that I have made in my life over the past two years and I honestly believe starting the day with a green smoothie has set the foundation for many other positive changes.

Fermented foods. My doctor prescribed fermented foods when it was found that I have a depauperate gut flora. She said two tablespoons twice a day. I have found this simple to implement and a good way of getting an extra serving of veggies. Do I occasionally recoil at the thought of my daily kraut, maybe. But gut bugs are good for your skin, good for your brain, good for your digestion, good for your mood. So I measure out my tablespoons and do my best to chew slowly and mindfully. Yum.

Outside time. My body was made to spend most of its time outside, smelling the smells in a forest, feeling sunshine and wind. I have felt most alive in my life during the periods of time when I have lived exclusively outside, bug bites, camp food, dirty clothes, handwashed underpants, and all. But my ten-minute task, while making sure I at least expose my body to the elements for a brief span each day, doesn't quite help me connect to those feelings. Sometimes ten minutes turns into an hour, and once this week I took a walk on a boardwalk through a wetland and saw two tortoises locked in conjugal embrace ("Mom, are they fighting? or hugging?"). I smelled the smell and felt that life is good and beautiful. So I'm keeping up the practice, but needing to refine it in some way.

Dancing turns out to be my toughest challenge (well, movement in general as I have yet to attend an exercise class). Here's what I've found with the three days I actually danced during the week: the first couple of times were fun, I listened to the music and kept the children from climbing on me like a jungle gym. The third time, my body remembered how much pleasure it can be to move. I guess what I'm saying is that the first two times my mind had a nice time and by the third time my body remembered what it felt like to be awake. I missed my friend Sarah. I thought of all the dancing we did. I thought about planning a dance-a-thon.

Playing an instrument. I remember more each day and it gets easier and more fun. This is pure joy for me and ten minutes is achievable.

Screens off at 9 PM has been a positive change. I definitely think it has helped me sleep better because the one night I stayed on until around 10 PM I had a much worse night of sleep—I just didn't wake up feeling refreshed. Yes, there could have been other factors. But for me less screen = more happier.

Exercise class. I need to sign up for a class and put it in my calendar! I have struggled with this for my entire adult life. I love yoga and would love to take a dance class too. I think it is making the commitment to a particular time that feels so daunting. What if something? So I need to just do it. Like right now. This minute.

Okay, I did it. It took about fifteen minutes because I had to read the class descriptions and decide whether to pay for a walk-in class or commit to the intro pack of four classes for $10 each (I committed).[25] I'm doing gentle yoga rather than hot yoga or anything called bootcamp. I'll try that and then schedule the next.

So that's my update. Overall I love my checklist and feel that it is a very positive presence in each day. It is just a tiny extra nudge from a good friend to do things that nurture me and build some healthy practices into each day.

---

25 Ended up paying $40 for one class because I didn't go back.

HOW TO MAKE ANY DECISION

September 29, 2017

I'm at loose ends. Again. Or still—I can't tell if it comes and goes or is more of a perpetual state.

This week I thought about applying for a job. I met with someone who has an open, full-time position for which I am qualified. I spoke with her about the responsibilities, the possibilities, the vision. What were they hoping to accomplish? How?

I didn't know what to do. The job would have me working with smart people who care about issues I care about to shift global systems. For instance, if one of the most important ways humanity can address climate change is to make sure that no more primary forests are cut down, this position would work with governments in developed and developing countries, major businesses (like huge oil companies), other NGOs, world-renowned academics to figure out *how can this happen*? And then work with the partners to get it to happen (and then throw a major party if it did happen).

I drove home. What am I going to do? I think keeping primary forests standing is super important. I love forests. They smell GREAT. I am scared about climate change. I am not a fan of multiple, massive hurricanes, I (in theory though I have never been scuba diving) love coral. I prefer that there continue to be massive glaciers and ice sheets.

This is an issue I care about. This is a job I can do. People have to go to war sometimes and it isn't that they want to go, but they have to because the times call for it.

Wait, what?

I said, people have to go to war sometimes....

You can't fancy about, doing only things that bring you joy. Sometimes you have to sit in work clothes, spend hours, years, in cold meeting rooms, sending emails, flying in airplanes to more meetings, writing reports, playing politics. Sometimes you have to do these things to make change. To save the world.

So, like I said, I drove home. How am I going to make this decision? I care about the world. I want to help. I sat down at the piano. I played some very elementary pieces, slowly, quietly. I felt the keys with my fingers. I heard two notes, or three notes, blending. My feet gently kept the rhythm.

I turned on some show tunes (Barbra Streisand "On a Clear Day" to be precise). I belted out some Barbra—about four songs worth. I pretended I was on stage performing.

I meditated. I did a fifteen-minute Deepak Chopra guided meditation on intention that I found on YouTube. At the end he said: *I place my intention in the vast ocean of possibility and allow the universe to work through me.* He said it three times, so I remembered it, and wrote it down afterwards.

And I knew this job was not for me.

I have been thinking about my 11th grade history teacher. She subscribes to this blog, which is both an honor and a source of some anxiety. Will she approve? Since you probably don't know my father's middle name, I will go ahead and let you in on the secret that she is the answer to the frequently asked security question: Name of your favorite teacher. Though I can never remember whether I put in just the last name or the full name—I try to be consistent with capitalization but I'm never sure.

I have been thinking about her because I have been thinking about impact. About one lifetime and choices we make. About the scale of what we try to do.

I was brushing my teeth earlier this week and I was thinking about wanting to say thank you. I don't know if she changed my life. I do know this: She taught me how to really work, academically. She expected me to work. I think, of all the teachers I was blessed to have, she taught me to examine, to think, to organize thought (she and Chauncey Loomis). She was the best writing teacher I ever had. And she loved me.

She was tough. *And she loved me.*

One teacher in one school in one town in one country teaching one subject. Thirty years later I am brushing my teeth and sending a silent thank you to the universe for her effort, her attention, her devotion, her love. For the difference she made in one life. For the love that she poured into one small, open heart.

She did not sit around with heads of state talking about forests. She came and watched me sing Barbra Streisand in the Samford University auditorium when I competed in the Junior Miss Pageant. She laughed when we gave her a box of Depends Undergarments as a 40th birthday present. She reads my blog.

I am glad that there are people who ask big questions and who sit in meeting rooms together trying to figure out how to move the big levers to take care of our beautiful world. I send prayers out to the universe for their success. I edit their (copious) documents and reports sometimes. It is a small thing, but it is a thing.

I will keep writing. And singing. And editing. And selling cosmetics. I will plant flowers for my butterflies and birds. I will post smoothie recipes on my blog. I will make up games and missions for myself and my friends.

And I will gently and carefully put my intention in the vast ocean of possibility and allow the universe to work through me.

EINSTEIN AND THE FIVE PEOPLE

October 4, 2017 unpublished

A number of months ago, my husband emailed me a quote from an article he had read online, I think believing I would feel validated, or at least be in complete agreement with the author:

> *Albert Einstein was asked once how we could make our children intelligent. His reply was both simple and wise. "If you want your children to be intelligent," he said, "read them fairy tales. If you want them to be more intelligent, read them more fairy tales." He understood the value of reading, and of imagining. I hope we can give our children a world in which they will read, and be read to, and imagine, and understand.*

The quote was the entire text of the email.[26] For some reason, who knows what I had had for breakfast or what was happening that day, the quote struck some sort of nerve. I did a (very little) bit of googling and promptly replied to my husband thus:

> *Very interesting. A) Is intelligence the highest value for a child? B) Why is someone asking Einstein about raising children? He was a philanderer with one schizophrenic son committed to an asylum, a daughter by his first wife that was given away and no one knows what happened to her, and one other kid with a wife he left to be with his two subsequent wives. I just don't see him as an expert in this particular area.*

I quickly added in a subsequent email:

> *not to say that this might not be reasonable advice, just ques-*

---

26   The full article, *Neil Gaiman: Why our future depends on libraries, reading and daydreaming*, a reprint in the *Guardian* of a talk on the importance of libraries, is quite nice.

tioning the rationale behind the author's sharing it and people thinking that because Einstein said it that it must obviously have some inherent value, with regard to children[27]

Why did I look up this particular exchange six months later and why am I sharing it today?

I am very very (very) confused. I am sad and confused and I don't know what to do and I don't know who does know what to do. Here's what I don't know. There are people in your life. You love them. You hurt when you think they are hurting. Your chest constricts. That spot, that band, that runs from your heart on the left side over to your not heart on the right side, the part that feels bruised and can't quite fill up with air no matter how many deep breaths you take, that part tightens up and you know there is someone you love deeply who is hurting.

You think about calling. You think about inviting them to go somewhere for a weekend. You think about a way to show you care, and especially think if there is anything you can do to help.

But, of course, you have your own life. Your own dreams. Your own needs. And you have read it—in so many places these days—that you are to surround yourself with people who support you. Strong people. People who fill you up (this seems to be the conventional wisdom if you seek to fulfill your potential / share your special gift with the world / live your extraordinary life).

Today, on Facebook doing some research into whether I should start a group or a page (or neither, I kind of hope the answer is neither), I saw an article somewhere with a headline along the lines of: "See the nanny who started a million-dollar business during nap times and trips to the park."

I sell cosmetics as a side hustle so I'm privy to the work lives of a number of women who have a job after they finish their other job. I hear them, on phone calls, cajoling their kids to be quiet while

---

27   yes, I am always this much fun to be married to.

they are on the phone. Bribing the little tots with candy, if they'll just shut up, or with some time to play games on their phone. Anything to get a transaction finished, to build the biz.

I love Einstein. I enjoy his essays and getting a glimpse into the way his mind works. Obviously he made huge contributions to humanity. As did Gandhi. I mention Gandhi because I recently read something about his taking a vow of celibacy and then asking a number of young ladies (including his niece) to sleep in the nude next to him, to test his will I guess.

These guys changed the world. The contributions they made are immeasurable. And they led human lives and had human flaws, whatever "flaws" means, we aren't dishes after all. They were people. People are people and they act like people and we shouldn't expect them not to.

But if you read about Gandhi, for instance, his kids didn't have the greatest lives. And then there are the Einstein family life details mentioned above. And without doing a thorough investigation of the greatest humans who have ever lived and their children or their families, I feel like it often surfaces that the ultra successful (rich, famous, celebrated, etc.) often have these statistically worse relationship histories than Joe Schmo. But that might be because we don't know anything at all about Joe Schmo and anyone in the world, anyone at all who you examined would have these personal life struggles because that's what happens in personal lives. Most people struggle and most families have folks who make it out and survive and others who don't.

So the question is: You love someone. They are in a dark place. You have things to do. Priorities. Responsibilities. You cannot be Einstein and take a break from the lab to take someone camping for a weekend to talk about life. You probably can't be Einstein anyway, I guess. So maybe that's the answer. If you think you can be Einstein, maybe just keep working at your thing. But otherwise, it seems like we all are having the work ethic of an Einstein.

Thinking that making a few more sales in our cosmetics business is going to move humanity's understanding of quantum physics forward and so it is okay to just push the kids off for a little while longer. To build our side business during the hours we are being paid to perform the service of a nanny and interact with children. To put off calling a friend in need today because the energy is so difficult and we've been cautioned that you have to secure your own life jacket first. Maybe you don't. Maybe when you love someone you just call, you feel the hurt in your chest, you make the call, you turn off your screen and walk away from your Twitter, you don't achieve that extra thing, you move to a smaller house.

Maybe I will die with the song still inside of me. Without making a statement or showing the world what I can do. Without living an extraordinary life or what have you.

But I will have loved someone. I will have taken a bit of my soul and a bit of my spark and, taking in as much air as I can, given my limited lung capacity under the circumstances, I will have tried to use that tiny spark to breathe fire back into a heart that my heart loves.

Maybe it will work. Maybe it won't. But I don't guess I will ever give up trying.

42 CANDLES

October 5, 2017 unpublished

When I was one year old there were four people who mostly made my world. My mom and dad, my mom's sister, Denise, and her son, my cousin Bill. Bill, born in February, was seven months my elder and was just about the best thing the world had ever made, in my opinion.

My cousin Bill was one of my life's great gifts. I don't see him much these days. He still lives in Alabama and I've been away from home for longer than I lived there. And as I get older and older, it seems less and less likely that I'll ever move back home. I still call it home though, even after twenty-five years away.

Bill was my playmate for seventeen years. Every birthday, every holiday—time with Bill was the highlight. He mattered to me *immensely*. He was like a slightly older brother who you love with all your heart, but one who is always kind to you, one who is always happy you are around.

Bill was kind. He was his own person. He never seemed to be swayed to be anyone else. And this was his gift to me. In admiring him, I saw that I could be myself too.

Now that I have my own children, who have their own friends and influences, I recognize what an incredible treasure my cousin was to me. We had mud fights, we pretended to be *anything* and made a game up around that, we didn't really play with toys—we used our imaginations, we invented games and stories, we were happy. He helped me learn to be nice. He helped me learn to have fun.

And deep down, whenever I might have felt lonely, or like I

didn't fit in, I knew that I had one friend. And that one friend felt like a rock.

Life is funny. And funny is a word to mean some other word that maybe doesn't exist. I see Bill once or twice a year now. We talk for an hour or two, I find out the basics, he finds out the basics, and then we go back to our grown-up lives. That's life I guess — we grow up and people and places that were our whole world stay an important part of the story, but aren't any longer the main characters.

My birthday is on Saturday. My 42nd. Growing up I had a large extended family — my mom is one of four girls and we celebrated family birthdays together. Three of the sisters and seven of the grandkids all lived in town, so there were twelve birthday celebrations each year and we would all get together at a house or restaurant, in later years frequently a Japanese steakhouse called Kobe, which is now closed.

I haven't been home with my family for a birthday since I turned thirty. And actually, I was living in England for my 30th birthday (I didn't have a cake that year so I put a candle in a hard-boiled egg with my then boyfriend, now husband). But before I went to England, in August, we had a 30th birthday party in Alabama. I invited some friends from home, so of course Bill and his wife were there. That was the last time.

I don't know what to do for my birthday this year. It has felt like a hard year, and a difficult few months, and a tough week. There's Las Vegas, and Puerto Rico, and all of the people struggling and suffering and trying to figure life out in the wake of all that happens and is happening.

And my aunt is dying.

She has had lung cancer for so long. They did not think she would live to 65 and she's 69 now. But the cancer has stopped responding to treatment and she's on hospice. She's been told six months and that was almost three months ago.

When my daughter turned one, I wondered if I should take the day off of work or what we should do. She was one. She would never know, never remember.

My mom had told me—it is one of those things your mom tells you more than once: *When you were turning one I wasn't going to do anything. You were only one. But your Aunt Denise said we should have a party. So she and Bill came over and we sang and had some cake.*

So when I wasn't sure what to do for Maggie's first birthday, my mom reminded me of the first birthday story and then said: *Invite your sister, get a cupcake, and have a party for Maggie. It's not just for Maggie—it's important for you too.*

My mom called today and asked what I'm planning to do for my birthday this year. I'd like to be with some people, I think. It feels like a lot of work though and I'm so tired. And so sad. My mom told me that she reminded my aunt that it was my birthday this weekend and my aunt cried. I asked my mom why. I wanted her to tell me why. I don't know why I asked. She said: *She loves you. She's remembering what has been.*

Now I am remembering what has been. I wish I could go home. I wish I could be with Bill and Aunt Denise and go to Kobe and have the ladies sing to me while I blow the candle out of my pineapple. I wish I could sit at their house and eat Fruity Pebbles. I wish Aunt Denise would bring me her tins full of coins and I could count them out for her.

I am so thankful for that first birthday party and all of the days in between. For the jello salad. For the time and the love—all the love. I miss you now. I will miss you later. I love you. And I thank you so very much.

In two days, when I blow out my 42 candles, I will say thanks and send my love 770 miles away to all of you.

I WROTE A SONG

October 11, 2017
I was sick yesterday and I recorded myself singing a song that I was writing. I wanted to share it with my family, but since I was sick I thought maybe I'd wait and try again later.

However: I live very close to the Pentagon and around 10 AM, right after I had recorded the song, an uncommonly loud jet plane flew over my house. As the plane was getting louder and louder and closer and closer, I thought: I would really like to share that song right now, just in case. I'd like them to have it. I'd like it to exist somewhere other than on my phone. So I sent the recording (made using my phone's voice memo app) to my parents and my brother and sis via text message.

And then my mom called and, because she's my mom, told me it was great. So I shared the recording on the blog too. I wrote a first draft (lyrics only) last Wednesday night and then my kids got sick. And then I got sick. I put music to the words yesterday, revised last night, and recorded it on my phone this morning.

Dear God
I know we don't talk much
but I need some help tonight
This day feels so dark and heavy
can't seem to see much light
There's a handful of hearts
that are woven into mine
when a string is pulled in one mine feels it too
and the chords feel stretched to break
worry how much more some hearts can take
and it isn't clear to my heart what I can do

Dear God
the ones that I hold dear
have sorrows of their own
and out there is the whole big world
and each new day another stone
with the storms and the guns and the bombs and the people
who could help make it better but they don't
with the right and the left and everyone's a person
who could talk to each other but they won't

Dear God
I'm just one lost soul
to help with the hurting, big and small
I wonder if I'm strong enough
and I know that I can't do it all
Should I pray or march or meditate or tweet or call or sign
Should I help my neighbor or write another song?
Read an angry post and share
help a friend who's in despair
plant a garden, take a breath and carry on?

Dear God
I know we don't talk much
thanks for listening tonight
Guess I know what a girl can do
and I promise to try and share some light
with the world full of hearts that are woven into mine
when a string is pulled in one mine feels it too
and when the chords feel stretched to break
remember there's a lot a heart can take
to just keep trying is all that I can do
To just keep shining
is the only thing to do

BASIC TRAINING ROUNDUP

October 20, 2017

My four weeks of Basic Training are about to wind up. In case you are good at math or paying close attention, *yes*, it has been more than four weeks since I started. The beautiful thing about Basic Training is that it is fully adaptable. If you have sick children, if you are sick, if you forget, if it becomes overwhelming, if you decide to rebel, *you can start from wherever you are*. If you decide, hey, I don't think dancing every day is a key to my well-being—*you can cross it off*! Leave the list on the fridge, with a line through dance every day. Dance if you feel like it.

For me, the most important lessons from my "four weeks" of Basic Training are that:

1) I can meditate! That "monkey mind" that won't be quiet when I try to meditate? Noticing the incessant chatter of my brain is the whole reason *to* meditate! If you try and your mind won't stop *thinking*, congratulations! You are alive! Just keep practicing.

2) Setting aside ten minutes each day to play an instrument is, essentially, another form of meditation and incredibly soothing to my body, mind, and soul. It feels like getting a brain massage every night after the kids go to sleep. And it usually turns into more than ten minutes.

3) Turning off electronic devices by 9 PM each night has been difficult to stick to, but I notice that my life feels better if I adhere to this practice. Not sure what to do after 9? [Insert joke about sex here.] I use my time after nine to read, play music, fill notebooks, have conversation with my husband (remember conversation?), organize stuff, or, if those all feel like too much effort, I go to sleep.

4) I am still struggling with wake times but am hoping to make a push in this area when the clocks change. I also notice that screens off after 9 PM makes a big difference with the ease of waking.

After completing Basic Training, the next stage is going to be focused on energy. Components of The Jenny Goodguts Super-ish Hero Training Program will be some versions of:

Basic Training

Module 1: Bad Guys 101—Loop-o

Module 2: Allies/Good Guys

Module 3: Lair/Hideout

Module 4: Secret Weapons

Module 5: Superpowers

In Module 1 we will modify the spreadsheet, but keep paying daily attention to most of the Basic Training activities, adding new tasks to specifically look at energy drains and try to plug some energy leaks. Module 1 should be ready to launch next week.

In other news, what I'm about to report is small beans in the world of the internet, but big beans for me. As of this morning, my song has been seen by 489 unique visitors—the most of any song I've written. I've had 2,796 page views this month, which is not my biggest month, but is a pretty big turnout for me.

So it seems like I've written a song that not only I like but some other people do too. I'm thinking about a way to record it as a music file instead of having to listen from the website each time. I have some other songs I've been working on. They are not all in the same vein as this song. I will share some of them. They are almost ready.

novel in progress

ONE WAY TO WRITE A NOVEL

October 26, 2017
PART 1: In which our heroine lays out the project and multiple objections

On Saturday night, we decided that I will write a novel. I stated my objections:

Objection the first/primary: What about money? Do I not need to exchange my time/life for money?

I have, on a notecard taped above my desk, a quote from Alan Watts recently sent to me from the universe via a wise soul: *Under all circumstances one should behave like the water, one should adjust to the requirements of the outer world, keeping safe his/her unchangeable essence in the meantime.*

Adjusting to the requirements of the outer world is a tricky thing. Which are the *requirements* and which are not? Food. Water. Shelter. Love. Safety. Belonging. Maybe we exchange time/life for belonging. For security. For experience. For freedom. For stability. Money can help provide some of these things, to some extent, but on its own cannot provide any of them. Lots more to think about here.

Decision: I have three months to write the first draft of a novel. I will sell cosmetics. I will accept editing contracts offered during this time, but will not pursue new ones.

Objection the second: A novel? An essay? A short story? A song? An album? If I spend time on one, I'm not spending time on the other. If I don't write music now, will anyone want to hear (me perform) it in five years when I finally make the time? If I pick the wrong project now, and it doesn't work, will I run out of time for trying and have to get a "real job" and the song/story inside will remain unsung?

Decision: You have an idea for a novel. Your songs are nice but (per counsel) your writing is better. Focus on the novel. Get a draft done. Find out if you can do it.

Additional note: National Novel Writing Month (NaNoWriMo) begins November 1st. The objective is to write a 50,000-word novel by the end of the month. There are tutorials, support groups, resources, and generally some community supporting creative endeavor so it seems fortuitous to begin at a time when there might be some human engagement more readily available (rather than sitting at home alone rocking and laughing at all the hilarious lines my amazing characters will be delivering).

Objection the third: Write a novel? Don't you know the world is kind of in trouble?

I was in the carpool line to pick my kids up from school yesterday. Before pick-up begins, cars wait along the right-hand side of the street in a long line, sometimes blocking driveways. This was the case yesterday. We all shifted, some forward, some back, to allow a highly incensed man to pull his truck into his driveway. I can relate to feeling frustration when you get home and there is something blocking your parking space. I sympathize and recognize that it would doubtlessly be annoying to have all these Audis and Lexi, and the odd Tesla, blocking your drive each day at 3 PM. So he said something rude to one of the ladies in the line, I believe it was a nanny, in an unpleasant and not totally unthreatening tone, and then went inside his house.

Directly after this incident I had pulled forward and there was a car parked on the side of the road next to me and so my car was about a foot more towards the left than most of the other cars. I was sticking out towards the center of the road when, from behind me, came a towering monster of a truck. Grey. Chevy? Or Ford? Who can say. I don't know much about motors or the mechanics of producing sound therein. I think, if you have your car in very low gear and you press the gas, say to the floor, you can create what turns out to be an unmistakably intentional and incredibly hostile sound. A chest-tightening, stomach-flipping sound that pretty clearly indicates to the lady in the car sticking out an extra foot from the line that you hate her and her private school brats and she should go f** herself. I think that's what the car was saying but I don't speak engine so I could have some particulars of the translation wrong.

If you are me, next you start thinking about people who are mad and about guns and about children and schools. And then you start thinking about solutions and what could change and what is making that person so upset and what can be done and misinformation and power and people profiting from being divisive. And then thankfully your kids get in the car so all you can think about is keeping their bodies separate, explain why it is too late to change their minds and both be Odd Squad agents for Halloween, try to give a lesson in economics and explain the difference in cost and value, explain that while some kids do, in fact, buy whatever costume they have in mind each year for Halloween that's not how it was when you were little and that's not how it is going to be for them but you are happy to help them make something out of the dress-up clothes and cardboard boxes at home. Explain that it is less about the expense than about disposability and the consumer aspect of buying new costumes on a whim each year. You know you are no fun. Why can't anything just be fun? So you spend the afternoon putting jewels on a crown with your daughter who has decided that she will use a dress she has[28] and be a queen, even

---

28   that brocade dress I bought on consignment on the last day of my thirties.

if the boys don't like things like princesses and all that. Son still undecided.

So anyway, there are problems and they are big and scary. There are helicopters flying to the Pentagon all the time I can tell you. Let's not get into this anymore here, I think we all know what I'm talking about.

So I'm going to write a novel. It's not going to solve anything. But there have been some pretty awesome people in history who have thought it was a useful idea to write a novel. I am, statistically if for no other reason more closely linked to ability, unlikely to join in their ranks in terms of longevity and impact, but if many of my heroes and soul mates have been writers, maybe I can be excused from saving the world for a few months and try my pen.

(*Silent and unspoken objection (the fourth)*): No, I don't think I'm Jane Austen, or Charles Dickens, or William Faulkner, or Umberto Eco, or Tolstoy, Forster, Byatt, Woolf, White (etc., etc.). I just want to write. Can I please just try?

PART 2: In which, after some slight delay, our heroine does, in fact, begin to write

Monday morning was my first morning for novel writing. I had it blocked out in my calendar. The hours of nine to twelve in the morning are for writing each day, five days a week (for three months, and if you can't do it then DOOM!). I sat down to write. I found the four handwritten pages I had started two or so weeks earlier, ready to type them into my laptop (still undecided whether to write by computer or hand), screens off after 9 PM as you know. I placed the sheets on the desk, directly next to the computer. And I had a thought. Maybe, just for a few minutes, I might have a quick peek at some Jane Austen. Just to get myself into the mindset. I selected *Persuasion* off of the shelf. I opened it to the first page. I read the first half of the book sitting at my desk. I got up and went to the bathroom. I sat on the pull-out sofa and read the second half with my eye on the clock noting I would have to leave to get the children by 3:00. I finished the book around 2:30. The whole book. And then I ate something, maybe some nuts.

The afternoon passed. The kids were fed, bathed, put in bed. Sam lay upstairs and sang himself to sleep (NSync's "Bye Bye Bye" his current lulla(bye) of choice). I was tired and a bit off kilter having read the entirety of *Persuasion* that day. Well (I thought), I'm not going to type now (screens and all), I will read a different author. I revisited the same shelf, selected *A Tale of Two Cities*, unopened (by me) since 1990, and read until just after Charles Darnay and Sydney Carton have had dinner after Darnay's reprieve from being quartered, meaning to be cut into quarters, your guts pulled out and burned while you're still alive (book the second, chapter 4)—about one-third of the book. I slept fitfully (this is not a "light" book being mostly about the human appetite for torture and beheadings and prisons, etc.).

The next morning, Tuesday, I *knew* that I could not spend another day in the same way. The novel must be begun! But I happen to own a two-volume biography of Charles Dickens. I have had these two volumes on my "to read" shelf for several years. The shelf containing over one hundred books (with new books frequently added and old books rarely subtracted), it was not clear when reading about the life of Dickens would become the top priority. It turns out Tuesday was the day. Just one chapter as I'm insatiably curious about his childhood when his dad went to debtor's prison and he was pulled out of school to work in a factory. I want to know a little bit about that. To imagine a mind like Dickens' sitting in a blacking factory, gluing labels onto pots and sealing them for twelve hours each day, at age 11, not knowing if he would ever have another opportunity to do anything else. So I read for two hours and then went to the doctor, had some lunch, read just a little bit more.

STOP! (I reprimanded myself.) *No more putting it off! Start your novel already.*

So I did. Tuesday after lunch. I reread the handwritten stuff, adjusted, and got to 1,268 words by 3 PM. Again got the kids, kept them alive, fed, bathed, read (we started reading *Stuart Little* on Monday night, so that's three of my favorite authors in one day). I then spent Tuesday evening reading more about the life of Charles Dickens.

Let me set the scene carefully for what next precipitated (ha ha, you'll get it in just a sec): In bed, Tuesday night, I was propped up against my (multiple) pillows, reading my little heart out, resting the book in an upright position against my body, most likely with one or the other eye closed (I rest them that way when I am tired) when something dirty fell out of the book and landed on my chest. Some brownish bit of grass or old leaves. I moved another page and more earthy material fell out of the book.

Four-leaf clovers.

About ten four-leaf clovers were either tucked into or had just fallen out of a page towards the middle of the book. The last person to have intimate contact with this particular volume before me had amassed a collection of four-leaf clovers and pressed them in between the pages. I don't know if this was my grandmother's book. Or my great-aunt's book. Or my great-grandmother's book (or some dude who liked to collect four-leaf clovers, it could have also been a man, of course). What I do know is that someone, and, knowing the tastes of my living relatives in terms of their likelihood of having read a Dickens biography in this lifetime, someone a long while ago, pressed a bunch of four-leaf clovers into this volume, sending me a message decades later.

Do you remember when I found that lucky quarter at Trader Joe's and stopped playing addictive iPad games and healed my gut flora? Just imagine how much more powerfully some 60-year-old four-leaf clovers found in a Dickens biography I had begun reading on the same day as starting my novel might affect me. It's a sign!

I wrote again on Wednesday (up to 2,993) and then Wednesday night began reading Zora Neale Hurston's *Their Eyes Were Watching God*. I want to reread *To the Lighthouse* but fear I gave my copy away in a clutter-clearing frenzy and so looked for fiction, by a woman, about the life of a woman. Slim pickings. There was only one choice on the "to read" shelf. I'm pretty sure I've read *Their Eyes Were Watching God* before but I recently took my sister's copy from a shelf at my parent's house—it feels familiar but I guess it would have been years and years ago that I read it. A little over halfway through with that one. Add it to the bedside stack.

So here it is Thursday and I'm writing this to update you on the latest and will move on to noveling next.

I like what I've written so far. I'm not sure what I'm doing exactly. I don't have a plan. I'm sort of trying to excavate the bones (as Stephen King describes in *On Writing*). I'm sort of trying to write what I know. I know there are things to say. So I guess I'll get to it now.

ON GLOW STICKS, AND GETTING
OUT OF A FUNK

November 17, 2017

You might be wondering (or not), what's up? Why no new posts in the last three weeks? How is the novel? Any chance I've reverted to certain addictive behaviors lately? Am I blaming Halloween for any minor life or habit setbacks? How's Basic Training? Still meditating? Still eating fermented foods? Have I been wearing the same shirt for a week? Do I have a not unwarranted but probably disproportionate rage against glow sticks? How is my cosmetics business?

It's funny you asked! Here are the updates, in brief:

Novel: I am up to 17,090 words on the novel. To get to 50,000 by November 30th (the NaNoWriMo goal), I am about 7,000 words behind where I should be. If I write an average of 2,194 words each day until the 30th, I'll get there. My biggest day so far has been 4,390 but we have to keep in mind that I will have family in town, Thanksgiving to host, children out of school, Black Friday and Cyber Monday (shudder), birthday parties to attend (etc.). So maybe I'll get to 40,000. I'm pretty happy about that. The main character is a mother of two who lives in Alexandria and takes issue with the status quo (I don't know how I think of these things either!). It is fun and challenging and sometimes it makes my heart feel like it is hurting but that may be muscular strain from sitting in one position for too long. It takes a lot of emotional energy to think about what you really mean, what really motivates someone. I think I like writing novels. But I'm not totally sure what is going to happen yet. There are some parts I love, that I read and feel like

I don't know who exactly wrote them. That's fun.

Confession: I played *the game*. About five days ago I played the cursed iPad game. I can't remember exactly what happened. But I did it. And then I kept doing it. For hours. Hours. And the next day, maybe for just one or two hours. And then I knew I would have to tell you about it. So yesterday I deleted the game (okay, the two games) from the iPad forever.[29] I had not touched the games since starting the blog last spring. More about this below.

Coffee: In the past two weeks I have unintentionally switched from being a tea-drinker who dabbles in an occasional weekend coffee to one who is functionally reliant on coffee. I did not have coffee on Tuesday and I woke up on Wednesday morning in excruciating pain that could only be taken away by sweet, sweet caffeine. So this will have to be addressed but for now I'm a coffee drinker. Again, don't know what happened. I just felt like being reckless so I started drinking a big mug of coffee every morning and—bam. I think I thought I was being kind of naughty because I know I'm super sensitive to caffeine. Well, what's done is done. I will have to figure a way out of this.

Halloween: Used to be my favorite custom. Now I kind of hate it (for multiple reasons, many of which are discussed in my upcoming novel). Also, I cannot resist a Kit Kat. So I get hooked on Kit Kats and then I become a coffee addict and play farming games until my arms hurt. I'm weak I guess. But I fight this battle every year and it is never pretty. The Kit Kats are gone now (and not in the trash) so it will be back to smoothies soon. I should mention that I haven't had a smoothie all week. Or any fermented food. Nor have I played the piano, meditated, spent time outside, danced. I have done a lot of singing in the past two days. And I've spent time with two friends, which was probably the only antidote I needed.

Glow sticks: Can we talk about glow sticks, just for a minute?

---

29   um, not exactly forever...

Glow sticks are one great example of something that is possible to make. Yes, human beings, ingenious creators, have figured out how to make a little plastic stick glow in the dark for a few hours before it becomes trash. Yay! Kids love these things for at least five minutes before they throw them on the ground and forget about them forever and then they are just garbage. YET, I do not rail against the glow stick because they are just dumb trash (I will save that for my Chuck E. Cheese birthday party favor bag rant). I rail against them because the chemical inside a glow stick that makes the glow is a phthalate, in most cases dibutyl phthalate, and these little chemicals are pretty horrid for human beings. True, most children do not eat glow sticks. But when you throw them away, they don't magically disappear! They go *somewhere*. And that somewhere is the water we drink. Pthalates are linked to asthma, attention-deficit hyperactivity disorder, breast cancer, obesity and type II diabetes, low IQ, neurodevelopmental issues, behavioral issues, autism spectrum disorders, altered reproductive development, and male fertility issues. People, it just isn't worth it. Twenty seconds of sheer glee (for a kid who, most likely, is way overstimulated already whether it is Halloween or not) versus a population exposed to chemicals that we know are making us all sicker. If I see you buying glow sticks (I'm so sorry, I'm working on this, truly, but) I will judge you. Maybe you're judging me right now. I know, all this judging is the worst, maybe I should just work on being at peace with the glow stick. I'm just being honest. It will make me feel sad. So keep that in mind.

Roadrage: We are all in agreement that watching a show on your phone while you are driving a moving car is not an okay thing, right?? I was so happy this morning, singing a song after dropping my kids off. Driving back home. And this lady was driving very erratically and I needed to switch lanes so I looked at her to see if she saw me signaling and SHE WAS WATCHING A SHOW ON HER PHONE—not at a stoplight (I do not condone this either)—she was driving on a road that has a 45 mph speed limit. She was driving and watching a show!?! I got upset. I tried to feel lighthearted again and sing my song, but it just wasn't in me. Then some other people drove like selfish jerks (I, meanwhile, drove perfectly, faultlessly). Then I saw a friend and felt much better.

Cosmetics: My Beautycounter business is going pretty well, thanks for asking. I like that they are trying to change the industry and to make products that don't contain known harmful ingredients. I have a thing about businesses that know—full well—that certain ingredients/behaviors/substances are seriously damaging to the population as a whole and they just don't give a crap. Please see my note below about the Sacklers.

The Sacklers: I have been very upset this week. I believe the iPad game relapse was due to an article I read in *The New Yorker* by Patrick Radden Keefe, "The Family That Built An Empire of Pain." He writes about the Sackler dynasty, well known as generous philanthropists who give tons of money to art museums all over the world (think the Met, Louvre, Smithsonian) and have their names on all this stuff and are knighted (etc.), but their names are strangely absent from the webpage of the pharmaceutical company they privately own, a company called Purdue Pharma that developed OxyContin and, it appears, knew pretty well from the start that it was extremely addictive but had a targeted campaign to convince doctors across America that it was safe to prescribe, even though the doctors voiced legitimate hesitations. The article posits that this drug is the primary driver of America's opioid crisis and the family now has $13 billion dollars (that number growing every day, along with the number of Americans dying from overdoses, the number of babies born addicts, the number of families destroyed, etc.). And now they are expanding to foreign markets (also there's a new pill for kids over 11)—even with all that is known. Read the article. You are probably not as soft as me so you won't fall into Kit-Kat fueled, virtual agrarian despair.

What next? By the fact that I am writing this post you can rest assured that I am now on an upward, rather than downward, trajectory. There are many possible explanations for why we get into "funks." Could be related to the time of year, could be you get a huge credit card bill, could be how you are eating, or not eating, could be that you are lonely and feel isolated, could be that you are reading too much news, or not reading or thinking or doing enough to remember all that you do have, could be you are super tired, could be someone you know is sick, could be you are sick.

I also don't know what it is that gets you out of a funk. Could be talking to a friend. Or just getting to the end of the candy and making a decision not to get more. Or making a decision to help someone else. I think usually (always?) there is a point where you make a decision and then you follow through with that decision. Maybe you have help or maybe you do it on your own. Well, once again I've made a decision to crawl out and, luckily, this funk was short lived (sigh of relief).

Children's literature: My kids have been discussing a book they are enthralled with, one I have never read. Apparently the main character is a cat who poops out cupcakes. There may be a great lesson in this book. It might be Shakespeare, or Beatrix Potter. I cannot help but wonder. Kids used to be told stories that helped them understand their place in the universe. To learn how humans behave, how we interact with other people, creatures, the Earth. Now people make money figuring out how to make characters that kids will think are funny. Give the four-year-olds what the four-year-olds want! I like that we value childhood more now than in, say, Victorian times. I love to laugh with my kids. I'm all about creativity and imagination. But I guess I feel like maybe there is a middle ground that we've missed. A cupcake-pooping cat? Call me old fashioned but it feels like somewhere we went a bit off the rails.

light up our backyard.
A bird that flew five thousand miles
is trilling six bright notes.
This bird flew over mountains and valleys
and tiny dolls and pencils
of children I will never see.
Because this bird is singing to me,
I belong to the wide wind,
the people far away who share
the air and the clouds.
Together we are looking up
into all we do not own
and we are listening.

— Naomi Shihab Nye, *Messages from Everywhere*

One thing that helps me get out of a funk is this blog. So thanks very much for being here. Now back to that novel.

NOTHING FANCY, JUST SOME UPDATES

December 12, 2017

When last we left our heroine, she had initiated work on her novel, reaching a total of just over 17,000 words in a bit over two weeks. Unfortunately, she had also reverted to playing addictive iPad games (only twice, or for two days, before deleting forever, she hopes), had developed a debilitating coffee habit, had said some pretty strong things about glow sticks (the people are just trying to have fun, can you relax?), judged, possibly unfairly, modern children's literature based on a cupcake-pooping cat, was, in the opinion of many, justified in her anger with the Sackler dynasty, and had just about pulled herself out of the annual mid-autumn slump, yearly heightened by overconsumption of Kit Kats or their close relatives.

And there we left her. On the edge of our seats. Will she write more? Will she keep going with the blog? The posts seem to be coming less frequently, with less regularity. Perhaps another creative project that's run out of steam? We wondered about her Beautycounter business—is network marketing really the best use of her time? We wondered if she had any thoughts about the crush of patriarchy, the potential election of Roy Moore in Alabama. We were curious as to why she didn't replace that uncomfortable sofa.

Well, trusted readers, wonder no more.

Sofa: WE GOT A NEW SOFA!! Call me up if you're ever in the neighborhood. There's somewhere to sit. Your feet don't even have to leave the ground.

Roy Moore: Shoot. This blog isn't close to long enough to say it all. I have been trying, with some effort, to understand the position of the people I know and love in Alabama who might consider voting for this man. They are not bad people. They are people who, like all of us at times, allow one particular issue to matter more than character. I think we all need to shake hands—all of us pretty good, hard working, loving people who try to live as decently as we know how—and we need to agree that we're going to vote based on character. Because I promise you there are a bunch of a-holes without character who are super happy to take lots of money from people who don't give a crap about you, about your kids (in utero, one month old, in elementary school, or at 14) and use that money to print fliers making you feel outraged about something and then laugh with their rich buddies all the way to the bank as they turn our beautiful country into a sh*t show.

That's probably not as eloquent as I would like to be.

THE PATRIARCHY: Shoot. This blog isn't close to long enough to say it all. Perhaps just one short note. Over the weekend I read an article by a woman who was seething, raging, about the patriarchy in which we all live. You see, she had hosted Thanksgiving dinner and had had about 20 people into her home. Men and women, all decent folk. Now, what I am about to tell you may shock you, but she walked into her own bathroom, in her own home, and there was a toilet seat raised. Yes, you read that right. The seat was UP. This woman, this abused and tortured soul, had to TOUCH THE SEAT to lower it. Well, I can tell you she was livid. Beyond belief. She furiously sought her husband, rending her garments, tearing her hair, who would dare to treat her thus! In case you are not familiar with the term, patriarchy is when a culture is designed around the needs of men. So her hypothesis was that a man, by not lowering the seat for her after his use of the commode, is assuming that the way men use the toilet is the way everyone uses the toilet, or he just can't be bothered to think about who comes next. My husband was quick to point out that every single time he uses the toilet he touches the seat not once, but twice. He must lift the seat before he uses the toilet and then replace it back again afterwards. So, to me, that sounds more like a matriarchy? I always assume the seat will be down. That works for me but not for the men in my house. So they, very courteously, both lift and lower, and then wash their hands.

I thought about women who still walk 10 miles a day to cart water back to their home on their heads so that the men can eat first and best, so that men can bathe themselves, so that men can sit and talk with their buddies, where women are forced at a young age to marry some gross old guy based on their father's wishes—and don't have a sink right next to the toilet (and probably some froufrou Beautycounter liquid hand soap) where they can wash their hands if there's a seat lid up once in a blue moon.

I'm not saying we don't have long roads to walk in this country. But I feel this kind of indignation, over a raised toilet seat, confuses things (confuses what, well, that's what I need to spend time writing more clearly! I have thoughts, lots of thoughts). [Significant text cut. Not ready to get all into this. Forgive me.]

Beautycounter: Promoted to manager in November. Yes, it does take time away from my promising career as a best-selling novelist. But, truth be told, when I sat down and did a vision board to figure out my life purpose, I realized that helping more people to have dewy skin was my true calling. Everything I've ever done in my life, from living in tents in Africa to organizing international teams to negotiate at UN Conventions, it was all leading to this.

(I do like it. It feels a bit like playing store and playing dress up at the same time and it gets me out of the house, meeting new people, and washing my face. Conflicted about the industry? Perhaps. Mad that companies are knowingly putting carcinogens in children's body care products? That's a yes.)

This blog will not run out of steam: But it may cut back to a twice-monthly schedule to keep up with the demands of my novel writing and cosmetics pushing. Maybe I will figure something out around the new year.

Novel: Current word count is 17,090 words. If you're paying attention and are even just adequate at math you will recognize that this marks an advancement of zero words since my last post. Yes, I do have a good excuse. It's that I stopped writing when my mom came to town before Thanksgiving and now I don't know how to get started again. That's not fair to you because it isn't the whole story (mom came, dad came, Dave got home, Thanksgiving, parents left, I don't remember a few days, Sam got sick, I stopped drinking coffee, I don't remember more days. I sold cosmetics. I listed coins on Ebay. I wanted to write. I volunteered in Sam's class. I saw a friend. I helped a neighbor. I cleaned some dishes).

I have committed to get to 25,000 words by the end of this month. A reachable goal. Also to write two blog posts (one almost done) and to finish reading *Don Quixote*. I'm only about a hundred pages in but I can see why people make such a fuss about this book. I mean, if you are a huge book nerd probably. You might not like it otherwise. I laugh out loud every night and profess my unending love for Cervantes. I *might* be more in love with him than with E.B. White. Let me get to the end first. I'm sorry E.B., I still love you. Forever. But… we'll see.

Parting words: I really like writing to you. Thanks for reading. I hope I haven't written anything too stupid or offensive. I'm trying to work some things out.

ON RESOLUTIONS

January 12, 2018

For Christmas, my husband bought me a magenta-ish Patagonia hooded sweatshirt (aka, a hoody). I unwrapped it around 8 AM on December 25, directly removed it from it's plastic bag, and put it on. At the time of the ham incident (see below), I had removed the sweatshirt to sleep and, briefly, for three other occasions. I did not wear it to Christmas dinner. I did not wear it one afternoon when some relatives came to visit. I did not wear it for an hour on New Year's Eve (but then I felt chilly so I put it on). As of January 5th, I had worn it for all but eight waking hours over the course of twelve days. I changed shirts daily, or nearly that, in case you are wondering.

Now, about the ham. In my family, it is tradition on New Year's Day to eat ham and black-eyed peas (for luck) and greens (for money). Not sure about the meaning of the ham. Our tradition was always turnip greens (the kind that come frozen in a rectangular solid) when I was living with my parents though I think, technically, consuming any kind of greens on January 1st ensures a steady flow of money raining down from heaven over the course of the year. Feeling compelled to instill a bit of tradition in my offspring (while quite aware that they would not approve of the menu), on the 2nd of January I bought a ham (and black-eyes and collards). (We were on the road on the 1st and I'm hoping there is not some other tradition that says if you eat greens and peas the day *after* the 1st you will have terrible luck and lose everything—I'll keep you posted.)

We baked the ham, the spiralized kind. We ate it on Tuesday

night. And Wednesday night. I ate it for lunch on Wednesday. School was cancelled on the 4th because of "weather conditions" so I think I ate whatever the kids didn't eat but much of the day goes by in a snow-day haze so I could have mostly missed lunch. So there I was, Friday January 5th, wearing my hoody and standing in the kitchen. It's lunchtime and I see the huge ham, about eight pounds remaining. I will freeze it and use it to make red beans and rice, I tell myself. It is healthy, inexpensive, delicious. But in the meantime I'll eat some ham for lunch. So I unwrap the ham, setting the two sheets of glaze-splattered foil on the counter, pulling off part of a slice and shoving it into my mouth. Not *exactly* like an animal, I did use my hands and didn't just put my face directly on the ham, but possibly like a monkey I guess. Like an ape. Except that apes don't eat ham and if you've seen the gorilla at the zoo regurgitate food, it wasn't like that. I put it in, quickly, chewed, sort of, and then ripped off another slice.

At some point during this luncheon, I recognized that I'm wearing my sweatshirt (certain household members may have mentioned that the sweatshirt may have become a sort of uniform, and maybe they mentioned this in a way that suggested such a uniform might not be considered a positive development). I'm wearing my sweatshirt for the twelfth day in a row and standing in my kitchen ripping slices off a spiral ham and shoving them in my mouth and I start giggling. People would think there is something wrong with me. This is the part of the movie where I'm deep down in a funk, not quite right. I should cut off some slices, put them on a plate, sit at a table. There should be a salad, or some veggies, a glass of water. Maybe even another person. I should go to a café, in my stylish clothing, with my hair and makeup done. My friends would laugh at some story about what we did over the holidays, I would listen intently, then I would go back to my desk to finish up an important memo about something that was going to make the world just a little bit better, or at least make my boss happy, and then I would get my paycheck.

Now, fast forward to today, January 12th, a week later. I have had some serious talks with myself since the ham incident. Here's the thing: I'm not in a funk. This is not the part in the movie where I make an appointment to get a haircut (I did make an appointment to get a haircut though), start going to the gym (we'll talk about that another day but it is definitely time that I start at least stretching regularly. Okay, we'll talk about it now. I think I've been thinking I'm super sneaky and I'm going to be that person who makes it through life without exercising regularly. And the thing is—I can be! I'll just make it through life a little bit more quickly, and less comfortably, than I would otherwise. So that suddenly doesn't feel like such a sneaky, or good, plan.) But back to the not funk.

My mom, over the holidays, suggested a couple of ideas for things that I might be good at doing, professionally. She meant well. She loves me. She has a lot of confidence in me. She said these things in front of other people which made me feel embarrassed. Like what I am and what I'm trying to do isn't enough. As if selling safer cosmetics and blogging when I feel like it isn't my destiny.

Here's what I'm saying back to her, to you, to myself. *This* is what I'm doing. I'm eating ham, with my fingers, wearing a sweatshirt. The sweatshirt is soft, clean, it keeps me warm. I don't need five sweatshirts. This one is great. It fits, is rip-free, is a beautiful color. It serves my needs. I'm eating a little bit of ham for lunch. I don't need to spend a ton of time eating lunch some days. Sometimes a little ham is enough and then I can get back to the things I'm working on: writing, reading, editing, seeing friends, selling cosmetics.

I think I've been feeling like I don't have a full-time job because I can't have a full-time job. I think that's what I've been telling people. We have no family nearby that can help with kids, my husband travels for long periods of time, we've both worked full-time before, with two kids and travel, and it felt unsustainable. But here's the truth: I don't want to work full-time in an office. I don't want to spend any more of my life that way. I have worked as a receptionist, as a data-entry intern, in accounts payable for Budweiser, in a greenhouse, as a waitress, as a nanny, cleaning hotel rooms, at two magazines doing research and writing, planning and overseeing scientific expeditions to Africa, organizing teams to negotiate at UN meetings, on organizational design and strategy for a large 30-country conservation NGO.

Now I am searching. I'm living a human life, awake. It is not always comfortable. It is not always clear. I do not have defined deliverables and I don't have anyone holding me accountable other than myself. My ego fights me. Financially it is not the easiest path. And *this* is what I choose to be doing. Could I improve in terms of how to structure my days? I feel confident saying yes, I could. Might I develop some deliverables for myself? Well, maybe. Eventually, for sure. Right now I am searching. I am giving myself time to look around. To wonder. To feel the feelings in my body. That little pain that pops up around my heart sometimes—is that muscular, or from my soul?

So I just wanted you to know that. I'm not in a funk. When I look at myself in the mirror, while there are certainly lines that I'm not excited about and spots that I wish weren't there and also consider a professional liability, when I see my red sweatshirt I feel happiness. When I look at my eyes I recognize myself.

In 2017, I started this blog, started writing three novels (and one has just passed the 25,000 word mark and is going strong), wrote two essays I think are very good but I need to finish, and started another 15 or so essays that have some potential. I started taking songwriting lessons and shared one song on the blog, I started meditating, started playing the piano regularly, planted a butterfly garden, took a trip to the ocean with my kids. I started a Beautycounter business, found a bunch of four-leaf clovers in a biography of Charles Dickens, and received notes of encouragement from unexpected sources. I learned that my gut flora is depauperate and took steps to address matters, learned I *can* eat cultured foods, I broke a debilitating addiction to iPad games, I saw a Democrat elected to an Alabama senate seat, I spent more time with some of my favorite authors (E.B., Cervantes, Austen), I wrote a couple of paid articles, edited some cool stuff, got paid to learn about some things I'm interested in. I spent time with some friends. I listened to them. They listened to me. I cooked and ate a lot of healthy food. I cleaned some toilets. I stressed about money. I tried to stop stressing and be thankful. I will try harder this year.

As far as resolutions go, here is what I'm thinking:

I will make more choices instead of letting things go undecided for so long. My husband found some cotton plants while he was in Alabama, he picked some cotton, he was very interested. I put the cotton, stems, and seeds in a ziplock bag. Maggie brought it to school to show her class. Then it sat in the bag, in my dining room, for two weeks. I looked at it every day. What will I do with that cotton? I composted it yesterday. Decision made. (There are a lot more to go.)

I will acknowledge the choices I am making. I won't sink into feeling done-to.

I will try to meditate every day. This is really good for me. I like the Headspace app and you can start with three minutes a day. You can do it.

There is more to share about *Swedish Death Cleaning* and Napolean Hill and *You are a Badass*, but I have to post this before 11 AM which means I have eight minutes to reread.

P.S. I'm going to start saying the New Year's ham is for persistence. Luck and money are very well and good, but I want to persevere.

Happy New Year!

HOW TO LOSE TEN POUNDS IN TEN DAYS

January 20, 2018

Reader, have I got great news for you!

A *proven* weight-loss formula. Guaranteed results.

Step One: Send your spouse out of town for a week. Make sure to have your identity stolen the day before he/she leaves and to have an Apple laptop ordered by a criminal using your credit card to be delivered to your home address. Make sure the criminal subscribes you to thousands of websites in Germany and Japan. When you go to sleep each night, think about this criminal, the information they have access to, and whether they are watching your house to pick up the computer, or if they're stupid enough to have figured out how to hack into all of your personal information but were in a hurry when it came to the address, maybe they were watching a show on Netflix at the time or something.

Step Two: If your child's school hasn't already planned to give your children extra time off for a teacher workday right before a three-day weekend (presumably in case you want to fit in a ski vacation less than two weeks after school has resumed after Christmas break), go ahead and take your kids out of school for that extra day. Heaven knows, with all of the snow days and delayed starts and early closings you certainly don't want to miss a chance for more together time.

Step Three: Maybe you want to get out of the house for a few hours over the course of the four-day weekend. Go for it! Make sure to visit someone who recently had an extra virulent strain of a stomach bug that took down every member of her family. Eat a meal there. Bonus points if someone in the family still wears diapers. Viruses live in poop for extra long and luckily diapers are nothing like Vegas, what goes on in a diaper…

Step Four: Wait 24 hours.

Step Five: Voila! Your children will start to vomit. It must be in your car, all over the seats that you could not imagine why you would ever have scotchguarded at the time of purchase (what could happen?). Let this be at night, and make sure the vomit smells strongly of parmesan, even though no parmesan was consumed. Drive home for 15 minutes while you breathe in the aroma/airborne vomit particles. You may roll the windows down, even if it is 10 degrees outside, as this will have no impact on either the smell or the eventual health outcomes.

Step Six: After your daughter vomits all over her sheets, and you've changed her bed, and then your son vomits all over his sheets, and you've changed his, after they've both vomited in buckets and toilets at the exact, precise, same instant, after your son has dry heaved all night and your bathtub is literally filled with dirty sheets, duvets, pillows that you will wash in the morning but are a little too scared to take down into the basement, what with the criminals out there and all, slip into at least three hours of blissful sleep.

Step Seven: While you are doing thirteen loads of laundry, given both the rank odor and the fact that you will definitely be touching some upchuck, you will not feel hungry. Luckily your kids can't keep anything down except water, so you won't need to cook for at least a day. If hungry, feed them applesauce.

Step Eight: Wait four hours.

Step Nine: Change your daughter's sheets again as the vomiting is ongoing!

Step Ten: It seems like so many steps, doesn't it! But you will get quick results—guaranteed. You're just about to hit pay dirt.

Step Eleven: I know that Step Ten wasn't a step, but if you stick with it, you're about to seriously lose some weight. It will be totally worth it.

Step Twelve: Your energy and resolve to complete the program may start to flag at this point. Make sure to have your credit card company send you notifications every time there is a foreign transaction. This way, even when you are using the lid of an old cashew nut can to scrape dried vomit off of a pillowcase, you can vicariously enjoy lovely meals out together with your beloved spouse, who you know is working really hard (and that is not sarcastic, it *is* hard work to have meals out with smart people who are interested in the same things you are). Did I mention that the vomit smelled so strongly of parmesan?

Step Thirteen: Make sure to keep your kids home from school for that fifth day since they still don't have the energy to sit up.

Step Fourteen: Clean like the dickens. Do the laundry. Wash the dishes. Put everything away. Make sure to finally clean the vomit out of the car. You won't know what to do because vomit will have totally soaked in to your non-leather seats. Just rub it with a cloth, rub and rub and rub, first with water. Drench it with peroxide (more of the rubbing) and then coat whatever is left with baking soda. This will inoculate you against ever smelling the odor in your car again, though you will be told in the future that it still smells, terribly. Look, when you've spent that long with your face that close to three-day-old vomit in a car, you really can't smell it anymore, it's just some white, chunky blueberries and other stuff that's very hard to identify that you're just rubbing, and rubbing, and rubbing into your car for what seems like a long, long time.

Step Fifteen: Definitely don't figure out how to order groceries to be delivered to your house. You'll just go to the store tomorrow, right? After all, you still have a gallon of milk, two cheese sticks, some wilted kale, a bag of carrots, and an old chicken carcass. Sure, having some groceries delivered would provide nourishment for you and your children, and there is snow forecast, you live at the top of a treacherous hill and don't have four-wheel drive. Better idea is to text your neighbors to see if anyone can drop off a pack of dry pasta. You're going to need it.

Step Sixteen: Dine—Feast!—on a scrumptious and decadent half-full bowl of plain Essential Everyday Thin Spaghetti. It is the only thing your kids seem to be interested in and, since none of you have been eating for days, even if you can still smell the vomit from cleaning the car out earlier, you haven't had a meal in 48 hours. Eat the noodles as—who knows—this may be your last meal for a while.

Step Seventeen: Get one night of blissful, uninterrupted sleep. In your exhaustion, you've forgotten about the nefarious criminals so you won't wake up each time an old board in your house shifts due to the bitter cold, and unless there's snow tomorrow the kids will be back in school. Your spouse will be home in just two more days. Hooray!

Step Eighteen: Now you're going to have to arrange for a snow day. Or at least a delayed start to the day. It is imperative that your kids not go to school for the sixth day in a row and that they be home with you.

Step Nineteen: Get out of bed. Start some more laundry. Make sure to wash your hands at least fifteen more times. Notice how raw and chafed your knuckles are from your newly compulsive behavior. Now, drink some tea. Isn't that nice? Warm, soothing. Hmm—that's funny, you don't usually feel so queasy drinking tea. Maybe you should sit down on the sofa for the first time in three days, just rest for a couple of minutes.

Step Twenty: Don't get up from the sofa, for any reason, for the next twelve hours. Curl up into a ball. Teach your daughter how to adjust the thermostat (from the sofa) because you can't get warm, even covered in the sleeping bag that was luckily shoved under a door to keep the draft from coming in.

Step Twenty-one: Remove the sleeping bag because you're

too hot. And so on, back and forth. Teach your daughter how to make an emergency phone call from the cell phone, just in case. Notice she seems eager for you to lose consciousness, so she can try it out. Try to keep your son from giving himself a concussion, all day long. Recognize that he was definitely ready to go back to school. Google "flu symptoms" and "norovirus." Note that you don't have a fever, so you're probably fine. Teach your children how to make their own lunch (again, from the couch). Shout (with all the strength you can muster—this is the exercise component of the plan) to/at your son that under no circumstance should he, as he proposed to his sister, get the big knife out of the drawer. They will eat bagels and apples.

(Step Twenty-one.five:) Resist any urge you might have to grab your children by the face. You might feel this. It can happen. Look, we all feel like grabbing our kids by the face once in a while, right? But grabbing a big handful of childface will not keep them from doing things that might lead to their doom. Plus, you can't get to them. They won't listen to what you are saying and you can't stand up to reach their faces. You can't even grab at their batman costumes. Instead, try watching more of the brilliant and compelling drama, *P.J. Masks*. Hope that your children quickly learn its delightfully melodic theme song.

Step Twenty-two: Let your children make dinner for themselves. Suggested menu: a granola bar, baby carrots, and a cheese stick. No knives!

Step Twenty-three: Take your temperature. Aha a fever! Perfect. This plus the aches all over your body will give you enough cause for alarm that you probably will not sleep all night. Not to worry, your son also will not let you sleep all night.

Step Twenty-four: Have your children put you to sleep. Talk them through their nightly routine from your bed. Don't remember what happens next.

Step Twenty-five: Wake up an hour later, sweaty. Lie there sweating all night. It will give your skin a rosy glow. Have your son call for you throughout the night. He's little and he's nervous that you're not okay. You aren't, but stumble dizzily through the dark, repeatedly, to reassure him anyway (Note: Coming into contact with his now runny nose is recommended for the 20-day program only).

Step Twenty-six: Wonder how in the world you are going to get your beloved children out of your house/to school in the morning. Think about this while you are trying to find the cool spots on the sheets that your fevered body hasn't already turned grossly warm.

Step Twenty-seven: Wake up very slightly improved. Pack two lunches, get breakfast for children, make sure they have underwear, hats, gloves, snow pants, backpacks, library books, favorite toy car.

Step Twenty-eight: Get in the car, don't notice any smell of puke. Do notice the low fuel light is on.

Step Twenty-nine: Last car in line before carpool ends. Success! Lean against car with eyes closed while filling gas tank, visibly counting over and over to ten. This "insane" look guarantees no need for chit chat. Drive home while listening to the same song on repeat for 20 minutes. Binge watch *When Calls the Heart* on Netflix all day long. Eat nothing.

Step Thirty: Get in the car to pick kids up. Drive down the street. Wave to a neighbor, like everything is fine. Poop in your pants. No, like really do it. Just poop in your pants. Wonder if that really just happened. It did. Turn around and drive home. Change your pants. Even though you are dizzy, and it takes a while, walk downstairs to put the soiled pants on top of the washing machine. It just would not be okay for your spouse to arrive home and find your poopy pants in the sink first thing. Gotta keep the romance alive. Drive back to school. Collect your children. Drive home. Lie down on the sofa, wrapped in your sleeping bag. Wait.

Step Thirty-one: Your spouse should now arrive home. He/she may notice that there is a jar of empty applesauce on the kitchen counter along with all of the breakfast/dinner/lunch dishes from the past 24 hours. He/she may or may not notice the blue bucket and handheld vac next to front door (one used for vacuuming baking soda before driving to school, other in case you vomited during the drive), or that every surface in the den is covered, overrun with stuffed animals, an exploded Life game, pieces of a marble run, calico critters, art supplies, pillows, blankets, matchbox cars, random mail everywhere (literally like mail confetti). He/she may make a comment—out loud—about the state of the household. This comment alone could burn off up to one of the ten pounds. But you are still too weak to care. And he/she is not wrong. It is a fricking war zone around here.

Step Thirty-two: Allow the spouse to take the children to the grocery store. Bingewatch more *When Calls the Heart* for as long as possible (it is about a handsome mountie and an heiress turned schoolteacher in a small mining town in Canada in the 1910s—super highbrow).

Step Thirty-three: Take sips of things that make you feel sick to remind yourself that you still are really, really not hungry. Get on the scale, because you have an idea for a blog post.

Step Thirty-four: Be grateful that it was not the flu. That your children did a great job making their own lunch and did leave the sharp knives in the drawer. That you had someone, albeit with a terrible, disgusting virus lurking in a diaper in her home, who loved you enough to endure a morning with your two plus her two kids so that you could have some relief (also that you had another friend to whom you gifted this special program on Sunday night, the ten-day-program pilot group?). That your spouse is back and that he does good work that you are proud of, and sometimes he gets to have dinner out while you are scooping vomit with a nut lid. That he has done his fair share of scooping vomit too. That you have neighbors that brought you pasta, and would have helped more if you had asked. That you didn't grab anyone's face and were too weak to yell (very much). That all that was stolen was some electronic information and the time it is going to take you to unsubscribe from thousands of random newsletters. That you successfully intercepted the laptop, cancelled your credit card, changed your Gmail password and Apple ID, and returned the laptop to the Apple store. That there is no snow forecast for at least two weeks. And that your jeans are going to fit really well for at least several more days.

MAGIC!

STILL WRITING THAT NOVEL?

February 21, 2018

It has been over a month since my last report. Yes, I am still wearing the sweatshirt (though it is warm today so I just opened the windows to let in some fresh air). The rest of the ham is in the freezer awaiting combination with red beans (mom, can you bring me some red beans when you come to visit?). Yes, we have been visited by another dread virus but this one was significantly less laundry-intensive. In other news:

Novel: Total count is 52,291 words at present. The goal was to reach 70,000 by the end of February but that's a pretty tall order on the 21st. I'm aiming for 8,000 additional words this week and think that is achievable (as a stretch goal) because I don't have another contract to work on and both kids are just getting over the most recent sickness so they will probably not be home from school again this week. The novel (and a recently concluded contract) is the reason you have not heard from me on the blog lately; I'm learning to prioritize and also to live in a bit of an artistic bubble. Apparently this is somewhat necessary to actually produce something.

I am really enjoying writing the novel and the exercise is completely different from what I would have guessed it to be like. You learn a lot about yourself. You pay attention to the world in a different way. It's not always comfortable because you have to *be* in a particular feeling to write about it well (to write well about it?). Or to be able to imagine feeling that feeling. And maybe it is your subconscious or what I'm calling "infinite intelligence" but you are typing away and stuff is happening in the story and then you go back and read it and think—who wrote that?—where did that come from? And it doesn't feel like it came from your mind, but you like it (or maybe you don't).

My original expected word count for the first draft was somewhere around 80–90,000 but it is looking like the first draft will be over 100K. I think about sharing excerpts sometimes, but I'm not quite ready for that.

Clean eating: Every year (for three years running), Dave and I spend three weeks in January/February eating "clean"—that means we don't eat gluten, dairy, sugar and a number of other foods (coffee, corn, soy, alcohol, it's a long list) during that time. We did this as an experiment three years ago and it fundamentally changed the way we eat. We found it to be sort of tough the first year (though much easier when you do it together) but after about a week we stopped craving sugar (and stopped craving much of anything really) and we figured out a few standard meals that we like that meet the criteria and now we eat this way 85% of the time until life gets too stressful or we are visiting friends/traveling.

We have finished our three weeks this year and as usual it was eye-opening and beneficial. This year, we followed the protocol in the book *Clean Gut* (with our own modifications) but for the two prior years we followed the protocol in *Clean* (again, modified).[30] Here's what I noticed: My mood and energy are significantly better while eating this way. You don't necessarily notice the improvement until you go out for breakfast and get a sausage, egg, and cheese bagel with a vanilla chai after the program is completed. You swim through that day totally exhausted and realize that you would rather spend your life feeling optimistic and energized.

French Food Challenge: We have started playing a sort of game with our kids to encourage them to approach new foods with

---

30 Both *Clean* books are by Dr. Alejandro Junger whose work is endorsed by the eminent nutritional scholar Gwyneth Paltrow.

curiosity and also to be more interested in the ingredients that go into different dishes. I call it the French food challenge because, as we've all heard, "French kids eat everything"—my kids are really enjoying it,[31] and soon I will share it on the blog. It's been a great thing.

Reading list: I've read a few books so far this year that have helped shift my habits and behavior in a positive way including *You Are a Badass* by Jen Sincero, *Think and Grow Rich* by Napolean Hill, *The Creative Habit* by Twyla Tharp. I'm still slogging through *Don Quixote* but not because it is not amazing, it's just dense and these other books have been from the library. I'm also currently reading *1491* (about the pre-Columbian Americas) by Charles Mann and I haven't quite finished my Dickens biography or my E.B. White. And I'm listening to Mark Twain's autobiography (20 disks) in my car when I'm on my own—I'm on disk 4.

The largest changes I've made so far in 2018 have to do with prioritizing fewer things instead of spreading myself too thin, being more decisive, and what I'm calling "living like a pro"—based on the concept of a pro in another great book, *The War of Art* by Steven Pressfield. It has always been easy for me to act when someone else is holding me accountable but difficult when I am only accountable to myself. But the things that I want to accomplish require me to hold myself accountable, so that's what I've been doing so far in 2018 and it's working pretty well.

My bulbs are starting to come up and a few perennials are barely peeking through. I'm definitely ready for spring!

---

31   As one example, they both voluntarily tried raw oysters.

WHEN BONO SAVED EASTER

March 30, 2018

I'm cold. Our house is under-insulated and old and it gets damp and I'm frugal/conscious of invisible gases in the sky. I sit with my hoodie hood up or a winter hat on and April starts on Sunday. I look out the window and the world is brown. There are a few blossoms hanging around but with the grey sky, the bare trees, and the mud, the blossoms look like lipstick on a corpse.

A devoted reader who, for the sake of anonymity, I will hereafter refer to as "Granny Goodguts" remarked that it has been a while since my last post. That my readers, given the arrival of spring (somehow this was especially relevant), might appreciate some further thoughts. Granny Goodguts suggested the topic of rebirth: an Easter reflection. Usually (you may be shocked to learn), I quickly dash off whatever I'm thinking about and publish the post before I lose my nerve. But this request, this assignment, has required a bit more thought, more emotional labor. I have a lot of words, but no clear way to arrange them in my mind. I have cultural norms and childhood teachings all jumbled together and I guess I haven't been able to hear, or to listen, clearly.

Enter Bono.

After some pondering, and writing words that sounded okay in combination but that didn't sit right in my guts, my epiphany came only moments after the children requested music during our morning commute. My phone randomly selected U2's "California," "Ghostbusters" (I ain't afraid of no ghosts), "Second Hand News," "King of Pain," "Endless Love," and "Renegades" on the way to school and back. Waiting at the exceptionally long red light,

Maggie requested that no one sing so she could listen.

So there we were sitting quietly and Bono sang:

At the dawn you thought would never come, but it did, like it always does (whoa-o-o-o-o). All I know, and all I need to know, is there is no, yeah there is no end to love

That was the moment when it all felt clear to me. I knew what I would come home and write. I might have even gotten a little bit teary, or even just a bit out of my body, unreal for a moment.

But to explain all that, I have to go back, way back, to January 1, 2018.

I am awake, eyes closed in a California king-size bed with one of those super comfortable memory foam mattresses at my friends' house. I can hear my children running up and down stairs, playing ninja or something else that is satisfyingly gender-inspecific. My husband is up and probably about to enjoy his first cup of coffee in the New Year. We have stayed up late eating fondue, an annual tradition. We have had more wine than I am used to these days. We have watched our yearly fill of Ylvis and searched for something else on YouTube that would make us laugh as much but come up empty-handed again and still Ylvis has made nothing new.

I lie in the bed. I hear the sounds. The heater has been on all night so the room is overwarm and the air is dry. I stretch and feel the coolness of the sheets. I wonder if I will have a headache later. I am definitely thirsty. I consider that maybe this is not the best way to begin, this slight dullness, the heaviness from overindulging in bread and cheese, maybe it is not auspicious. But my optimism, or maybe just a survival instinct, kicks in and 2018 again feels precious, like a crisp, empty notebook in September. I think to myself: *In 2018, I am kind to others and to myself. In 2018 I tell the truth, or rather, I don't tell untruths. In 2018, so far, I am patient, I don't shout or scowl to get my way. I don't say things I don't mean. I keep my commitments.*

If I'm being honest, that is more of an idealized script. That is what I might think if I hadn't over-cheesed and drunk wine without counting the number of glasses. What I actually think is more like: *It's a new year and so far you haven't made any mistakes. You haven't lost your temper. You haven't been unsupportive or said anything rude. You haven't said things you don't mean. And so far you haven't gone a single day without washing your face* (or insert habit that I've struggled with for 40 years and still haven't managed to instill). Then I think something along the lines of: *Let's just try to keep this streak for as long as we can.* And I go on to have a few good days. This little talk I give myself works, if only for a short while.

When asked about rebirth, this scene was what first came to mind. New beginnings. Starting fresh. A second (or fortieth) chance.

January's possibility infuses me with a pleasant energy, like a small cup of good coffee without sugar, a healthy buzz. I can grow. I can choose. I can set some intentions and make plans. I love to get out empty sheets of paper and write down some things to accomplish (*in 2018 I will finish drafting a novel*), some practices to make habitual (*in 2018 I will meditate five days each week*), some themes for the year (*in 2018 I will "ship my art" or "live like a pro"*). I have a whole year ahead of me. A whole unknown year to be lived, a blank notebook to be filled with bold strokes and delight.

February is a bit more ho-hum. Still cold. Someone is probably sick. But the hopefulness, the momentum of January remain. Eleven more months to make this a great year.

Then March hits. Still cold. Someone is probably sick. The end of the school year looms. It is time to plan for summer. Summer? How could it already be time to plan for summer? Once summer comes the year is half gone. How could the year already be half gone? I'm still not living like a pro. I've missed a lot of days of meditation. The novel? It's going to take a bit longer than expected. Probably not *this* year anyway.

Now we get back to where we started. It's the end of March. My hoodie hood covers my ears but my feet and hands are still cold. I have made my plans. I have worked and I have tried. This year will come to an end, like all of the years before, and some things will change and some things won't change and I might never write that novel.

I look out the window at the grey sludge. Life is hard. Bad things happen. Scary, sad things. What can I do? I don't feel like I can work any harder. I don't think I can change any faster. I want to do my best but I'm tired. I want the world to be different, kinder, safer. And I'm still cold, my shins, inside my bones (*maybe if you could finally stick to that exercise goal, warm you from the inside out* I gently chide myself…)

The Easter parade begins, very subdued. Tiny snowdrops are first to emerge from drifts of collected leaf debris, little white faces peeking over the decay of last summer's growth. Then the crocuses, purple, gold, white. Thin green spikes barely supporting a few slovenly arranged petals that last only days. The trees are bare, their branches like arthritic hands reaching for the light. The daffodils open, cheerful yellow in the midst of the still, brown deserts. Weeping willow, apple blossoms, cherry blossoms emerge, and those dark red blooms, unexpected, appear on the maples. Then one day you walk outside and it isn't dead, cold winter anymore. The birds are the first to tell you, but you can also feel it in the wind, a damp coolness that whispers to your skin. Your body, which you had been sheltering from the cold for five long months, feels something different. A yearning to stay out, to be gently caressed by this misty breeze for a few minutes more.

There may be nothing (excepting my children, my spouse, my parents, my siblings, my good friends, chocolate soufflé, tree frogs, my piano, and my magenta sweatshirt) that I love in this world more than perennials. They are like magic. The ground is flat dirt.

Cold. Hard. And underneath there is this surprise waiting. There is no hint except sometimes some dried old stubs left from last year. I start watching in February. My eyes hungry, methodically scanning for even one small green tip. And one day, something is there. A tiny green shoot. A small red bump. A hint of life. And as it slowly emerges, day by day, I worry that it will get too cold again and it will die, but it doesn't. It is prepared for the cold. It has a little jacket or it waits just long enough, until just the right moment on just the right day. And it turns into a whole plant. Maybe a coneflower, maybe a black-eyed susan, maybe a poppy (I always hope it's a poppy), or milkweed or salvia or foxgloves or bee balm. The point is, they are all there, waiting under the flat, brown mud. All that cold winter they were under there and one day you look and see them popping up that first tiny shoot, that first small green leaf pushing through the remnants of last year.

That tiny shoot of green, that hopeful sprout—it's the same plant. It isn't a new plant. It isn't reborn, it was alive—living— all the time. Sometimes it was drinking water, sometimes it was drenched in sun, sometimes it was sweetly singing to the honeybees and the butterflies, sometimes it was blown by a harsh wind, sometimes a kid picked all of its flowers or stepped on it, sometimes it was spreading roots under ground, sometimes it was protecting itself under a blanket of mud. And here it is, the same plant, in a new season.

We humans, mortals, we plan, we work, we strive. We tell ourselves that we are not enough—that we need to be reborn, start again. We hack ourselves to be more productive, more intentional, more beautiful, more (fill in the blank).

Night comes. Darkness. We can't see clearly. Not because we didn't work hard enough, not because we are flawed.

Because the sun has moved.

And we can't bring it back.

Easter is named for Ēostre or Ostara, a Germanic goddess of dawn, the dawn which arrives at the end of each night. Always. No matter how poorly you slept, if you stayed awake all night, crazed, disconnected thoughts holding you hostage, forbidding rest and peace, eventually, the color of the sky will start to shift. The sun returns bringing light, warmth, life.

The concept of a new year, a new you, a do-over is so seductive. I can be better. I can do better. I need to be different from yesterday's me. But what we need, what I need, is not rebirth, but endurance. Acceptance. Faith. Humility.

Faith that even when I can't see it, life is welling up underground, fed by what it was before, fed by all the life that was before, the leaves of last year, the same water that has trickled through every pore of this earth for billions of years.

Acceptance of what has been. Of what is. That the power to bring back the sun is not mine. Nor is the responsibility.

And Love.

My second moment of insight during the morning commute came towards the end of "Endless Love" (ironic?) when Lionel and Diana are keying up for the power punch and he sings (and I with him, while simultaneously wondering what it is that makes this particular part of the song so irresistible, so potent):

CAUSE NO (no) ONE CAN DENY
THIS LOVE I HAVE INSIDE
I'LL GIVE IT ALL TO YOU
MY LOVE (my love, my love) MY ENDLESS LOVE

Acceptance, surrender, not being able to bring back the sun on command. These are difficult things. So what do we do? We know the dawn will come, we know life is beautiful. We know we are a part of the whole. But there's still the waiting, the uncertainty, the dark, the cold. We have to do something, we can't just sit there and wait for the world to sort out all of the problems on its own, humming fancy mantras. Jesus taught two basic rules for living:

Love God. Love your neighbor. Not wipe your own slate clean. Not secure for yourself a fancy reward at the end. Not check all the boxes or make yourself into something you think others will admire.

All I know and all I need to know is there is no, yeah there is no end to love.

Maybe the power to endure comes from the endlessness of love.

And maybe that Endless Love is found in connection. Merging with another. Recognizing one's relationship to the whole. Not smoldering, not wanting, but a bond strong enough to enable releasing, giving away.

We are alive and we are reaching for light, just like everything else that lives, and the path is not clear. The cells in me right now, made of sun, water, and stardust, different to the cells from last year but part of the same organization, would like to write a novel. Want to practice patience. Feel good when I meditate. So that is how I will organize my time in this season. Not because what I am needs to change. But because when the dawn came today, I woke up, alive, myself.

My dear Granny Goodguts, you have asked me about rebirth. Your question raises so many others and, even with Bono's assistance, I still can't quite work it all out. But to honor the importance of your question and in summary:

Spring, Ēostre, Easter, Ostara reminds me that the dawn always comes no matter how long and dark the night. That I don't bring the dawn of my own accord, through my hard work. Instead, I acknowledge the night, I surrender to what is, I accept what has been. I share my light with others when I can, I appreciate the light that others shine for me. I wait. And when the dawn, Ēostre, comes I see the signs of life that were there underground all the time. I don't need to start from scratch. I don't need an empty notebook. I'm not an empty notebook. I'm an annotated, dog-eared notebook, loved, one tiny, rich volume in an unfathomable library.

EATING AND OTHER PROBLEMS

May 18, 2018

When I was 22, I lived for a short time with a family of four above a butcher shop in the middle of Delhi. I remember that you couldn't see the stars there, the sky was too thick with exhaust. Just after arriving on the plane, and before meeting this family, I had used a pair of scissors in a hostel bathroom to cut off all of my hair. Most people shave their head with an electric razor, giving it a somewhat even appearance, assuming one has a somewhat evenly shaped head. But I didn't have access to such a device. I had, the month before, cut my hair boy-short, but now it needed to come off, all off, urgently I guess.

I wonder what that family thought about an American girl with the privilege of traveling across the world who had apparently had her hair forcibly removed, gashes of scalp showing here and there. They certainly were not particularly warm towards me.

The butcher shops in Delhi did not have a refrigerated meat counter with carefully arranged steaks and chops, pink, just-ground chuck, little packets of breasts and wings wrapped tightly in plastic. They had animal carcasses, skinned and hanging from hooks, in the air, bloody, right there in the street as you walked by. No window, separating meat from passerby. I remember the overly rich smell, and the strong scent of iron. I remember the flies. I would walk past the shops on my way to hail a rickshaw to take me to class where a holy man dressed in all orange taught me that every grain of rice is sacred. That he is always careful never to step on an ant. This was not a hallucination. Though, all these years later, it seems like it could be.

In my class, we visited a village. I use the word village so that you will understand it was an organization of people in a centralized place. The children had those puffy bellies that you used to see on commercials asking you for just the price of a cup of coffee a day. I remember someone pulled down a child's lower eyelid so we could see evidence of some parasite or disease, like the kid was a mannequin. These people had been living somewhere else but that place had been flooded to make a hydropower dam to generate electricity, so they had been sent here instead but apparently here was worse than there. That was the story anyway. I didn't ask if they would have had parasites and swollen bellies had they stayed where they were. I just took away the lesson: The path of progress is deadly and its victims are innocent babes. Or maybe: hydropower electricity is used by bad guys to make money and here we see the victims of their greed.

A few years later, I went to Africa for the first time. My assignment was to coordinate a group of scientists to survey a few of the remaining forest patches left in the southeastern corner of Guinea, a tiny country on the coast of West Africa. A mining company was interested in the iron ore found in the Simandou range of mountains and we were to document any particularly interesting or important ecological information to make sure they didn't do too much damage, kill chimps or wipe out the whole population of a group of toads that live nowhere else on earth.

Driving across Guinea for two days there didn't seem to be very much "pristine" nature left. We arrived at the Pic de Fon, the peak of the mountain we were to survey, in the dark, in the rain, in four 4x4s laden with equipment and we tried to drive up steep mining tracks, red with iron dust. That same iron I had smelled in Delhi, veins of it running thick and deep under my feet.

That was my first month in a tent in West Africa. I held an olive sunbird in my hand, hiked 17 kilometers to see chimpanzee nests and find evidence (some cracked nuts) of their feeding. I learned how to look for tree frogs and shrews, I petted bats, looked for pygmy hippos, unwittingly stepped in piles of driver ants, bathed in a river, woke up each morning to birdsong, fell asleep each night to frogsong and sometimes to the sound of rain on a tent.

Today, a mother of two, I live in a suburb outside of Washington, DC. My street is full of lawyers, Hill-workers, secret service agents, and folks who are in/closely related to the US military. And us, some tree-hugging hippies with a dirty compost pile in the front yard. People are nice enough to us though I'm never sure what they think about my vegetable garden in the one sunny enough spot right next to the street, my let-it-live approach to clover and dandelions.

Tuesday morning is trash day in my neighborhood. Everyone has one large bin for trash and one large bin for recycling. I drive down the street in the morning before the trucks arrive to cart it all away and it seems that every trash can at every house is overflowing. This is one street. I don't dare do the math.

I came back from India with a lot of information. A lot of pictures in my head and a lot of explanations. I knew that families were being displaced, towns being flooded, I knew that children were filtering green-revolution chemicals out of their drinking water using their t-shirts, I knew that invisible gases were changing the climate, I knew that Coca-Cola was everywhere.

To provide one example of the story of the global economy that I internalized via my global education, let's consider food: To make food, the teaching goes, you start with clearing some land (so deforestation or just land degradation). In the case of plants (or animal feed), multinational corporations sell seeds that can only be grown with patented chemicals to a poor farmer whose family filters these chemicals out of their drinking water using their t-shirts (the ones they are wearing) and, even using the fancy, highly productive seeds, the farmer still has to borrow money the next year to buy more seeds and chemicals (incidentally, if you meet this farmer he is a nice guy and his kids have hearts that burst right out through their eyes). The land is irrigated (taking water from someone, somewhere) and fertilized (requiring mining for petrochemicals) and the requisite herbicides/insecticides are applied (poisoning the water supply, killing pollinators, decreasing biodiversity). Once he sells his crop for nearly nothing to a crop distributor, they store it (refrigerant chemicals, pesticides killing more pollinators and infusing food supply), package it (solid waste), and ship it (invisible gases into the air). It then goes to trucks or trains (more invisible gases), gets sent to a factory to be turned into something (water pollution, invisible gases) that no longer looks like a plant or animal (poor health outcomes, obesity), packaged further (plastics, solid waste), shipped again to a store (more gases, asphalt damage, car accidents), stored there (energy from cooling, energy from lighting, energy from people driving to store, deforestation for making bags, energy for shopkeepers to drive to store, petrochemicals for cashier's lipstick), some proportion of that goes straight to landfill because of sell-by dates (methane, waste of life energy) and some goes to someone's house to be refused by her five-year-old because he had cupcakes six times at school that week (future me editorializing).

I think the lesson was supposed to be that I needed to plant an apple tree and barter with my neighbor who had chickens.

Coming back from this experience, this "education," my most immediate problem was what to eat. With every bite, I was hurting something. Every spoonful a ladle of misery. Animals were suffering in appalling conditions, people were losing homes, the shroud around the planet was thickening, the rivers were silting, the fish were growing extra eyeballs. All because I wanted some breakfast.

I just wanted some breakfast.

I remember driving with my mom and my younger sister to take my sister to summer camp. On the way, we stopped at a

Walmart to buy some batteries. I remember studying the carts there. I had been taught that Walmart was destroying the earth, killing communities. But in the store I saw people with lives and wishes, just people, buying the things they felt they needed. In my memory, the bulk of what was in those carts was soft drinks. I walked back to the car, stony faced, silent. Crying turned laughing turned sobbing—I could not reconcile what I had seen, what I had felt—over there—with what I was seeing and feeling now.

I imagined an international tribunal, some kind of court of inalienable human rights, weighing the right of a child to not grow up in a dried out riverbed filled with literal trash versus my right to have six Diet Cokes a day. I know it is a totally ridiculous thought experiment. Candy apples to rotten, worm-infested oranges shipped from Mars. Not real. But these were the kinds of calculations my mind was making. Every day. About every thing.

And then I went to Africa where I met a mountain covered with tree frogs and sunbirds. Again, I returned home to the land of warm showers and dishwashers and cheese anytime you want it. Water from a tap. A land where my car, my pots, the train, my office, my spoon were made from iron cut out of mountains just like the one I loved.

When I see a Halloween-themed tablecloth, I feel sadness. I feel that something sacred has been rended from deep in the earth and transformed into a macabre festival of disconnected, unintended, destruction. You're just trying to make something nice and festive, I understand.

If a lion does not eat, he will die. If a lion does eat, something else will die. To remain alive, you have to fill your body with energy from the sun, and you can't photosynthesize. You have to protect yourself from the elements, and you can only grow so much hair in so many places. And you have to be able to breathe.

I don't know if I can ever make peace with that Halloween tablecloth. I live here—but I don't exactly know how to be alive here. I feel so many feelings, a lot of guilt, a lot of anger, a lot of fear. And when I watch the news, or read emails from well-meaning organizations, or look in my mailbox, I find plenty of information, words, images to feed all of these feelings.

I had to leave home to be shown the damage that my life was causing to other lives. To take on the burden of knowing. The internet was brand new, my camera had film, you couldn't make a video with your phone (plus your phone was attached to the wall of your house in America). But my children, my little ones, five and seven, have not had to leave home to learn these lessons. These lessons are around them every day. In books they read, at school, from my lips. My seven-year-old, who had a lesson in climate change at school last month, asked me why people are hurting the earth, why people do bad things to damage, to injure, Mother Nature.

It is important to have information. It is important to understand unintended consequences and how things are connected. But, at twenty-two, I did not make this world. For twenty years, instead of singing a lovesong to my home, instead of embracing, and celebrating, and shining a light on beauty and connection, I have fretted about tablecloths. I have seen life as damage.

There are problems to solve, shifts to be made. But you don't teach a child by calling her bad. You wrap her in your arms. You tell her that people love the Earth and people work hard to take care of what they love. That people are a force for good. That her life is not a burden, but a gift. That there are things we have not understood but that we are learning all the time, and once we learn then we can figure out how to take better care of our home and of each other.

You hold her close, you feel her warmth, her questioning, her aliveness, her care. You close your eyes. You hope, you pray, that what you are telling her is the truth.

365 DAYS

May 19, 2018

Adventures with Jenny Goodguts is my fourth blog. My first, *Cheapa$$ Jen*, begun in 2001, survives as a few printed sheets in a file in my basement. My second, *75 Small Steps for Change*, circa 2008, concluded abruptly after 20 steps when I was unable to maintain the planned pace of one post a day. My third attempt, *Jenaissance*, begun in November 2014, lasted for 2.5 years with periods of intense activity and months of silence. The *Jenaissance* blog had no organizing principle, other than the survival of my soul—it was a matter of writing something somewhere for someone. And here we are, one year into blog number four.

It's strange to think that it has only been a year—365 days. I think back over the year, what has happened, what is different. We have a new sofa. I meditate now, sometimes. I've written about 80,000 words of what was planned as an 80,000-word novel. And I think, sometimes, that I've learned how to hear my own voice.

Please remember, when we first met Jenny Goodguts, I (Jennifer, an aspiring super-ish hero) had been struggling for some months with a debilitating addiction to farm-building games on the iPad. I had been told that my guts hosted no flora save for a vast colony of *E. coli*. Donald Trump had recently concluded his first hundred days as President. I was watching too much news. I was scared, I felt lost, and I was way down depressed.

For the sake of clarification, Jenny Goodguts is not the author of the blog. 'Tis I, Jennifer, who wields the pen. Jenny Goodguts is the superhero—the alter ego who lives in my imagination. She's the one who is full of ideas about how I should act—for good.

245 DAYS / 245

If I'm not taking my vitamins, she helps me make a checklist. If meditation would be good for me, she helps me make a checklist (it turns out Jenny is a big fan of the checklist). Jenny is the voice in my head whispering that there's always something I can do to make things better. Who reminds me that I have the strength to do what needs to be done. Who helps me make a plan when the chips are down.

Jenny is the one who told me to tape the lucky quarter onto my kitchen wall and reminded me that I would lose 25 days of good luck if I played that damn game one single time. And she was right. I stopped playing the game. I ate some sauerkraut. And life changed.

I once wrote that Jenny Goodguts saved my life. I wrote that to get your attention I guess. Now I feel it sounds a bit overly dramatic. I would have gone on living, and things would have happened, good and bad. But starting this blog has changed the trajectory of my life. Why do I say that? What do I mean?

What started out as an idea to share games, quests, adventures has, yet again, turned into an outlet for me to say whatever I want about whatever I want to whoever is reading. Except.

Except with this blog I figured out how to send each post as an email, automatically. There's no choice, no planning involved. I write. I hit publish. My words magically appear in inboxes around the world.

And people subscribed. Not a lot of people. Some people I thought would subscribe, just to be nice, did not. And other people, who I would not have expected to subscribe, did. You did.

And not only did you subscribe, but you read and you kept reading and you said things like: *that post really spoke to me* or *that post helped me* or even *have you thought about stand-up comedy?* One note, seven words, from one person on one day. It makes a difference.

There have been artists throughout history who have been so

certain, so clear in their vision, that against all odds, against all criticism, they have gone on to make their thing and we celebrate them today. I'm not that type though. I am brave. I have done things, and tried things, that some others would not have done or tried. But I needed you. To read, to react, to nudge, to support, to appreciate, to notice. And your eight words here, your comment there, were enough. I felt brave enough to try new things. I felt safe enough to be real, to not hide behind cutesy attitudes and tired figures of speech. And here I am on the other side. With this year behind me and however many more to come. My voice feels clearer to me and more authentic and I look back on the words I've written here—to you—and I feel like I've made something that I want to make. I've said something that I want to say. I've found something that I wanted to find.

When I started this blog I imagined that I had it in me to write. I thought, I have had some interesting experiences, or I have had an unusual constellation of experiences. I also thought I had the ability to share the perspective derived from those experiences through writing. And that doing so would bring me some pleasure.

If I'm being honest, I also thought that the world was/is full of huge, daunting problems and that maybe I could do something, some small thing, to change minds, or to propose solutions, or to make change fun. I think I thought I was going to make games and challenges that in their way, small or large, would help people "do the right thing." Help us all be a little more super.

Did I want my writing to save the world? I think I could only give myself permission to write if there was some small chance that it might. I felt that my obligation was to exchange my life energy to help stop the damage, or to compensate for my share of damage, my accumulated share going back generations—that was the only arithmetic that seemed defensible. If I get to be alive, here, in these circumstances, there is a debt to be paid. I think that was the deep down truth.

After 365 days, I have a different view.

After 365 days, today, I will sit down with my friend, Jenny Goodguts, who set me on a path that changed my life. And I will tell her this:

My dear, beloved Jenny Goodguts, thank you for always being there, for your dedication, your persistence, your frightening ability to organize, your compulsive lists. Thank you for not giving up and for helping me when I needed you. That idea, taping the quarter to the kitchen wall, was invaluable to me and turned out to be the oar I needed to get back to shore.

But Jenny, I'm not so sure anymore about this theme song business, all this aspiring, or the obligation of my one life to make everything right.

You, Jenny, have so many ideas about how to fix things. Ideas about how the world could be different. But an alternative world, just like you Jenny Goodguts, is not real. And I am determined — determined — to love this real world. And its real people, every single one a wabi-sabi bowl, broken, chipped, glued together. Every single one.

Do you know what I'd like to do Jenny? I'd like to be awake in this real world, be myself, and I'd like to tell some stories. I think we could use some new stories and I think I have some inside me. But to do that, it turns out, I don't need to be a superhero. And it turns out I don't think what people need is fixing. My own Jenny, I love you, but I'm not on the path to super-ish anymore.

And Jenny, who is not real of course, will scrunch up her face and look at me oddly. She'll blink a few times and kind of curve her eyebrows like she's really disappointed in me. I'll look down because I'm a little embarrassed, but I won't change my mind. After a minute, she'll say back to me:

Jennifer (she won't say darling, because she's a superhero), you *are* real. And, try as I might, you still have not developed the rigid discipline, the focus at all costs, the regular exercise habit needed to save the world. I know sometimes you feel confused. Sometimes you feel—inadequate.

She'll pause for a minute, considering something, then continue: Maybe it's not inadequacy, maybe it's love that allows you to show people what's behind the curtain, in case it helps. Just in case that's what they needed.

She'll pause again, and she'll say, a bit more quietly this time: Maybe what people need most isn't another list. I guess... (and then she'll start to slightly nod her head, up and down) you should keep being... real. (Now she looks me straight in the eye) And try not to be scared. To be honest, I'm a little tired myself always devising these checklists and spreadsheets. If you're sure about this stories thing, maybe it's time that I put away my mask and my cape and learn to live with some clutter and eat chocolate soufflé and sit outside, my own two arms, my own two legs, my face, sit them outside feeling the wind and not try to fix anything for a little while. Just be.

Maybe, Jennifer, eventually, we can both learn to sing that lovesong to the world.

There is work to be done. There are good guys to help, banks to stop banking with, parabens to outwit. I've been around for what is scootching closer and closer to half a century and I'm darned sure that even if Jenny takes a break she isn't going to let me forget about all of this. I can't unlearn and I don't guess I would want to.

But on the one-year anniversary of the launch of this blog I am announcing, I am proclaiming, that while Jenny Goodguts might have had some great checklists to share, while she could put together a kick-ass resource list, while she really knew how to organize activities, she's on a sabbatical of undetermined length.

I don't feel like being super, I feel like being real. And I feel brave enough to be real thanks to you.

just me

IN WHICH THE UNIVERSE FORCES HER HAND

One heartbroken dummy

June 27, 2018 unpublished

I want you to understand why I'm not calling you. Why I haven't sent a quick message to let you know what's up, what happened.

I am not calling because there is only one thing you could say.

You won't say it. But you can't help but think it: *I'm sorry for your loss, it really stinks. But we both know that with a bit of precaution, just a modicum of common sense, dare I say professionalism, this would not have happened.*

You would sit there on the other side of the phone and feel pain for me. You'd shake your head and ask hopeful questions: *Have you tried...? Have you looked...? Maybe...??*

No, I would say in an empty voice. *50,000 words. Five months of work. Deleted and emptied from the trash.* I might start crying then. You would wish you could go back one month and make me take ten seconds to email a copy of the document to myself, or to you, for safekeeping. You would promise not to read it. Maybe you'd suggest I take another ten seconds to back up my file in Googledocs. Set up Time Machine. You would explain that the iCloud is not a backup in the sense that I had in my mind. It's just another copy of whatever currently exists in a different location: a flat and cold mirror, polished daily, not a musty old trunk full of mouse poop and memories.

But neither of us can go back and do the very simple things that

I should have done in May, or in April, heck—even in February. Who writes a novel in one Word file that she keeps consistently named the same (ridiculous) file name and never renames it or makes a duplicate or prints or stores it anywhere?? Oh, oh—me! You're talking about me!

I have asked my computer-savvy friends (the uber savvy ones)—there are gossamer threads of hope. I'm following these up.

I lash myself again. *What a flipping idiot.* Then I start to question. Maybe what I had written wasn't so good anyway. I knew I was going to have to cut a lot. This makes that easier. I can take the story in a new direction, I can remove characters, add that crazy lady who likes to make things out of trash, the one I've been thinking of.

I did not lose everything. When my mom was here (in April) I printed the first 20 pages for her: my first (and so far only) reader. I sat upstairs while she read at the kitchen table. I could hear her laughing. She also cried in those first 20 pages. After she had finished, when I had walked, crept, into the kitchen, not quite breathing with hopefulness, she read parts of it aloud to me. Like she couldn't resist doing it. My own words, my characters read by another voice, shared with another soul. It was an amazing feeling. I have those 20 printed pages. I also have a saved version from the last time I changed the file name—in January. So 30,000 words remain.

I still have the ideas that came to life, that bubbled through the portal as I sat there channeling from the great beyond onto the blank page. I had not gone back to read much of it—trying to dig up the bones first and then go back and edit later. It was hard not to reread, but I anticipated with such pleasure sitting down with my giant stack of printed sheets, reading what the universe, the infinite mind, and I had created together.

All is not lost from the hours spent writing those 50,000 words, 100 single-spaced pages. I remember when Jack slapped his mother, and the man with the beard at the coffee shop. But I don't remember the part about the Helvetians and I don't remember the story about God and the candy store. Or rather, I don't remember the language, the distillation of thought I liked so much that I broke my rule and read it aloud to Dave.

I spent about an hour and a half last night, while the kids tossed and turned not quite asleep though they were totally exhausted, reading 20,000 of the printed words. *I'm not going to quit* (I told myself). *I can make it even better.* I have never put as much love, soul, heart, effort into any piece of work in my life. This was the proof to myself that I can finish something that I start. Something that I choose, that's not an assignment. A promise kept to myself that I can take one small step at a time to make something, to contribute something that I love. It was my best work. And I lost it. I did not protect it.

The more I think about it, it occurs to me that maybe I didn't give it enough value, or didn't understand what it meant to me. I thought of it as just, you know, an experiment. A little thing I'm trying that might work and might not and, shrug, smile, not a big deal. If it doesn't work I'll be fine. This is not something I'm taking seriously so you don't need to be embarrassed for me if it isn't good. Just say it: if I fail.

I did not treat it like a treasure.

I loved reading those 20,000 words and am so thankful that I did not lose those too. But when I put the pages down and turned off the lamp and lay there in the dark, I missed my 50,000 words. I felt such deep sadness that they are gone and that I will not be able to read them again. That I can't share them with you. That I didn't share them with you already. If only I had shared them with you. Or just pressed print at the end of each day.

It feels strange to mourn an electronic document. People lose far more tangible and irreplaceable things every day. I am #blessed (please note the ironic use), healthy, the sun is shining, I have electricity, I'm not in a cage, I had a good breakfast, my kids are at camp.

But it hurts. I keep looking around the house, on the counter, on the bookshelf. Every room I go into I'm looking around for something and I can't remember what. Like I've misplaced the keys and I'm sure they are here somewhere, I know I put them down inside the house and eventually my eye will see something vaguely out of place and—voila!—my electronic file will be sitting there or I will remember that I got drunk one night and decided to print the whole thing and I forgot and there it is—not gone! Right there!! I will kiss the papers and dance around and have a celebratory cup of coffee (as opposed to the consolation coffees I am currently overconsuming).

It really hurts to lose it. It hurts because it was unnecessary and because I loved it and was proud of it, proud of myself. And I'm scared that this punch to the guts is all it will take to knock me off the course. It wasn't easy to stay on course when I had the momentum of an almost-finished novel motivating me to carve out the hours needed to sit down and thoughtfully write. Where will I get those hours? They are so precious and so hard to find.

Last night I had Popeye's fried chicken for dinner (three pieces) followed by a generous portion of Girl Scout Thin Mints and two glasses of milk (I did also have a couple of pieces of broccoli, so you know I'm not totally off the rails). I also played one of the iPad games for about 30 minutes while I let the kids take super leisurely baths. I know that's not the right trajectory.

I have some contract work to do to pay the bills. Correcting some unclear technical documents. I try to feel thankful to have work to do to earn income. It is hard to concentrate. I want to find a cabin and sit there and not feel scared of being out in the woods alone and write and write and write my novel back to life.

I want to show myself that I can do it. I want to share it with you. I want to not be beaten and to not give up.

And then I find myself fighting the same, relentless demons. Who do you think you are writing a novel? What's even the point? You're no Tolstoy or Vonnegut. You aren't going to change the world.

People lose things—big things—and start again or keep going all the time. This is just a few months of work, of practice. I feel stupid and it was unnecessary. But I also feel determined and I can see more clearly how much this means to me. I knew it, logically, but now I feel it too. Right in the guts.

I'm going to finish my novel. You're going to hold a copy of it in your hands. I hope you will laugh. And maybe even cry.

And, As God Is My Witness, I am going to print every single word I write between now and then.

HOW TO SING THE SONG

July 2018

I feel like I'm letting you down. Like you've read this far, waiting to see how it turns out, what words of wisdom, big statements about life, I might be able to elucidate in exchange for the time you've invested. But I have been thinking and writing and writing and thinking and talking and reading and rereading and wanting to make proclamations and they are just not there.

Something has changed. It feels like a good change. But I can't exactly tell you what it is. As far as I can make out, there isn't a replicable secret formula. And anyway, if you took the same path as me, or changed the same things as I did, it wouldn't turn out the same way for you. Even if I did the exact same things over again, but started today, it would turn out differently. That's the magic and mystery of being alive I guess.

I'm drinking coffee again. For breakfast and again at noon. Four ounces of coffee, with an ounce of heavy cream and three ounces of foamed milk. I whisper, wickedly and with longing, to the coffee grinder each night before bed *see you in the morning my friend.* I look forward to noon when the volume of coffee decreases and the volume of cream makes the difference to fill the cup. For the past few weeks coffee has been the majority of my breakfast. Then I'll have the second cup at noon. Then I will grab a snack-sized bag of Trader Joe's Kettle Cooked Potato Chips (sea salt) and eat them in the car on my way to get the kids at 2:30 or so. The bag is always empty too soon and then I'm hungry and grumpy when the kids get in the car, exhausted from a day at camp and grumpy about their own things. We muddle through the afternoon. If Dave is in town we eat something healthy for dinner. If he is not we have fried chicken or pizza or some combination of wheat and dairy, heavy on the dairy. As I write this I am eating a pack of Lance Toast Chee Sandwich Crackers (peanut butter flavor).

I have not meditated since May 15. I specifically remember thinking about meditating, probably on May 16, and deciding that I did not have a lot of available time and that I wanted to get some writing done so I chose to write instead of meditate and here it is two months later.

I've been on my computer after 9 PM almost every night this week, almost every night since I lost my 50,000 words. Usually until about 11 PM, then I sleep (not especially deeply) and then I wake up, tired, my skin a bit less dewy than usual, a random breakout on my neck or some extra lines particularly around my top lip that I think are due to dehydration more than anything else.

I have not danced (except for drunkenly once at 4 AM to four songs, including Toto's "Africa" twice, during my 20-year college reunion), I have not attended an exercise class, I have not spent ten minutes playing an instrument, I have not taken my supplements, I have not eaten any cultured food, I have not been out of bed by 6:30 AM once. I've been working in my garden at least, to water since there's been no rain for three weeks.

And I played the iPad game last week. Only very briefly. I also ate half a bag of Cheese Curls *past 7 PM.*

Jenny Goodguts went on sabbatical and—poof!—everything she taught me seems to have disappeared.

This is not a momentary blip as I mourn my lost words. The change started before then. Here's what happened: the one-year anniversary of the launch of the *Adventures with Jenny Goodguts* blog was fast approaching and I was writing a post to celebrate the year, to reflect, as I am wont to do.

I sat down one morning to finish the one-year piece—it was

nearly done but something didn't feel quite right. I opened a new, blank document and this swarm of words that had been bumping around in my brain for a few weeks flowed, erupted, out onto the page. I looked at what I had written, about my time in India, in Africa, my struggle to live life in America after that.

I felt like laugh-crying, and then I started thinking about the Greek story of Echo, who could only repeat the words of others, and I was nervous to share, as always, but I did share, as I do frequently, but not always, and I felt...I felt powerful. I felt that I had said something that was important for me and that I had said it in a way that was authentic, that got at the heart of something that hadn't been clear in my own mind, hadn't been acknowledged, until I read my own words.

I still wanted to do the anniversary piece, mostly to say thanks to my readers, because I wouldn't have grown in the same way without your encouragement. But, as I was writing what was meant to be a thank-you letter, I realized that Jenny Goodguts needed to go. It wasn't a planned thing. It sort of wrote itself.

After writing those two pieces, I knew something had changed for me. I felt I had come to a new jumping-off place. I wasn't sure where it was that I was jumping, but I felt energized, strong, focused, ready (significantly more than I had felt before—who ever really feels ready?).

And then I lost my words. I have consulted with former and current CIA and NSA staffers and there is nothing more to be done.

While waiting to see if the novel was recoverable, I began to consider compiling my past four years of blogging into a book, adding a few bits that were not posted on the blog. I've reread all of my written thoughts from the day I wrote about my pants before deciding to start the *Jenaissance* blog in November 2014, to when I left my job and stumbled through building a life structure as someone whose structure had been defined by externals for almost forty years and suddenly is not. Reviewing and remembering has been a frequently enjoyable and seriously sobering journey. Oh, there I am confused about life again. And there I am making another checklist! Oh, look, there I am promising to deliver something else that I never finished. And now there's the novel, the one project I felt I was undertaking with a reasonable amount of focus and discipline, and two-thirds is now bytes in the wind.

This walk down memory lane, in combination with recent adjustments to my daily habits, has led to some further introspection about sending Jenny away. What could I have been thinking?

Early on in the life of the *Jenaissance* blog I wrote down a quote from *Walden*: "Most men live lives of quiet desperation and go to the grave with the song still in them." I think when I started to blog I thought: My song, still undetermined in nature, is unsung because I've been doing something wrong. There are examples, success stories, there are tricks and tips and systems and habits and practices and, if I can figure out the right combination, if I can identify my own little light, work out the most unique, the very specialist contribution I can make—the gift to the world that only I can give—if I can hold myself accountable and keep my eyes on the prize, I will not go to the grave with the song still inside me.

If I can learn to meditate, eat only foods plucked directly from the bosom of the green earth, if I learn patience, develop a healthy daily routine, if I get enough sleep, if people like me, if I have a healthy local network of friends, if I am a supportive wife, if my children play well with others, if I don't offend anyone but am still honest, if I curate all of my possessions so that each item I encounter fills me with a gratitude and joy in being alive, if I seek out a supportive network of peers who uplift me daily, if I identify a path from point a to point z, where each step is individually fulfilling and, taken together, they lead me to my life's opus, a perfect match of my skills and passion, I will have earned the privilege of not going to the grave with the song still inside me.

So I set out to build my extraordinary life. I read books and blogs, I thought about mentors, I evaluated relationships, I analyzed myself, I cleared clutter, I bought magnets.

But of course life is not a road trip where you have a clear and correct map to your chosen destination, hand-select appropriate fellow travelers, purchase the perfect gear, exactly what you need and nothing else.

It's a random tour bus, crammed full of people, that you are dropped into in the dead of night, heading somewhere but a lot of the signs are written in a language that you can't understand. You hope there's a benevolent driver—or at least a thoughtful algo-rithm—rather than a madman behind the wheel. Everyone has different interpretations of what is happening and what should be done. Some people are dropped in the bus with a bulging wallet, and some people are dropped in the bus addicted to crack. You don't get to choose which you'll be. You were assigned a seat next to someone, you didn't choose that either but you're stuck together, though later, you do get to change seats and pick a new partner. But you don't know what's coming next and you've never sat beside them during a hailstorm, so you just pray you made a reasonable choice. On sunny days, when you can open the windows, the breeze feels great. On rainy days the toilet reeks and you wish you were sitting closer to the front. You aren't all heading to the same place and you don't all see things the same way. But there's just one bus.

You *are* unique. But your uniqueness isn't something inside you that is precious and hidden. Your uniqueness is how you treat others on the bus, and whether you share the song or keep it to yourself.

I have been hung up in wondering for a lifetime now, what is "my" song? How can I sing it? But there is no "my" song. I don't have a song without the rest of the world. The song is being part of the world-song, seeing the world, the imperfect, beautiful world and sharing what you can do, what is possible for you—today— not in your mind's eye when you finally have the skills or the network or the whatever. You see the world that is, know you are part of the flow of life, of life and a world that is not in your control, you look for where you can shine a light, today, and you shine it. As brightly as you can.

You can't sing the song by humming silently in your own head day after day. Making sure you have mastered every note combination so that, no matter what happens, you'll be ready. You can't wait until you are so well prepared that there's guaranteed success. A guarantee that you won't feel embarrassed. A guarantee that you won't feel scared. The tour bus doesn't offer guarantees. Not for anyone. And it is never predictable. No matter how thick the walls of your bubble, you're on the bus with everyone else and it can bump over a pothole at any point. No checklist, no routine can prevent that.

You don't need to change your life, fix your life, in order to sing the song. You don't need a perfect set of habits or a bulletproof routine. I love my checklists, and I'm sure when life allows it I will get back to many of my habits. But I've been writing for nine hours each day for two weeks straight on coffee and potato chips. I don't have to wait until everything feels right, and ready, and safe.

What I have to do is to acknowledge the uncertainty, the fear (*I don't know where this bus is going*)—to feel the love—and then to sing. Out loud.

To close my eyes, to feel my heart beating, to breathe in and to sing—out loud—and listen to hear the world sing back.

THE 100 REJECTIONS PROJECT

November 30, 2018

The plan: I am setting out to collect 100 rejections.

Timeline: We have to be flexible in life but I'm thinking four years which equals about two submissions per month.

Rationale: A focus on collecting rejections encourages me to seek situations outside of what is known and comfortable, to reach a little further than feels probable, to try what seems unlikely and to grow into it. By celebrating each rejection, it makes it easier to try, it adds a fun element to the trying, there is victory in defeat, which isn't even really defeat but a stepping stone to the next thing, a way of learning, and so much better than just sitting here wishing.

Parameters: I have to submit the best work that I can, the objective is to have my writing published. With respect to the best work I can, I can't just sit on something for three years because maybe I can make it better someday. I have to finish a piece to the best of my ability and send it off—not all of the perfectionism(ing).

Types of submissions: I have written pieces in mind. But I will be flexible. Anything that I am willing to try where there is some felt risk of being rejected can count as a rejection. So if I approach a local bookstore and ask them if I can do a reading from this book and they say no, that's one rejection. It is feasible that I could get to 100 rejections a lot faster than four years.

264 / THE RISE AND FALL OF JENNY GOODGUTS

When will I start? Truth be told I've already started. I submitted my first piece, a poem, to *The New Yorker* in October. I sent it off and felt excited, immediately, about getting my very first rejection, and the first one being from *The New Yorker*. I am looking forward to printing the rejection email and putting it into the empty spot on my wall where right now there are no rejections because I have never submitted my writing to anyone for publication.

Well, I had one poem published in junior high. I also had a few poems published in high school. The junior high poem, about cats, was cute. The high school poems were embarrassing, not because they were bad (they were) but because they were thoughtless, insensitive, just flexing my clever muscles and nothing else. I have had other writing published, but in those cases I was employed by a company to write something for their in-house publication.

How will I track it? You know that I already have a spreadsheet.

What will change between now and the one hundredth rejection? I don't know. I'm excited to find out.

Can I submit the same rejected piece to a new place? Seems like I could get to 100 pretty quickly in that case. I was thinking I'd have to write at least 100 different things but of course that isn't true. If I wrote just one mediocre thing and submitted it to 100 publications that would do the trick. Well, let's stick with 100. It's a nice-sounding number. If I get to 100 and haven't learned something interesting then I can make it the 1,000 Rejections Project. E.B. White's birthday is July 11th. So if 100 turns out to be a cinch then maybe I'll go for 711. But perhaps I should just get started.

Note: The 100 Rejections Project is underway and ongoing progress is tracked at www.jenniferhole.com.

THE STUFFED PROJECT

December 4, 2018

Dear sofa,

I want you to know that I love you. We dreamed of having you for a long time, but it was so hard to let go of your predecessor (who will receive her own letter in time, but since that is a break-up letter, it is more emotionally complex). I love that your springs are intact. That my feet don't leave the ground as my tired derrière slides towards the pit at the back of your cushions. You have no pit. May I long protect your integrity as a couch.

Sofa, I love that you are big enough for three people, four good friends, or up to six children to sit comfortably upon. It is nice to imagine inviting a friend over for a cup of tea. I know I've been promising something like this for a long time, and someday it will be more than just a dream.

I apologize and recognize that you were not sold as a trampoline. I am working on it and he will get older. We, you and I, will be happy that he is older. And also sad. I think we will both miss the jumping.

Thank you, dear sofa, for sheltering my body, covered, and uncovered, and covered, and uncovered with that sleeping bag when I could do nothing but roll into your embrace and hope my children didn't pull the knives out of the knife drawer while my husband was away and I had that undetermined dread virus last winter. I will never forget those 24 hours my dear friend.

I am so glad, so thankful, that your cover is washable. I promise that someday I will remove the old chocolate from your corner, the orange marker, deposited to your main cushion the very day of your arrival/assembly. Today will not be the day. But it will, eventually, come.

I remember when we met you, just three separate cardboard boxes too heavy for me to lift but that somehow fit into the back of our SportWagen. And now here you are, a part of the family.

Sofa, I know that you were once a towering tree, cleaning the air, feeling the breeze. That your cover is made from plants that felt the sun and drank the rain. That your joints came from within mountains, your stuffing from aged dinosaur bones. I honor your provenance and will do my best to treat you with the respect due to your sacred heritage.

May I take one moment, each time I rest upon your Flodafors beige threads, to cherish the comfort that you provide to me and to my loved ones.

I know the jumping is ill-advised. And you need a bath.

With love and gratitude,

Jennifer

ANNOUNCING: *Stuffed: One woman's odyssey to reimagine our relationship to the material world* (working title)

This project (and eventual book) might be for you if: You see heartbreaking videos about palm oil and chimps, read about ice sheets crumbling and the link to your daily commute, or some girl at Starbucks gives you the evil eye for using a disposable straw. Maybe you should have remembered to bring your cup but you live in suburbia juggling children, work, parents, community, broken appliances, holiday prep. So you buy things on Amazon and feel guilty/remorseful afterwards when the local toy shop goes out of business.

Unless you stop living, you use stuff. But you are surrounded by messages that the stuff you use is damaging someone or something else. You feel bad for wanting things, for buying things, and for feeling bad about the things that you've wanted and bought. And it is piled up around you, you spend so much time sorting it, moving it, organizing it, donating it, replacing it, repairing it, arranging it, selecting it, wanting it, not wanting it.

You know you can "vote with your checkbook" for the kind of world you want. But it feels like each choice takes so much effort, so much research. So you vote with your checkbook at The Container Store.

Your child asks you what a Pez dispenser is and you tell him it is just a piece of plastic that will turn into trash, and some sugar pellets. You overhear yourself and know you are no fun. But you're also right.

Your parents are/soon will be downsizing or no longer able to maintain a lifetime of material accumulation. And they are even more attached to things than you are as evidenced by the hurt look on the maternal face when the offer of a silver-plated candy dish, a wedding gift unused since the 60s, is politely declined. And how many conversations will you have about that broken candelabra? I know it was your mother's. I know. Something will need to be done with their stuff, and the thought of all of the decisions – and emotions – is difficult.

Holidays come that are focused on buying stuff, giving stuff. Most of the people you know have more than enough. And you know that lots of other people don't. But, in the name of love, you buy your parcels and wrap them. It feels fun, sometimes, (stressful and expensive, often) but you also wonder. What is the lesson to the little ones from all of this getting and giving? Giving is a fundamental joy of being human – can we do it differently (but, not just substituting with homemade certificates for quality time)?

You have read or heard about numerous clutter-clearing strategies and tried to KonMari your home but the birthday party favors never stop coming. You are also somewhat uncomfortable with the ethos of just getting rid of what you don't want to purchase different stuff, recognizing that every object equals nature transformed, life energy spent. You aren't going to give up your trash can, but could there be a benefit, some joy dividend you might gain, from creating less trash?

You want a balanced, joyful relationship with material things, not the possibility of a nervous breakdown every time you walk into the basement.

And it's not just your home and storage spaces that are overflowing. Your schedule, mind, and list of shoulds is rammed full too. You may vacillate between super healthy/restrictive eating and binging on cheese and crackers or Quadratini Dark Chocolate bite-size wafer cookies.

And yet, in the light of all of this over-fullness, there is a feeling that something is missing.

Maybe you need to redecorate.

Maybe you need to minimize.

Maybe you need to spark joy.

Do I have any guiding principles in this work?

Yes, thanks for asking. I am looking for joy and light. I will not focus on the harm done through acquiring and using stuff, but will look to describe a relationship with the material world that is connected and life-affirming.

I want to explore what's been written, what is helpful, how it works in real life, in my real life. My current plan is to read a lot, to do experiments with popular stuff-management approaches, to write a mix of personal essays, notes on history and culture, and a bunch of letters to my stuff, and hopefully write a few songs on the nature of glow sticks and Chuck E. Cheese. I want to shine a light on good alternatives and help you to see more beauty and feel more connection to the world through stuff, but less of it.

I'm excited about this project and I think it is going to be a lot of fun. I also think – I hope – that it can be healing, because the guilty feeling, and occasional paralysis, that accompanies your choices is weighing you down to the ground. Because you don't want to spend all of your time organizing, curating, making decisions about all of the STUFF that surrounds you, but the indecision, lack of clarity, and conflicted values that all the stuff represents is draining your life energy.

So I'm going to chat with you about it, to help you laugh about it and think about it in new ways. I'm not going to get too heavy, focusing on harm and doom. You can trust me, because I understand a lot about harm and doom, I promise to be a thoughtful and thorough advisor. But I'm not going to get into the nitty gritty of what is hurting the world and how. I'm going to talk about how we can protect and restore and nourish and love through more connection. I will be an understanding friend, not a purveyor of judgement, I will talk in real language about real life and not an idealized, spiritual nirvana.

So that's the plan. I figured December is the most Stuffed month of the year, a perfect time to announce my intentions.

Note: The Stuffed Project is also moving ahead. Updates and further thoughts are shared on my website.

THE END OF BOOK THE FIRST

April 2, 2019

Four years ago I walked outside to buy a sandwich to eat at my desk in my windowless office. Not pregnant, I was wearing maternity pants although my son, my youngest child, was almost two years old. When I arrived back to my desk, I wrote a few paragraphs, my own thoughts that, for once, insisted on taking form.

Today, I'm sitting at home. I ate lunch, some reheated leftovers, hastily at my desk where I can see the buds on the dogwood outside of my window, almost ready to open. I'm wearing my hoody sweatshirt and sweatpants, the same ones depicted on the front cover of this book. The sun is shining.

Nothing has changed.

I'm not a published author. I haven't finished a novel. I haven't figured out a master plan, I haven't found a pot of money, I still feel scared every time I share my words.

Everything has changed.

I have allowed space, I have listened, I have asked for help, I have studied, I have done what scares me anyway, I have sat uncomfortably and waited, I have practiced, and I have learned.

Later this month I am singing, I have a two-hour show at a local bar with a band. We practice every week on Tuesdays after the kids are in bed.

I've submitted my writing and received my first rejection. I am practicing every day.

I'm trying to love the world that is. I'm trying not to hide.

I see that I was confused by the certificates. I thought I needed permission. I thought approval provided some guarantee.

This book, the one you are reading that is now at its end, was not the plan. Having read this far, you won't be surprised to know that there wasn't a plan. But compiling and publishing all of this introspection was not what I would have imagined as my first big splash (or tiny ripple) into the world of letters.

If I had not lost (most of) the novel, things would be different. But I did lose it. And that led me to a sad but resolute place. And that led to a conversation with my husband about finishing things. And that led to a decision to finish *something*. And that led to telling a lot of people I was going to publish this book. And that led to revisiting all of these words, and considering them as a whole. And that led to a few minor revelations. And that led to more conversations and questions about why I had not yet taken action to share my writing in the usual ways. And that led to exploring the usual ways to share writing, and to submitting my work for publication, and to more writing, and reading, and waiting, and learning. I believe the novel will be better for all of this. I hope, one day, to say many useful things beautifully and with humor.

But now here I am, with a book all about myself, ready to share with any living human who decides to open the cover.

I can tell you, that's a scary place to be.

This is why people write novels. And fiction. And non-fiction about things other than themselves. This is why diaries are published when people are dead and why memoirs are told in hindsight, sharing what you want to share, rather than your often tortured and sometimes embarrassing inner thoughts.

But its done. This is what I have made, what I've finished. So now it is time to share it. Time to *place my intention in the vast ocean of possibility and allow the universe to work through me.*

And then I will be ready to make what is next.

SOMETHING DIFFERENT,
BEGINNING PART TWO

Note: I have been advised that this might make more sense to readers with a tiny bit of background. First, hopefully it will be obvious but this is fiction. My real sister was not actually punished by Hera, as far as we know. It may help readers to be reminded of the Greek myth of Echo, the mountain nymph who had her voice taken away by Hera, as a punishment for her long-winded stories (and, more specifically, for not exposing the whereabouts of Zeus), and afterwards could only repeat what she heard others say. Echo fell in love with Narcissus, who fell in love with his reflection in a pond and then turned into a flower, and afterwards Echo faded to nothing but a sound.

My sister was a shadow. Her skin no longer felt the brush of wind. She had become the breeze.

I never met her. But my first stories held her transgression. Conveyed her punishment. Her suffering.

Zeus, King of the Gods, sought my cousins. He loved their strong, laughing bodies. Their husky, smooth songs. Their sharp, glittering eyes. He followed them, hungry, into the mountains, into the rivers, blue-green, teeming with life.

His sister-wife, Hera, came looking for him—Hera, older than Zeus, tricked into being Queen of the Gods. Trapped into a life she had not asked for, Hera asked my sister for an answer my sister had been forbidden to give.

Where is Zeus? she asked.

I was told that Hera was jealous, vengeful and my sister verbose.

Both of these — crimes. My sister, with her long, rambling stories and beautiful voice, keeping secrets from the Queen of the Gods.

Hera, in her rage with her brother-husband, the one who had hung her from the stars, stole my sister's voice. Cursed my sister so that she could no longer share her own words but only repeat those of another. My sister who fell in love with a flower, her beautiful body withered, her bones became rock.

I listened closely to my mother, my cousins. I was a quick study. I had my sister's way with words, her lovely voice. And I knew these things were a danger to me. I knew to speak these words, to use this voice, could lead to losing everything: My very body, the feeling of waves washing over me, the taste of a ripe peach.

I learned to give Hera what she demanded: A dutiful echo.

But I was plagued by dreams.

I woke up, sweating, in the night. Hera beside me, I cowered. *I have done what you wish. I have said nothing but what I have heard from others. Please, spare me.*

Too afraid to look in her eyes, I looked away.

From the Queen of the Gods I heard the sound of ancient tears. I turned and saw deep grooves, canyons, where sorrow had carved a centuries-long path.

With weary tenderness she spoke. *He had already robbed her when he forbade her to speak the truth. I only made obvious what was already so.*

I don't want to become a shadow.

An echo is already a shadow.

But I can feel the wind. I can taste a peach.

Can you?

I'm afraid, I said. *I don't want to lose everything. They said I would lose everything.*

And Artemis the hunter and Athena the wise warrior were there. Aphrodite the lover. *We are with you.*

I slept fitfully.

Sunlight. I am breathing, alone in my room. I whisper the truth.

I am awake. It is morning.

Nothing happens. Birdsong.

I pull back the covers, my feet touch the ground. I look in the mirror, speaking slowly. *I am strong.*

Dust dances in a beam of light. Nothing happens.

I walk outside, the symphony of limbs, light and dark, warm, cool.

She was forbidden to speak the truth.

I speak this to the trees, to the sky. I say it clearly. Repeat it. Nothing happens. The branches do not seem to mind.

My legs start to move, before I know where I am going. I am walking, running. My lungs are filling with air, reaching for more air, not enough air. I am afraid I will run out of air before I get where I am going.

But there is Theia, the shining light, mother of the sun, the moon, the dawn—my lungs are renewed.

And the Muses, dancing with Apollo—more breath.

And then I see Alice Walker up ahead with a bag of air. And E.B. White?

There is so much air, I am full, to the brim, of all the air I need and I'm running, flying until I reach the cave.

I stand outside, looking into its depths.

I gather my strength and with all of the breath left to me I call, sending my words as far into the recesses as they will go: *He is here.*

I hear my sister's voice reverberating back: *He is here—here—ere.*

I feel the sun on my arms, a swirl of wind. Birdsong.

And my sister, blinking, steps out of the cave.

My sister became a shadow. But I am not. I have hands and a tongue and a still-beating heart. I am afraid. I am alive.

ACKNOWLEDGMENTS

Chronologically I should start with the higher powers. Then my ancestors, the people who grew the food I've eaten and built houses to shelter me, and my first dogs who taught me non-human love.

Ms.(es) Nolan, Hall, Reese, Boutte, Angwin, Lawrence, Swoger, Stephens, Sanders, Manley, Trafton, Phares, and Mr.(s) Reynolds and Sloan, and to Sally Furse and Donella Meadows. Thank you for your work to light so many candles.

My parents, there is nothing I have done or will do that is not a result of your love. Thank you for my life and everything that came after.

Yes, this book has inconsistent numbering and use of the serial comma. All my fault. Special thanks to Debby McCullough, Becky Chacko, Patricia Malentaqui, and Leigh Dameron for providing feedback and encouragement on various drafts, to Lisa and Matt, for a jacket that fits just right, to Sarah and Lani, for the cactus song, and to the 35 original blog readers, and all of my readers since, for the gift of reading and responding.

This book would absolutely not exist without the friendship and encouragement of Adam Meyer whose patient listening and thoughtful advice helped me to imagine myself as a writer.

Maggie and Sam, thank you for looking at the world with joyful hearts and reminding me to do the same.

Dave, I know that what came inside the package turned out to be different than the description on the box. Thank you for your trust, acceptance, encouragement, patience, and love.

SOME HOUSEKEEPING

At jenniferhole.com you can find updates on:
    The Stuffed Project (now in full force)
    The 100 Rejections Project (now meagerly underway)
    The Happy Atmosphere Challenge
    The French Food Challenge (possibly renamed)
    A smoothie recipe (though I advise you to look elsewhere)
    All songs mentioned in this book (except for possibly the mom
        opera if I have to take it down) and any new songs
    Grown-up star chart (not currently, but at some point)

What happened to the novel?
The dominant hypothesis is that my son accidentally deleted the
file while using my wireless keyboard as mission control, but this
can never be confirmed and he, as a small child, was not responsible. Mommy doesn't blame you sweetheart.

Note: Because the sun has moved
Yes, the earth moves around the sun. But, relative to our lived
human experience the sun moves across the sky according to its
own rhythm, not our demands.

Good news note
Remember how horrified I was about the volume of trash being
carted away every week? This summer, in Alexandria, they distrib-
uted smaller trash cans to every home. Small steps, but steps.

Climate change and snakes
I mentioned my intention to write this piece in my very first post.

Here's the basic premise: scientists have found that one unexpected consequence of a changing climate is increased predation of ground-dwelling bird eggs. The culprit? "Active, hungry snakes." This alone was enough to ramp up my commitment to living off the grid. I feel that the environmental orgs and activists have their messaging all wrong. They should just show us lots of pictures of *active, hungry snakes*. That alone could drive sales of electric cars through the roof. Now you know.

And a few notes that I wrote to myself as I was working on this book:

Tough Love Note #1: Justin and Taylor
You don't start off at the top of your game. Everyone starts somewhere and if your first efforts are a little embarrassing, you will get another chance. Just make the best stuff you can and be willing to share it. Then make it better.

Tough Love Note #2: Control
You don't get to make life your way. You don't choose your mom or dad, your brother or sister, your son or daughter. You don't have a clue when you choose who to marry. You don't get to choose the weather, or the laws of physics. You don't get to choose history. You are a tiny speck of the present and you will be gone in the future. Sure, make a spreadsheet, eat your vegetables—it does matter. But you live in the flow of life.

Tough Love Note #3: Other people
It is way better not to do everything alone. Ask people for help.

The best books I read over the four years covered in this book:
    Free Play: Improvisation in Life and Art, Stephen Nachmanovitch

One Man's Meat, E.B. White

The Creative Habit: Learn It and Use It for Life, Twyla Tharp

On Writing: A Memoir of the Craft, Stephen King

The Gift: Creativity and the Artist in the Modern World, Lewis Hyde

The Wave in the Mind: Talks and Essays on the Writer, the Reader, and the Imagination, Ursula K. Le Guin

The War of Art: Break Through the Blocks and Win Your Inner Creative Battles, Steven Pressfield

Man's Search for Himself, Rollo May

Irresistable: The Rise of Addictive Technology and the Business of Keeping us Hooked, Adam Alter

The Power of Myth, Joseph Cambell with Bill Moyers

This Phenomenal Life: The Amazing Ways We Are Connected with Our Universe, Misha Maynerick Blaise

The Little Prince, Antoine de Saint-Exupery

The Secret Garden, Frances Hodgson Burnett

Forget-Me-Nots: Poems to Learn by Heart, Mary Ann Hoberman and Michael Emberley

ABOUT THE AUTHOR

Jennifer Hole once had tea with the Queen of Bhutan. A species of katydid (it's an insect) has been named named for her. She has lived in tents, wet and dry, in Africa, eaten a lot of hot dogs in the Philippines, and sat at rapt attention inside UN negotiations. A debutante, she was formally presented to southern society in a white dress at 21. She was once selected from the audience to ride behind dolphins in a boat at Sea World. She entered and lost a pageant, three times. She once climbed almost to the top of Mount Rainier. She ate raw eggs and sushi while pregnant in Japan, but not without hesitation. Her dad used to copy her photo onto two-dollar bills.

This is her first book.

To follow her ongoing adventures, to learn about the next book, or to present her with fabulous writing opportunities or a recording contract, visit: www.jenniferhole.com

Made in the USA
Middletown, DE
18 May 2019